THE HUMAN RESOURCES GUIDE TO MANAGING DISABILITY IN THE WORKPLACE

First edition

2010

By Nancy J. Gowan,
B.H.Sc (O.T.), O.T. Reg (ON),
CDMP
President
Gowan Consulting

CARSWELL®

Canadian Cataloguing in Publication Date

A cataloguing record for this publication is available from Library and Archives Canada.

ISBN 978-0-7798-2213-3

Printed in Canada by Thomson Reuters

THOMSON REUTERS

CARSWELL, A DIVISION OF THOMSON REUTERS CANADA LIMITED

One Corporate Plaza
2075 Kennedy Road
Toronto, Ontario
M1T 3V4

Customer Relations
Toronto 1-416-609-3800
Elsewhere in Canada/U.S. 1-800-387-5164
Fax 1-416-298-5082
www.carswell.com
E-mail www.carswell.com/email

ACKNOWLEDGMENTS

Over the past 25 years I have had the privilege of working with many inspiring, dedicated and knowledgeable individuals and organizations. It has given me the ability to pursue a career that I love and an opportunity to learn something new each day. I would like to acknowledge the contributions of so many colleagues that supported me, employees that made my work look easy and corporations that gave me the opportunity to assist individuals in being able to perform meaningful and productive work.

This book is borne out of years of learning important ideas. I would like to give credit to the corporations that support their employees through adversity and focus on ability. Pieces of each corporation that I have worked with are contained in this book; some in what they did right and some in what we learned when disability management went wrong.

Above all I want to thank my family . . .my mother who taught me about working hard but for the right things, my father who taught me about the importance of independence, my husband who taught me that it isn't all about work, my children who taught me the importance of respecting everyone's differences and my sisters who gave me inspiration.

Introduction

Over 14.3% of Canadians reported having an activity limitation in 2006. With the changing demographics in Canada, employers will have an increasing difficulty in finding skilled workers to meet their needs. This book focuses on the tools that will allow an employer to recruit and retain employees with disabilities. As you use the tools in this book it is important that you understand the following principles and concepts:

- Work is healthy and allows each individual to contribute to society and each corporation to be globally competitive;
- Work helps an individual to express themselves and develop a unique self-image;
- Suitable and safe work is in the best interests of both the employee and the organization;
- Everyone has unique abilities and skills. If you focus on capabilities instead of limitations you will find a fit for these abilities;
- Focus on function and not the "illness" or diagnosis. Taking a functional approach to disability allows you to find a suitable work match;
- It is up to the employee and employer to determine the best fit in the organization. Having an employee centered approach will allow you to maximize the potential options and reduce lost time durations;
- Open and transparent communication is essential to working together and finding the solution. Although there are legal statutes that guide the communication process, focusing on function and work demands will lead to suitable and reasonable solutions;
- The spirit of your approach and following a fair and consistent process for all employees will be important for both success in finding solutions and legal compliance;
- Supervising support is one of the key ingredients to a successful program, so spend the time to train supervisors well.

All the tools in this book can be modified and adjusted to match your corporate culture, but maintaining these principles will lead to improved success.

TABLE OF CONTENTS

CHAPTER 3: HUMAN RIGHTS AND YOUR DUTY TO ACCOMMODATE

CHAPTER 4: WORKERS' COMPENSATION ACTS

CHAPTER 6: RECRUITMENT PRACTICES FOR INDIVIDUALS WITH DISABILITIES

CHAPTER 7: PREVENTING DISABILITY IN THE WORKPLACE

CHAPTER 13: MANAGING COMPLEX RETURN TO WORK ISSUES

CHAPTER 14: ACCOMMODATION FOR SPECIFIC DISABILITIES

CHAPTER 1: DISABILITY MANAGEMENT IN CANADA

INTRODUCTION

1.1 — Introduction to Managing Disability in the Workplace

Managing disability in the workplace is a challenging yet rewarding component of any Human Resources Professional's skill set. Recruitment and retention of employees allow businesses to outperform the competition through financial and productivity improvements. For the Human Resources Professional, optimally matching employee abilities to job demands occurs throughout the employment life cycle. This book will provide the Human Resources Professional with the knowledge and tools to manage employees with disabilities proactively in the workplace. The book is divided into several components including accessibility, prevention of disability, return to work planning and supporting individuals with disabilities in the workplace.

a) — Defining Disability

Disability is defined by the World Health Organization's (WHO) framework of disability provided by the International Classification of Functioning, Disability and Health (ICF). Disability is "any restriction or lack (resulting from an impairment) of ability to perform an activity or task in the manner or within the range considered normal for a human being."[1] This framework defines disability as "an umbrella term, covering impairments, activity limitations, and partici-

[1] World Health Organization, International Classification of Impairments, Disabilities and Handicaps, A manual of classification relating to the consequences of disease. Geneva: WHO, 1980, 47.

pation restrictions. An impairment is a problem in body function or structure; an activity limitation is a difficulty encountered by an individual in executing a task or action; while a participation restriction is a problem experienced by an individual in involvement in life situations. Thus disability is a complex phenomenon, reflecting an interaction between features of a person's body and features of the society in which he or she lives."[2]

It is important to understand that work is a part of health and that having a disability does not diminish the person's ability to contribute to society and to your workplace. The initial cause of the disability may be varied i.e. a congenital condition, a workplace injury or illness or a non-work related illness or injury. Whatever the cause, disability is determined by the gaps between the individual's capabilities and the core demands (physical, cognitive, emotional, sensory) as required by the role. One must examine the barriers to function, the role's tasks and the environment in which the role is carried out and not just the "medical condition/diagnosis." Focusing on function allows the workplace to understand what an individual is able to do and what that person may require to support the individual in being able to perform safely and productively in the workplace.

The individual with the disability is the key information source when defining gaps and determining strategies to overcome those gaps in the workplace. For best success use an employee-centred approach to disability management.

1.2 — Rationale and Objectives for Managing Disability in the Workplace

The overall objective is to provide a structure for employers to manage the needs of their workers with disabilities, so that workers' employability is protected, costs of disability (both human and financial) are controlled and global competitiveness is enhanced. Through the creation of policies and procedures for managing disability issues the employers' ability to maintain employees in the workplace is enhanced, and the incidence and costs associated with work disruption are reduced, positioning the employer to remain globally competi-

---

2 *Ibid.*

tive.[3] Further objectives are to: decrease the incidence and severity of illness/injury, reduce the duration of disability-related absences, promote early intervention and prevention strategies, increase the use of internal resources, improve the management of external resources, improve labour relations through joint labour-management collaboration, promote direct involvement of the worker, and comply with all related legislation.[4]

1.3 — Principles of Effective Disability Management Programs

According to the National Institute for Disability Management and Research,[5] effective disability management programs are deemed successful when they can demonstrate the following:

- Decreased injury/illness rates
- Reduction in presenteeism
- Improvements in stay at work potential
- Increased rate of returns for workers off due to work related or non-work related illness/injury;
- A decrease in the length of time ill/injured workers are off work;
- Measurable decrease in costs associated with workplace disability;
- Improvements in worker morale;

[3] This concept is addressed in each of the following sources: Towers Watson, "2009/2010 North American Staying@Work Report: The Health and Productivity Advantage" December 2009; Don Shrey, et al "Disability Management Best Practices and Joint Labour-Management Collaboration" Int. Journal of Disability Management Research VOL 1 Number 1 2006 at 52–63; Mercer; "The Total Financial Impact of Employee Absences" October 2008.

[4] Towers Watson, "2009/2010 North American Staying@Work Report: The Health and Productivity Advantage" December 2009; D.E. Shrey and Michel Lacerte (1994). Principles and Practices of Disability Management in Industry. Winter Park, FL: GR Press, Inc.

[5] National Institute of Disability Management and Research (1995). Disability Management in the Workplace: A Guide to Establishing a Joint Workplace Program. Port Alberni, BC: NIDMAR.

- Increase or maintenance of productivity levels.

1.4 — The Economic and Social Benefits of Managing Disability in the Workplace

Despite the fact there are societal and legal requirements to accommodate persons with disabilities in the workplace; a comprehensive disability management program has many economic and social benefits. Simply being off work can be bad for your health.[6]

Health Benefits: The statistics are stark. One in 13 of the working population claims disability benefits. If someone is off sick for six to 12 months, there is a 90 per cent chance they will not be returning to work in the foreseeable future; if they are off for more than two years, they are more likely to retire or die than return to work.[7]

Worklessness (being off work due to injury or illness or inability to work) leads to poorer physical and mental health, loss of self-worth and self-confidence, poorer social integration and more medical care. A study completed in the United Kingdom has calculated that worklessness has the same negative health impact as smoking 10 packs of cigarettes a day.[8] Gordon Waddell indicated that "what really matters in work is the social context. We need to change the culture of work, stop focusing on the potential toxic impact of work and understand that long-term worklessness is one of the greatest risks to health."

Reports in the literature have shown that people who are out of work as a result of disability or unemployment are more likely to have other diseases develop, and, ultimately, their lifespan is reduced when compared to people who are employed.[9]

---

6 Secretaries of State of the Department for Work and Pensions and the Department of Health by Command of Her Majesty, "Improving Health and Work: Changing Lives." Presented to Parliament: November 2008.

7 Dame Carol Black, "Working For a Healthier Tomorrow Dame Carol Black's Review of the health of Britain's working age population." Produced by the cross-government Health, Work and Well-being Programme: 17th March 2008.

8 Gordon Waddell & A.K. Burton, "Is work good for your health and well-being?" (2006) Dept for Work & Pensions, UK.

9 U. Janlert, "Unemployment as a disease and diseases of the unemployed." (1997) Scand J Work Environ Health 3:79–83.

Social Benefits: Disability management programs demonstrate that the organization values its workers and is able to retain valuable workers. Experienced workers are familiar with the workplace and the specific requirements of their job. Considerable time and resources have been invested in the training and orientation of workers so that they can provide the quality of service that is demanded. When a worker is ill or injured, they may not be able to provide the same level of service and in addition, replacement workers may be needed, or perhaps other workers will have to work short-staffed. Either way, quality of service may be affected. It is in the best interest of the company to have injured /ill workers back as soon as it is safely possible to maintain production and quality. This in turn will lead to an increase in worker morale and employee productivity. For the worker, it will reduce the negative effects of disabling injury/illness and individuals can regain their former income levels and a chance to perform meaningful work thus promoting both the individual and the individual's family's social well-being.

In the past, recovery would occur at home and the individual would remain off work until they were completely recovered. Unfortunately many often would not be able to return to work. We now know that performing work activities is a key component of rehabilitation. The ill effects of remaining off work can cause iatrogenic health concerns and social illness.

Financial Benefits: For employers, injuries, illness and disability can have significant costs. Estimates in the United States and Canada, for example, are that employers spend up to 8 per cent of their payroll on disability and disability insurance.[10]

A survey of Canadian employers found that employer's short-term disability costs on average were 2 per cent of payroll costs while long term disability costs accounted for 1.2 per cent of payroll. Workers Compensation costs accounted for 2.4 per cent of payroll for a total of 5.6 per cent of payroll going directly to disability costs.[11] This

[10] M. Campolieti & J.N. Lavis, "Disability expenditures in Canada: Trends, reform efforts and a path for the future." (2000) Canadian Public Policy Vol. 26(2) at 241–263. Barton Margoshes, "Disability Management and occupational health." (1998) Occ. Medicine: state of the art reviews. Vol 13(4).

[11] Watson Wyatt (2000/2001) Staying at Work Report; Watson Wyatt Worldwide.

same survey repeated in 2003 reported a doubling of short term disability costs in less than 5 years.[12]

Time lost from work due to injuries has a financial cost in terms of both direct and indirect costs. Direct costs are the costs that are most easily tabulated. They include medical costs, compensation and insurance. Indirect costs are also costs to an organization, although they are a little less obvious. Indirect costs include costs related to time spent investigating incidents and injuries, re-training staff, overtime costs for replacement workers, reduced service, sales and production.

It is estimated that the indirect costs of a workplace injury could be as high as four times that of the direct cost of an injury.[13] The average cost of a workplace claim in 2006 was $98,000[14] a more than 20 per cent increase since 2002. This significant increase in costs has been attributed to the increased complexity of disability and needless disability in the workplace. Needless Disability[15] is disability caused by delays in the systems, stakeholder competing agendas, delays in communication, lack of accommodation in the workplace and loss of "occupational bond".[16] These are disabilities caused by gaps in the system not the original injury or illness. Occupational Bond is defined by Don Shrey as the connection between the worker and the workplace. When a worker is away from the workplace due to injury or illness the worker becomes less attached to the employer and more attached to the medical system that is treating the impairment[17]. The role identification as a worker is lost and the employee becomes a "patient".

In 2008 a study to determine the cost of mental health in the workplace noted the final tally was between $11 and 33 billion in costs to

[12] *Ibid.*

[13] WSIB Annual Report 2004.

[14] WSIB Annual Report 2006.

[15] The American College of Occupational and Environmental Medicine "Preventing needless disability by helping people stay employed." 2005.

[16] D.E. Shrey & Michel Lacerte, *Principles and Practices of Disability Management in Industry*. (Winter Park, FL: GR Press Inc. 1994).

[17] *Ibid.*

Canadian businesses.[18] This is for mental health conditions alone. The total cost of physical and mental health disability for employers is estimated to be 8 per cent–19 per cent of payroll depending on what the employer includes in this equation.[19]

Direct costs of disability in the workplace include:

- wage replacements weekly indemnity, sick leave, short term disability, long term disability and workers compensation costs;
- replacement workers or overtime costs;
- training costs;
- recruitment costs;
- administrative charges and time.

Indirect costs of disability in the work place include:

- lost productivity;
- lost sales;
- supervisor and support staff time and frustrations;
- coworkers morale;
- turnover;
- employee pain and suffering.

While many organizations are tracking and seeking to control the direct cost of these issues, they are generally not tracking the indirect costs, particularly productivity losses due to illness/disability. Despite the impact that workforce productivity has on profitability, this issue is often overlooked when organizations calculate the cost of employee absences and the value of health and productivity policies designed to improve employee effectiveness.[20]

---

[18] J. Samra, M. Gilbert, M. Shain & D. Bilsker, "What is Psychological Safety & Health?" Consortium for Organizational Mental Healthcare (COMH, 2009).

[19] These concepts are supported in: Towers Watson, "2009/2010 North American Staying@Work Report: The Health and Productivity Advantage" December 2009; Don Shrey et al "Disability Management Best Practices and Joint Labour-Management Collaboration" (2006) Int. Journal of disability Management Research Vol. 1 Number 1 at 52–63. Mercer; "The Total Financial Impact of Employee Absences" October 2008.

[20] Watson Wyatt (2007) Staying at Work Report, Watson Wyatt Worldwide.

The Watson Wyatt Stay@work survey completed in 2007 noted that there was an "increasing concern for management processes for health and disability management programs with less confidence in external programs but more confidence in supervisor support being the key to managing health." The 2007 Staying@Work Canada report found that "mental health issues are the leading cause of both long- and short-term disability claims (72 per cent and 82 per cent respectively)". Despite the prevalence of these claims, "only 15 per cent of responding companies conduct mental health risk assessments and less than 20 per cent say that addressing the stigma associated with mental illness is a priority."[21] A unique resource is now available to assist employers in having a psychologically safe work environment to prevent these costs.[22]

A survey completed by Gowan Health Consultants in 2008 found that over 25 days lost per employee per year was still common in 16 per cent of workplaces. Only 15 per cent of employers had less than 5 days lost per employee per year.

Statistics Canada indicated a total of 8.1 days per employee per year was lost to disability in 2007.[23] The following chart outlines the trends in days lost per employee per year across Canada over a 5 year period due to illness or disability.

---

[21] Gowan Health Consultants: Disability Management to Practice Survey Report 2009.

[22] www.guardingmindsatwork.ca

[23] Statistics Canada 2008: Statistics Canada, CANSIM table 279-0029.

Days lost per worker due to illness or disability, by sex, by province (Both sexes)

	2003	2004	2005	2006	2007
			Both sexes		
			number of days		
Canada	*7.5*	*7.5*	*7.8*	*7.6*	*8.1*
Newfoundland and Labrador	9.1	8.8	8.1	8.2	8.2
Prince Edward Island	6.4	6.0	6.9	6.9	6.8
Nova Scotia	8.1	9.1	9.0	8.9	9.9
New Brunswick	8.8	8.0	8.5	9.7	8.8
Quebec	9.3	9.4	9.6	9.3	9.8
Ontario	6.5	6.7	6.7	6.6	7.2
Manitoba	7.8	8.0	7.9	8.1	8.7
Saskatchewan	8.6	8.1	8.9	8.7	8.3
Alberta	6.2	5.6	6.5	6.6	6.9
British Columbia	8.1	7.3	8.5	7.6	8.2

Note: Includes full-time paid workers only.
Source: Statistics Canada, CANSIM, table *279-0029*.
Last Modified: 2008-05-22.

1.5 — The Prevalence of Disability in the Workplace

Individuals in your workplace may be dealing with many types of disabilities. Disabilities may result from many causes. A Statistics Canada Survey completed in 2006 provides an outline of the number of individuals who have disabilities reported in Canada:[24]

Hearing	689,370
Seeing	258,150
Communication	26,140
Mobility	1,186,800
Agility	412,800
Pain	984,920

[24] Statistics Canada: Statistics Canada, Participation and Activity Limitation Survey, 2006.

Learning	168,250
Other	433,890

The Participation and Activity Limitation Survey in 2006 reported that "4.4 million Canadians living in households reported having an activity limitation yielding a disability rate of 14.3 per cent. This is an increase from the 2001 disability rate of 12.4 per cent, when 3.6 million Canadians reported limitations in their everyday activities due to a physical or psychological condition or to a health condition. The increase is due to a number of factors, including aging of the population and changing reporting behaviours.[25]

Overall, the disability rate increases with age for both men and women. Nevertheless, women were, in general, more likely (15.2 per cent) to report an activity limitation than men (13.4 per cent).

Problems related to pain, mobility and agility affect the largest number of adults 15 years of age or older. Close to 3 million Canadian adults (approximately 11 per cent of the total population aged 15 and over) reported one of these limitations.

People with activity limitations posted strong growth in their employment rate, from 49.3 per cent in 2001 to 53.5 per cent in 2006, narrowing the gap to the population without activity limitations with an employment rate of 75.1 per cent in 2006.

Labour force participation for people with activity limitations rose from 56.9 per cent in 2001 to 59.6 per cent in 2006, again reducing the gap with people without activity limitations.

The unemployment rate for people with activity limitations dropped from 13.2 per cent in 2001 to 10.4 per cent in 2006, narrowing the gap by roughly one-third with those without activity limitations."[26]

These statistics demonstrate that more individuals are working with disabilities then in 2001. Individuals with disabilities still tend to be underemployed and there is potential for recruitment of skilled employees by tapping this underemployed population.

---

[25] *Ibid.* 2006.

[26] *Ibid.* 2006.

1.6 — Employment and Disability Myths and Facts

Attitudinal stereotypes about people with disabilities are still pervasive in the workplace, causing them to be hired less and fired more than workers without disabilities. These stereotypes have often been shown, through research and reports from employers who employ individuals with disabilities, to be false.

MYTH: All people with disabilities require job accommodation and those accommodations are expensive[27]

FACT: Studies have shown that less than one-quarter of employees with disabilities need accommodations, and about 70 per cent of such accommodations cost less than $600 per employee. Almost one-third cost the employer nothing. Of employees who responded to a JAN survey, 56 per cent said the accommodations cost absolutely nothing.[28] In many instances, the refinements prove beneficial for able-bodied employees who happen to be shorter, taller, less agile, older, or depart from the norm in other ways. Ergonomic changes can reduce the number of future workplace injuries while assisting individuals with disabilities to safely function in the workplace.

A large percentage of individuals with disabilities in the workplace do not need any workplace modifications. Most of the adjustments may involve different approaches to the work or work processes. This can cost the employer nothing but can improve the efficiency of the process for others performing the same work.

MYTH: Individuals with disabilities are not reliable, punctual or efficient

FACT: Surveys have shown that people with a disability: on average, have a better attendance record;[29] have an average or better pro-

---

[27] A. Cantor, "The Costs and Benefits of Accommodating Employees with Disabilities" (Toronto: 1996), online: http://www.cantoraccess.com/publications/accomm_1996_worksitenews_2.shtml

[28] JAN (Job Accommodation Network): "Work Accommodations: Low Cost High Impact Fact Sheet" September 1, 2010.

[29] http://pubsites.uws.edu.au/ndco/employment/employer/information/myths_stereotypes.htm

ductivity rate than other workers; and have an average or better job retention rate[30]. In 1990, DuPont conducted a survey of 811 employees with disabilities and found 90 per cent rated average or better in job performance compared to 95 per cent for employees without disabilities. The Job Accommodation Network reported that accommodations, (1) allowed employers to retain a qualified employee, (2) increased the worker's productivity and (3) eliminated the costs of training a new employee.[31]

MYTH: Individuals with disabilities will have more work related injuries

FACT: A 1990 study by the E.I. DuPont Company that assessed the safety records of employees with disabilities found that 97 per cent rated average or above average in safety. Similarly, a Marriott International, Inc., study revealed that the 6 per cent of self-identified workers with disabilities had safety records that equalled or exceeded their non-disabled peers.[32] A research study conducted by Noel in 1990 demonstrated that disability has no measurable effect on workers compensation insurance premiums.[33] Many work related injuries are related to a poor job match. When accommodating individuals with disabilities one of the goals of an accommodation is properly matching capabilities and job demands. This will help to prevent future injuries.

1.7 — Defining Workplace Programs that Manage Disability

There are many distinct processes that must be understood when controlling the impacts of disability in the workplace.

1. Stay at Work Programs — This process involves the simple day-to-day management of impairments/injuries/illnesses as they occur at work. Every employer should have a process in place for

---

[30] *Ibid.*

[31] JAN, above note 28. *Ibid.*

[32] http://pubsites.uws.edu.au/ndco/employment/employer/information/myths_stereotypes.htm

[33] *Ibid.*

workers and their supervisors to manage an injury/illness as it occurs to shorten the length of time an individual is unable to perform work activities. This involves a simple worker and supervisor discussion to determine how to adjust the job in order to allow the employee to safely continue to work. E.g. an employee with back pain may ask to have lifting reduced during a shift. This can be reassigned and the employee continues to work on other tasks.

2. Return to Work Programs — This applies to an individual who has an injury or illness and requires time away from work. It may require a case management approach to assist the employee in working through the administrative/healthcare and insurance processes in order to return to their own work or to alternate work activities. This will involve not only the worker and supervisor but now includes benefits carriers/workers compensation, union, and the human resources professional to assist with return to work planning. E.g. an employee is off work for surgery or rehabilitation and a return to work plan must be developed to safely reintegrate then into the workplace temporarily or gradually.

3. Accommodation — This describes an individual who has a permanent disability and requires adjustment to the work, work processes, or work environment in order to reduce the gap between abilities and job demands. This may involve consideration of a duty to accommodate process. This will now include not only the stakeholders above but may include senior management, health and safety, legal advisors and specialists in accommodation. E.g. an employee who has permanent restrictions may require permanent changes to work or alternate work options.

All of these processes require an understanding of disability and may use the same tools but become more complex and involved the longer an employee is unable to perform their own work duties.

1.8 — Key Components of Effective Disability Management

The goal of Disability Management interventions is to protect the employability of workers with disabilities, regardless of the cause of their disability. Key components of successful Disability Management programs are:[34]

- *Stay at Work Process*: early intervention for individuals with symptoms or concerns prior to losing time from work is an important step in preventing long term disability issues;
- *Early intervention, early return to work values*: early considerate and genuine contact with workers with disabilities assists with monitoring the effectiveness of medical care & treatment received by the worker, allows for offering of appropriate modified work accommodations, prevents chronicity of injury/illness and identifies social, financial and personal factors which may impact recovery, and prevents worker from assuming a "sick role";
- *Prevention strategies*: focused on identification and elimination of work place hazards or factors that contribute to the occurrence of injury or illness;
- *Joint labour management collaboration and commitment*: management & labour working together to develop policies/procedures for Disability Management and actively support the program;
- *Multidisciplinary interventions*: involving medical, social, ergonomics to ensure that all issues that affect workers with disabilities are addressed;
- *Case management*: to co-ordinate medical, functional, psychosocial aspects of disability, which may occur following injury or illness;
- *Education of workers/management*: regular and ongoing education through workshops, sessions or written materials to promote the benefits of the Disability Management program;

---

[34] These concepts are supported in: D.E. Shrey. and Michel Lacerte, above, note 17, National Institute of Disability Management and Research (NIDMAR); Disability Management in the Workplace: A Guide to Establishing a Joint Workplace Program. Port Alberni, BC: 1995; R.L. Franche, et al. "Workplace-based return-to-work interventions: A systematic review of the quantitative literature" (2005) J Occup Rehabil.. Vol. 15(4) at 607–631; Dianne E. Dyck, *Disability Management: Theory, Strategy and Industry Practice, Second Edition*. (2002, Butterworths Canada).

- *Access and utilization of employer and community based resources*: to promote wellness and recovery;
- *Policies and procedures to support accommodation and modified work*: written policies developed with labour management input and which comply with legislative mandates;
- *Formal process/system to ensure accountability of all involved*: step by step process to follow from onset of injury or illness to return to work or recovery, with roles of all involved clearly defined;
- *Information management system/program evaluation*: data management process, computer based where possible that tracks all experience with injury, illness, and disability and associated costs and return to work outcomes.

a) — Best Practices for Managing Disability

Many studies have been done in the last twenty years about how to manage disability in the workplace and the key components of a disability management program. A comprehensive research literature review completed by the Institute for Work & Health,[35] addressed what workplace based return to work interventions are effective. Overall, the literature review found that workplace-based return-to-work interventions have a positive impact on duration and costs of work disability. Out of this research the Seven "Principles" of Successful Return to Work, were developed. Tailoring and implementing these evidence-based strategies for successful return to work into your workplace takes collaboration. There is a need to educate appropriate workplace parties, and create the confidence in this complex process in order to maximize the Return to Work (RTW) outcomes.

The following seven key principles in workplace disability management were produced from this literature review:[36]

- The employer makes an early and considerate contact with the injured/ill worker;

[35] E. MacEachen J. Clarke, R.L. Franche & E. Irvin, "The process of return to work after injury: findings of a systematic review of qualitative studies." (2006) Scandinavian Journal of Work, Environmental & Health, 32(4) at 257–269.

[36] *Ibid.*

- With the worker's consent, employers and health care providers communicate with each other about workplace demands, as needed;
- Someone has the responsibility to coordinate RTW;
- The employer makes an offer of modified work (also known as work accommodation) to injured/ill workers so they can return early and safely to work activities suitable to their abilities;
- RTW planners ensure that the plan supports the returning worker without disadvantaging co-workers and supervisors;
- The workplace has a strong commitment to health and safety which is demonstrated by the behaviours of the workplace parties;
- Supervisors are trained in work disability prevention and included in RTW planning.

The chapters in this book will examine the management of disability throughout the employment life cycle. Each chapter will provide you with a rationale, principles, with steps to implement change, and tools so that you can develop a comprehensive disability management program in your workplace.

1.9 — Levels of Disability Management

Every disability management process involves three layers that must be considered in order to be legally compliant and successful in implementing return to work.

MEGA Level: This is the overarching layer of legal statutes that guide disability management to which every organization within the jurisdiction must adhere. For example it includes the laws and society codes i.e. Health and Safety Acts, Employment Standards, Human Rights Codes, Workers Compensation Acts, etc.

MACRO Level: This layer is company specific but allows the company to provide consistent and fair processes to all employees with disabilities i.e. benefit programs, collective agreements, policies and procedures, etc. These policies and programs must be legally compliant with the Mega Level.

MICRO Level: This is the individualized level of disability management. Every return to work initiative must be individualized according to the individuals' abilities, restrictions, job demands, skills and work environment.

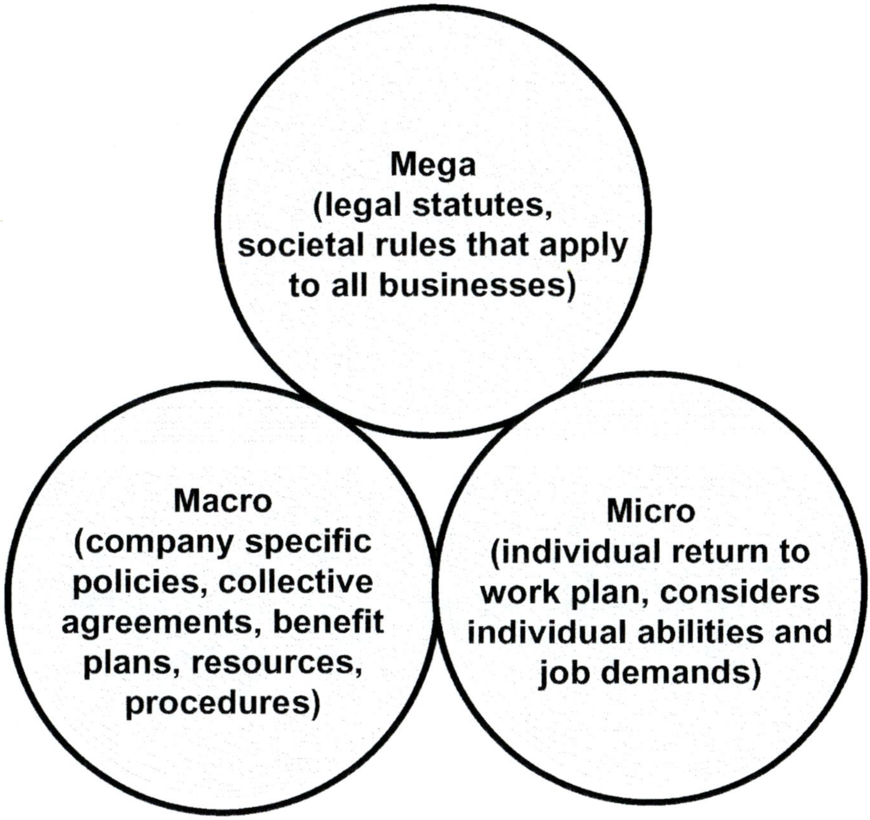

Disability Management Processes in the workplace can be effective in managing the individual, organizational and societal impacts of disabilities in Canada. This book will help the human resources professional understand the various components and tools that will make these issues manageable. Successful programs are those that will manage each component in a structured way but also ensure that the employability of the individual worker is protected through sound accommodation principles.

CHAPTER 2: LEGAL ISSUES ACROSS CANADA

LEGAL ISSUES SURROUNDING MANAGEMENT OF DISABILITY IN THE WORKPLACE

2.1 — Employment and Disability Legislation and Regulations

There is key legislation that guides and regulates the employment of persons with disabilities. In planning for a disability management program the human resources professional must have general knowledge of all international, national/federal and provincial employment and disability legislation.

a) — International Legislation: Bill of Human Rights and Declaration of Disabled Persons

The Declaration of the Rights of Disabled Persons[1] (United Nations 1948) defines a person's right to employment, right to equal pay for equal work, the right to just and favourable remuneration and social protection and the right to form or join trade unions. It also defines the rights of disabled persons — right to measures that encourage self-reliance; right to treatment, rehabilitation, counselling, placement and other services to promote integration into the community and work environment; the right to employment and the right to have special needs taken into consideration.

---

1 United Nations http://www.un.org/en/documents/udhr/ United Nations, Declaration of the Rights of Disabled Persons, proclaimed by General Assembly resolution 3447 (XXX) of 9 December 1975.

b) — National Legislation: The Canadian Charter of Rights and Freedoms and Human Rights Legislation

Canada supports international covenants and agreements that support and protect human rights, including the rights of persons with disabilities. The *Canadian Charter of Rights and Freedoms*[2] expresses the values of Canadians and sets the agenda from which the government determines policy and legislation. The two sections that deal with the rights of persons with disabilities are sections 15(1) and 15(2). Human Rights legislation at the federal and provincial level pre-dated the Charter of Rights and reflected the principles that were laid out in Canada's first Bill of Rights.

c) — Human Rights

The Canadian *Human Rights Act*[3] protects persons with disabilities from discrimination in employment. The Act applies to those organizations under federal jurisdiction such as federal departments, agencies and Crown corporations. The Act was passed in 1977 with further amendments added in both 1985 and 1992. (1985: clause added prohibiting discrimination against people with disabilities; 1992: reasonable accommodation and undue hardship clauses added).

Provincial Human Rights legislation are moral laws put in place to protect individuals who may otherwise be discriminated against and not provided fair and equal treatment in employment. Under the human rights acts there are protected areas for which the act applies i.e. in Ontario the protected areas include race, ancestry, place of origin, colour, ethnic origin, citizenship, creed, sex, sexual orientation, age, marital status, family status, disability or the receipt of public assistance. Employers have a duty to provide reasonable accommodation to disabled workers.

2. (1) Every person has a right to equal treatment with respect to the occupancy of accommodation, without discrimination because of race, ancestry, place of origin, colour, ethnic origin, citizenship,

---

2 Canadian *Charter of Rights and Freedoms* R.S.C. 1985, App. II, No. 44 En. Canada Act 1982 (U.K.), c. 11.

3 Canadian *Human Rights Act*, R.S.C. 1985, c. H-6.

creed, sex, sexual orientation, age, marital status, family status, disability or the receipt of public assistance.[4]

Generally all provincial human rights legislation includes a prohibited grounds for discrimination clause and a commission to deal with complaints and breaches of the code. The impact on the employer of the various human rights codes and the duty to accommodate will be discussed in detail in the following chapter.

For additional information on human rights acts within your jurisdiction visit:

Province	**Website**
Alberta	http://www.albertahumanrights.ab.ca/
British Columbia	http://www.bclaws.ca/EPLibraries/bclaws_new/document/ID/freeside/00_96210_01
Manitoba	http://www.gov.mb.ca/hrc
Nova Scotia	http://gov.ns.ca/humanrights
New Brunswick	http://www.gnb.ca/hrc-cdp/
Newfoundland and Labrador	http://www.justice.gov.nl.ca/hrc/
North West Territories	http://www.nwthumanrights.ca/
Nunavut	http://www.canlii.com/en/nu/laws/stat/snu-2003-c-12/latest/ snu-2003-c-12.html#history
Ontario	http://www.ohrc.on.ca
Prince Edward Island	http://www.gov.pe.ca/humanrights/
Quebec	http://www2.cdpdj.qc.ca/en/pages/Default.aspx
Saskatchewan	http://www.shrc.gov.sk.ca/
Yukon	http://www.yhrc.yk.ca/
Federal	http://www.chrc-ccdp.ca

4 *Ibid.*

d) — Worker's Compensation

Workers' compensation is a no-fault social insurance program administered provincially by independent boards. The disabling injury or illness must be work-related. It protects the employee from a legal suit for the injury. It protects both workers and their dependants by providing compensation and other benefits to workers and/or survivors of deceased workers. One of the other key functions is to promote health and safety in workplaces with the goal of preventing illness and injury and to facilitate the return to work process and worker recovery. Other services include payment of health care costs, rehabilitation services and vocational rehabilitation. Services can differ from province to province. Each province will have a specific law and regulations that must be followed. To find out more about your provincial laws and regulations visit the following websites:

Province	Website
Alberta	www.wcb.ab.ca
British Columbia	www.worksafebc.com
Manitoba	www.wcb.mb.ca
Nova Scotia	www.wcb.ns.ca
New Brunswick	www.worksafenb.ca
Newfoundland	www.whscc.nf.ca
North West Territories	www.wcb.nt.ca
Nunavut	www.wcb.nt.ca
Ontario	www.wsib.on.ca
Prince Edward Island	www.wcb.pe.ca
Quebec	www.csst.qc.ca
Saskatchewan	www.wcbsask.com
Yukon	www.wcb.yk.ca

e) — Provincial Occupational Health and Safety Acts

The Occupational Health and Safety Acts apply to all organizations provincially regulated and operating in that province or territory. It covers health and safety regulations that must be followed by all employers. The main premise of the legislation is that the employer takes "every reasonable precaution to ensure the safety of its employees". To find out more about the health and safety legislation in each jurisdiction review the following:

Province	**Act**	**Website**
Alberta	*Occupational Health and Safety Act*	http://www.qp.alberta.ca/570.cfm?frm_isbn=0779749200&search_by=link
British Columbia	*Workers Compensation Act* (Regulations under WCB Act)	http://www.bclaws.ca/EPLibraries/bclaws_new/content?xsl=/templates/toc.xsl/group=W/lastsearch=/
Manitoba	*The Workplace Health and Safety Act*	http://web2.gov.mb.ca/laws/statutes/index.php
Nova Scotia	*The Occupational health and Safety Act*	http://www.gov.ns.ca/legislature/legc/statutes/occph_s.htm
New Brunswick	*The Occupational Health and Safety Act*	http://www.gnb.ca/0062/acts/acts-e.asp#GlossO
Newfoundland and Labrador	*The Occupational Health and Safety Act*	http://www.assembly.nl.ca/egislation/sr/statutes/o03.htm
North West Territories	*The Safety Act*	http://www.justice.gov.nt.ca/Legislation/SearchResults.asp?Option=Title &DBTable=LegReg&Parameter=S&Page=1
Nunavut	*The Safety Act*	http://www.gov.nu.ca/hr/site/healthsafety.htm
Ontario	The Occupational Health and Safety	http://www.e-laws.gov.on.ca/html/statutes/english/elaws_statutes_90o01_e.htm

Province	Act	Website
Prince Edward Island	*The Occupational Health and Safety Act*	http://www.gov.pe.ca/law/index.php3
Quebec	*The Act respecting Occupational health and Safety*	http://www2.publicationsduquebec.gouv.qc.ca/dynamicSearch/ telecharge.php?type=2&file=%2F%2FS_2_1%2FS2_1_A.htm
Saskatchewan	*The Occupational Health and Safety Act, 1993*	http://www.qp.gov.sk.ca/
Yukon	*The Occupational Health and Safety Act*	http://www.gov.yk.ca/legislation/
Federal	Canada *Labour Code* (Part II — Occupational Health and Safety) *Government Employees Compensation Act* (see Accident prevention activities and safety program)	http://laws.justice.gc.ca/en/index.html

f) — Canada *Labour Code*[5]

The Canada *Labour Code* applies to federal organizations such as federal departments, agencies and Crown corporations. Part II covers health and safety legislation. Part III covers minimum employment standards intended to ensure fair and equitable conditions of employment such as minimum wage, hours of work and overtime, equal pay,

5 R.S.C. 1985, c. L-2.

weekly rest days, vacation, stats, leave of absences and termination of employment. It sets out standards that include provisions requiring employers to retain jobs for workers who are absent from work due to injury or illness.

g) — Employment Standards Act[6]

This legislation is administered provincially and covers most workers and employers with the exception of those workplaces governed by federal jurisdiction such as transportation, postal services and other crown corporations. This legislation ensures fundamental rights of workers are not threatened. It governs such items as hours of work, minimum wage, annual vacations, statutory holidays, maternity/childcare, sick/bereavement leave, emergency leave, severance, garnishment and protection from dismissals and layoffs.

h) — Employment Equity Act[7]

This legislation was passed to address the unequal representation of workers and to ensure that there is adequate representation for those persons who may be subject to discrimination at the workplace. It is designed to remove barriers to employment by applying a concept of reasonable accommodation. It applies to employers and Crown corporations with 100 or more workers who are regulated under Canada *Labour Code*. Provincially, this is addressed in the *Employment Standards Act*.

i) — Accessibility for Ontarians with Disabilities Act, 2005[8]

This legislation governs all businesses operating and providing goods and services within Ontario. The purpose of the legislation is to reduce barriers within the organization for individuals with disabilities to access goods and services. There are five areas of accessibility: customer service, transportation, information and communication, employment and the built environment. Businesses within Ontario will need to consider these standards and comply according to each regulation. The first regulation that has been passed is the

---

6 http://www.hrsdc.gc.ca/eng/labour/employment_standards/index.shtml

7 S.C. 1995, c. 44.

8 S.O. 2005, c. 11.

Accessible Customer Service Regulation 429/07. All public organizations were required to comply by January 1, 2010 and all private organizations must comply by January 1, 2012.

In other provinces there is not specific accessibility legislation but it is expected that the AODA may be mirrored in future legislation across Canada.

This book does not intend to be a comprehensive legal guide to every applicable piece of legislation and it is important for the human resources professional to understand the legislation that guides the business. The legislation will vary according to the organization and the nature of its business. There are other specific legislations that may impact disability management in organizations such as the transport of dangerous goods, food handling, policing and emergency services, health care and operations in various provinces and countries.

The following chapters will examine some of the most significant legal issues that impact the employer when managing disability in the workplace.

2.2 — Benefit and Compensation Systems Related to Managing Disability

Canada has a complex policy and program framework to fund and to support individuals with disabilities. Many of the government programs involve a partnership between federal and provincial departments. These programs offer employers and persons with disabilities, who meet the eligibility requirements, support in terms of income replacement and other supportive programs and services. It is important for the human resources professional to have a good understanding of these programs to be able to provide explanations to injured/ill workers and their dependants and facilitate the process for workers to apply for benefits to which they are entitled.

There are also private benefits schemes that support individuals with non-compensable illness and/or injuries who cannot attend work or who cannot perform their essential duties. It is important that the Human Resources Professional understand the organization's benefits plans and how they interrelate.

a) — Worker's Compensation

Workers' compensation is a no-fault, government insurance program administered provincially by independent boards. Approximately 80 per cent of workers across Canada are covered by workers' compensation insurance. It provides "no fault" insurance protecting the employer from potential law suits. Workers' compensation is funded through premiums paid by employers and compensation levels are calculated as a percentage of net earnings and benefits are tax-free. Services and earnings differ from province to province. If an employer has employees in various provinces they must follow the workers' compensation policies in the province in which the employee works. Therefore it is important to understand each of the province's processes and obligations.

The employer is obliged to report a work-related injury to WCB by completing the appropriate "Employer's Report of Injury" form. The worker also has a responsibility to seek medical attention from their treating practitioner, to participate in the recommended treatment and to participate in the return to work process. The employer pays premiums or direct costs of the claims. Most of the province's programs incentivize early and safe return to work after an injury and therefore it is important to not only prevent an injury but also to offer suitable return to work options early in the process.

b) — Employment Insurance Sickness Benefits[9]

Employment Insurance Sickness Benefits covers those persons with non-compensable illness or injury. An individual must have paid into EI through payroll tax. To be eligible, the worker must be incapable of work through illness, injury or quarantine and have worked a specific amount of hours in the last 52 work weeks or since the last EI claim. The period which the individual can collect will vary depending on the reason for need, i.e. illness or loss of employment. There also exists a maximum benefit per week based on earnings. Other services provided include job training, career counselling and vocational rehabilitation services. Some employers ask employees to use this benefit instead of having coverage for weekly indemnity or short term disability.

---

9 http://www.servicecanada.gc.ca/eng/sc/ei/benefits/sickness.shtml

c) — Canada Pension Plan (CPP)[10]

This benefit has strict eligibility requirements. The disabling condition must be considered "severe and prolonged" and can be either physical or mental. "Severe" is defined by the plan to mean that the condition has prevented a person from engaging in work at any job. "Prolonged" is defined as a long-term condition or one that could result in death. To be eligible a person must contribute to the plan four out of the last six years, be under the age of 65 and submit a written application. Payments are based on the worker's income and contributions made through payroll deduction. CPP allows persons to earn small amounts of money without being disqualified but must be "regularly incapable of substantially gainful employment". CPP also offers vocational rehabilitation services (case management and career counselling) and workers can collect benefits for up to three months while trying a return to work plan.

d) — Disability Tax Credit and Medical Expenses Tax Credit[11]

The Disability Tax Credit and Medical Expenses Tax Credit support persons with disabilities by providing tax relief for persons with disabilities. This government program reduces the amount of tax paid and is available to persons with disabilities that are considered severe and prolonged. The disablement, which can be either physical or mental, must be for a minimum period of 12 months. Employers can also apply for tax relief for workplace accommodations made for persons with disabilities.

e) — Employment Assistance for Persons with Disabilities (EAPD)[12]

The Employment Assistance for Persons with Disabilities (EAPD) was established by Human Resources Services and Development Canada with the goal of increasing employment for persons with disabilities and supporting persons with disabilities in the workplace.

---

[10] C.R.C. 1978, c. 385.

[11] http://www.cra-arc.gc.ca/disability/

[12] http://www.servicecanada.gc.ca/eng/epb/sid/cia/grants/ead/desc_eapd.shtml

Each province has their own program but generally have the following types of services — career counselling, provision of assistive technology to persons in vocational crisis, assistive services in sign-language and interpreters, training/education, assessment and job placement services.

f) — Opportunities Fund[13]

The Opportunities fund is operated by Human Resource Services and Development Canada (HRSDC) and is designed to help private and public sector organizations, including disability organizations to assist people with disabilities who do not qualify for Employment Insurance benefits. Eligible activities include encouraging employers to hire persons with disabilities; help persons with disabilities start businesses, employment skill training, and personal supports.

g) — Social Assistance[14]

Social assistance is a "needs" based benefit designed to support persons with little or no income. Rules differ from province to province. If persons are collecting CPP, EI or WCB benefits — this would be deducted from social assistance amount.

h) — Short Term Disability (STD) and Long Term Disability (LTD)

Both short-term disability (STD) and long-term disability (LTD) plans are private insurance plans that are purchased by organizations for their workers. They provide income replacement for non-compensable illness/injury. Each organization has their own policy for these programs and some may have chosen not to have these programs supplied to their employees. It is important for the human resources professional to review the organization specific policy to understand the coverage and procedures for STD or LTD.

STD coverage comes in a variety of formats ranging from weekly indemnity (accumulated sick leave plan), to either a percentage or full income replacement for all non-occupational related illness and or injuries. Eligibility requirements can vary with each plan; how-

[13] http://www.hrsdc.gc.ca/eng/disability_issues/funding_programs/opportunities_fund/index.shtml

[14] http://www.canadabenefits.gc.ca/f.1.2ch.4m.2@.jsp?lang=eng

ever, generally, the worker must be incapable of either 100 per cent of their job or cannot perform the essential duties of their job.

LTD provides benefits to workers who are disabled and who meet the eligibility requirements and have exhausted the elimination period (generally 26–52 weeks). Generally, LTD plans pay 60–70 per cent of wages, depending on the plan. With policies which have an own occupation/any occupation definition change, following a two-year period, a person must be deemed incapable of any occupation for which they are "reasonably qualified". In most situations, LTD programs are administered by outside carriers. STD can be self administered or administered by an outside party. The use of third party administration services is a popular method to allow employers to have these delicate decisions about benefits managed outside of the organization.

i) — Auto Insurance

All provinces except Newfoundland have compulsory auto insurance plans that provide certain benefits to people based on a no fault insurance scheme. Benefits range from rehabilitation cost to income replacement and coverage of expenses varies from province to province. Quebec and Manitoba have pure no-fault insurance — benefits come from the employee's own insurer and individuals cannot sue. Ontario has threshold-no-fault insurance which means that an individual cannot sue unless a threshold definition is met. All other provinces have tort systems, which allow an individual to collect benefits and to be able to sue another person. To find out more on the Auto insurance program in Ontario log onto www.fsco.on.ca (Financial Services Commission of Ontario). For the human resources professional, it is important to understand the role of the auto insurance program in your province and how you will work with the auto insurance carrier in managing return to work and benefits. In Ontario the legislation indicates that the employer's benefit program pays first prior to use of the auto insurance funds but in many cases auto insurers will have the ability to fund rehabilitation and ergonomic equipment to support return to work.

j) — Canada Revenue Agency[15]

Under the *Income Tax Act*, 20(1)(qq) and 20(1)(rr), the Federal government allows businesses/commercial building owners to deduct the amount they paid during the taxation year to make renovations or alterations to a building that enables individuals who have a mobility impairment gain access to the building or to be mobile within it.

Businesses are also allowed to deduct prescribed disability-related devices or equipment, such as:

- elevator car position indicator, such as a Braille panel or an audio signal for individuals having a visual impairment;
- visual fire alarm, listening device for group meetings or telephone devices for individuals who have a hearing impairment.

For further information, contact Canada Revenue Agency:

Tel: 1-800-959-5525

Website: www.cra-arc.gc.ca/menu.html

k) — Industry Canada[16]

Industry Canada's FedNor program provides funding for programs and services which bring economic benefit to northern and rural Ontario communities. FedNor delivers funding through three key initiatives:

- Northern Ontario Development Fund;
- Community Futures Program; and
- The Eastern Ontario Development Fund.

For more information and office locations, visit FedNor's website at http://strategis.ic.gc.ca/epic/internet/infednor-fednor.nsf/en/Home

l) — Collective Agreements

In unionized environments each union will have a separate and distinct collective agreement. Many collective agreements will include the benefits available to ill or injured employees. Some collective agreements will include sections on rehabilitation and return to work

---

[15] S.C. 1999, c. 17.

[16] http://www.ic.gc.ca/eic/site/ic1.nsf/eng/h_00140.html

which will guide your management of disability with unionized employees. More unions are becoming involved in the return to work process and the research supports the involvement of unions in the development and implementation of any disability management program.

2.3 — Application of Policy and Legislation in Arriving at Decisions

The Human Resources Professional must stress to their employees that decisions surrounding benefit payment and entitlement decisions are based on policy, law and the consideration of the related objective information (medical, history, applicability) available to the adjudicator. It should be stressed that the employer does not have any part in entitlement decisions. It is recommended that any internal adjudication processes be outsourced to a third party administrator to avoid conflict of interest issues in the workplace with benefits decisions.

CHAPTER 3: HUMAN RIGHTS AND YOUR DUTY TO ACCOMMODATE

3.1 — Human Rights Legislation

When accommodating an individual with a disability the human resources professional will need to understand the federal or provincial human rights codes. This portion of the book will provide an overview of the human rights legislation and case law which has developed with respect to this legislation.

When a human resources professional is developing hiring, promotion, termination and return-to-work policies this legislation prevails over all other legislation. The employer has an obligation to ensure that there is no discrimination, either inherently or blatantly, in any policies or procedures for employment.

For organizations that are federally regulated the *Canadian Human Rights Code* applies whereas those that are provincially regulated must be guided by the applicable provincial human rights codes. The main principles of human rights apply across jurisdictions in Canada and therefore case law from all jurisdictions should be reviewed. This chapter will review the main principles of the human rights legislation and duty to accommodate.

Human resources professionals should develop a systematic approach to managing disability in the workplace to address the duty to accommodate and to ensure that policies and procedures in the workplace do not discriminate against employees with disabilities.

3.2 — *Canadian Human Rights Code*

The *Canadian Human Rights Act* provides that the special needs of a person relating to a prohibited ground of discrimination must be accommodated unless the employer or service provider can prove that to do so would be an undue hardship.

Section 2 underlines the importance of this principle by incorporating the duty of accommodation directly into the Purpose section of the Act. It states:

> The purpose of this Act is to extend the laws in Canada to give effect, within the purview of matters coming within the legislative authority of Parliament, to the principle that all individuals should have an opportunity equal with other individuals to make for themselves the lives that they are able and wish to have and to have their needs accommodated, consistent with their duties and obligations as members of society, without being hindered in or prevented from doing so by discriminatory practices based on race, national or ethnic origin, colour, religion, age, sex, sexual orientation, marital status, family status, disability or conviction for an offence for which a pardon has been granted.[1]

A person who is denied accommodation can file a complaint with the Canadian Human Rights Commission. Complaints can be made in relation to any aspect of employment, including pre-employment testing, the working environment, training and promotions.

> 7. Employment[2] — It is a discriminatory practice, directly or indirectly,
>
> (a) to refuse to employ or continue to employ any individual, or
>
> (b) in the course of employment, to differentiate adversely in relation to an employee,
>
> on a prohibited ground of discrimination.
>
> 8. Employment applications, advertisements[3] — It is a discriminatory practice
>
> (a) to use or circulate any form of application for employment, or
>
> (b) in connection with employment or prospective employment, to publish any advertisement or to make any written or oral inquiry
>
> that expresses or implies any limitation, specification or preference based on a prohibited ground of discrimination.

Protection against discrimination is particularly important in cases where an employee has a medical condition/disability and is planning a return to work. Research has shown that many of the complaints filed with the CHRC arise from these situations. In return-to-work cases, disability is the ground most likely to be at issue.

The following sections of the CHRC indicate what is considered discriminatory practice in the employment realm. It is important to

---

1 Canadian *Human Rights Act*, R.S.C. 1985, c. H-6.

2 Canadian *Human Rights Act* R.S.C. 1985, c. H-6, c. 33, s. 7.

3 Canadian *Human Rights Act* R.S.C. 1985, c. H-6, c. 33, s. 8. Canadian Human Rights Commission (2000). Bona Fide Occupational Requirements and Bona Fide Justifications under the *Human Rights Act*. Ottawa.

note that beyond the CHRC there is case law that will be considered as to whether discrimination has occurred and whether the employer has offered reasonable accommodation. This case law will be outlined in this chapter.

3.3 — Ontario *Human Rights Code, 1990*

Provincially regulated employers will be guided by the provincial legislation. The premises of the Human Rights Acts in the various provinces are the same and therefore this section will take the Ontario *Human Rights Code* as an example. It is important for the human resources professional to review the specific provincial human rights act and the definitions included in that Act.

The *Human Rights Code* has primacy over other Acts as described in Section 47(2):[4]

> Where a provision of an Act or regulation purports to require or authorize conduct that is a contravention of Part I, this Act applies and prevails unless the Act or regulation specifically provides that it is to apply despite this Act.

The *Human Rights Code* provides that every person has a right to equal treatment with respect to employment without discrimination because of protected grounds, including, disability.

Disability is defined in the *Ontario Human Rights Code* as follows in Section 10(1):[5]

- *Any degree of physical disability, infirmity, malformation or disfigurement that is caused by bodily injury, birth defect, or illness and, without limiting the generality of the foregoing, including diabetes mellitus, epilepsy, any degree of paralysis, amputation, lack of physical coordination, blindness, or visual impediment, deafness or hearing impediment, or physical reliance on a guide dog, or on a wheelchair or other remedial appliance or device*;
- *A condition of mental retardation or impairment*;
- *A learning disability, or a dysfunction in on or more of the processes involved in understanding or using symbols or spoken language*;

---

4 Ontario *Human Rights Code*, R.S.O. 1990, c. H.19, s. 47(2).

5 Ontario *Human Rights Code*, R.S.O. 1990, c. H.19, s. 10(1).

- *A mental disorder*;
- *An injury or disability for which benefits were claimed or received under the insurance plan established under the* Workplace Safety and Insurance Act, 1997 .

Accommodation and undue hardship are defined in Section 17(2) of the Ontario *Human Rights Code*:[6]

> The Commission, a board of inquiry or a court shall not find a person incapable unless it is satisfied that the needs of the person cannot be accommodated without undue hardship on the person responsible for accommodating those needs, considering the cost, outside sources of funding, if any, and health and safety requirements, if any.

An employer who decides not to hire an individual due to his/her disability or decides to terminate an employee for lack of performance or absenteeism could, in certain cases, create a violation of the *Human Rights Code* and this could lead to a human rights complaint or grievance under a collective agreement where the employee seeks reinstatement.

The *Human Rights Code* applies throughout the employment life cycle. The existence of the human rights legislation does not, however result in an eradication of the employment contract. The right of the employer to receive its part of the employment bargain, namely, the employee's performance of his or her work is inherent in the employment contract. However, the right to terminate or end the employment contract will be subject to the right of the individual to be free from discrimination as required in the *Human Rights Code*.

Even where discipline and even termination is based on a prohibited grounds under the *Human Rights code* (i.e. disability), the employer may defend its decision by establishing that the employment essential duties and attendance rules are *bona fide* and reasonable and that the employer has attempted to accommodate the needs of the employee to the point of *undue hardship*.

The Human Rights Commission (Ontario) Policy and Guidelines on Disability and the Duty to Accommodate indicate that the duty to accommodate holds tripartite responsibilities.[7]

---

6 Ontario *Human Rights Code*, R.S.O. 1990, c. H.19, s. 17(2).

7 Ontario Human Rights Commission. Policy And Guidelines On Disability And The Duty To Accommodate. Toronto, ON: The Commission; 23 Nov 2000. Available from:

The **person with a disability** is required to:

- Advise the accommodation provider of the disability;
- Make her or his needs known to the best of his or her ability, preferably in writing, in order that the person responsible for accommodation may make the requested accommodation;
- Answer questions or provide information regarding relevant restrictions or limitations, including information from health care professionals, where appropriate, and as needed;
- Participate in discussions regarding possible accommodation solutions;
- Co-operate with any experts whose assistance is required to manage the accommodation process or when information is required that is unavailable to the person with a disability;
- Meet agreed-upon performance and job standards once accommodation is provided;
- Work with the accommodation provider on an ongoing basis to manage the accommodation process; and
- Discuss his or her disability only with persons who need to know. This may include the supervisor, a union representative or human rights staff.

The **employer** is required to:

- Accept the employee's request for accommodation in good faith, unless there are legitimate reasons for acting otherwise;
- Obtain expert opinion or advice where needed;
- Take an active role in ensuring that alternative approaches and possible accommodation solutions are investigated, and canvass various forms of possible accommodation and alternative solutions, as part of the duty to accommodate;

---

http://www.ohrc.on.ca/en/resources/Policies/PolicyDisAccom2/pdf. Accessed: 2008 Sep 16.

- Keep a record of the accommodation request and action taken;
- Maintain confidentiality;
- Limit requests for information to those reasonably related to the nature of the limitation or restriction so as to be able to respond to the accommodation request;
- Grant accommodation requests in a timely manner, to the point of undue hardship, even when the request for accommodation does not use any specific formal language; and
- Bear the cost of any required medical information or documentation. The employer should pay for example, doctors' notes and letters setting out accommodation needs.
- Take an active role as partners in the accommodation process;
- Share joint responsibility with the employer to facilitate accommodation; and
- Support accommodation measures irrespective of collective agreements, unless to do so would create undue hardship.

Unions and professional associations are required to:

- Take an active role as partners in the accommodation process;
- Share joint responsibility with the employer to facilitate accommodation; and
- Support accommodation measures irrespective of collective agreements, unless to do so would create *undue hardship*.

3.4 — Satisfying the Duty to Accommodate to Undue Hardship

The concept of Duty to Accommodate has become more prevalent and better defined in the past few years as arbitrators and the Supreme Courts have attempted to define the Duty in more practical terms. The duty to accommodate applies to all of the employment life cycle from the application process to termination or retirement. It is important to understand the application of this concept in each area of employment.

The general rule is easy: *The duty to accommodate involves investigating whether existing positions can be adjusted, adapted, or modified for the employee or whether there are any other positions in the workplace that might be suitable for the employee.*

The employer has the responsibility to look at ALL reasonable accommodations.

1. Determine if the employee can perform his/her existing job as it is.
2. If the employee cannot, then determine if he/she can perform his/her existing job in a modified or re-bundled form.
3. If the employee cannot, then determine if he/she can perform any other job in its existing form.
4. If the employee cannot, then determine if he/she can perform another job in a modified or re-bundled form.
5. Determine if modifications or adjustments constitute "undue hardship."

In all situations the employer must make a "good faith" effort to accommodate the individual within the workplace.[8]

The most meaningful and now considered a prominent document in considering accommodation is the decision reached by the Supreme Court of Canada referred to as the "Meiorin Case" or *The Public Service Employee Relations Commission v. BCGSEU* (1999). This case defines the process expected for an employer when determining if there has been discrimination. The employer must ask a series of questions when considering employee accommodation:[9]

1. Have alternative approaches been investigated that do not have a discriminatory effect, such as individual testing?
2. If alternative standards have been investigated and found to be capable of fulfilling the employer's purpose, why have they not been implemented?
3. Is it necessary to have all employees meet the single standard for the employer to meet its legitimate purpose? As well, could

---

8 *Miele v. Famous Players Inc.* (2000), 37 C.H.R.R. D/1 (B.C. Human Rights Trib.)

9 *British Columbia (Public Serv ice Employee Relations Commission) v. BCGSEU*, [1999] 3 S.C.R. 3, Sept. 9, 1999.

standards reflective of the group or individual differences and capabilities be established?

4. Is there any way to do the job that is less discriminatory while still accomplishing the employer's business objectives?

5. Is the standard properly designed to ensure that the desired qualifications are met without placing an undue burden on those to whom the standard applies?

6. Have other parties in the workplace — the union and the individual employee seeking accommodation- fully assisted in the search for the solution?

When the Supreme Court of Canada released the *Meiorin* decision in the 1990s there was a fear that the pendulum had swung too far towards employee rights and promised to change the way that employers would be held accountable for accommodation.

On June 27, 2008 the Supreme Court of Canada handed down its decision in the landmark case of *Keays v. Honda Canada Inc.*[10] In this case a wrongfully dismissed employee who suffered from chronic fatigue syndrome was awarded a record $500,000 in punitive damages by an Ontario Superior Court judge, an amount later reduced to $100,000 by the Court of Appeal. On appeal, the Supreme Court overturned the lower court's award of aggravated (Wallace-type) and punitive damages and indicated that the employer does indeed have a right to manage employee accommodation and attendance.

Lower courts and levels of the judicial decision making seemed to follow that lead with the publication of the courts decisions in *Keays v. Honda Canada Inc.* Employers wondered if they had rights to question the medical community and ask employees to be in attendance at independent medical examination. The Supreme Court of Canada in *Keays v. Honda Canada Inc.* seemed to finally balance this fear and acknowledge that the employer does have a right to have information in order to accommodate. They continued to emphasize the importance of the employer's communication with the employee throughout the process and the duty to accommodate.

[10] *Keays v. Honda Canada Inc.*, 2008 SCC 39 (S.C.C.). http://scc.lexum.umontreal.ca/en/2008/2008scc39/2008scc39.html

a) — What is Undue Hardship?

The Supreme Court of Canada in *Central Alberta Dairy Pool* (1990)[11] and *Renaud* (1992)[12] laid out important factors to be considered in what might constitute undue hardship. More recent accommodation decisions have commented on the strength of each of the factors.

Undue hardship under the Ontario *Human Rights Code* is based on three factors: costs, outside sources of funding and health and safety considerations. These others factors have been considered in more recent case law:[13]

- Financial hardship — if the financial hardship will effect the long term viability of the company;
- Impact on collective agreement — only when no other accommodation is possible should a proposal that would interfere with collective agreement rights be adopted;
- Problems with employee morale — not given strong weighting — applied with caution
- Interchangeability of the work force and facilities — usually linked to size of the operation but looks for flexibility of operations, schedules, and work assignments, re-bundling of workload;
- Size of the employer's operations — the larger the operation the more likely that accommodation would not pose undue hardship;
- Health and safety — safety of other workers is given more strength than safety of the employee himself. The employee may understand and accept a small amount of risk within the legal bounds of the law. The employer will require substantial evidence to prove that the accommodations will effect others safety.

---

[11] *Central Alberta Dairy Pool v. Alberta (Human Rights Commission)*, [1990] 2 S.C.R. 489 (S.C.C.)

[12] The Supreme Court of Canada's decision in *Renaud v. Central Okanagan School District No. 23*, [1992] 2 S.C.R. 970 (S.C.C.) [hereinafter "Renaud"] sets out the obligations of unions.

[13] Canadian Human Rights Commission (2000). Bona Fide Occupational Requirements and Bona Fide Justifications under the *Human Rights Act*. Ottawa.

In *Renaud*, the Court dismissed the claim of undue hardship and stated that "More than mere negligible effort is required to satisfy the duty to accommodate. The use of the term 'undue' infers that some hardship is acceptable; it is only 'undue' hardship that satisfies the test . . . Minor interference or inconvenience is the price to be paid for equal treatment in society.

Several decisions *Calgary District Hospital Group* (1995), *Greater Niagara General Hospital* (1995), *Canada Safeway* (1998), and *York County Hospital* (1992) all dealt with employer's not providing sufficient exploration of reconfiguring jobs, retraining the employee, introducing job aids or searching for productive alternative duties.[14]

Employees who seek accommodation of their disability have an obligation to be forthcoming in terms of providing information to their employer. Once the employee has established that he has a mental or physical disability that requires accommodation, the burden then shifts to the employer to prove that every reasonable effort was made to accommodate.

The foundation of the conclusions in all cases on accommodation is the interpretation of the evidence, which in turn depends to a great extent on the clarity and thoroughness with which the facts can be presented. Therefore, an essential part of dealing with human rights implications of disability management is to record discussions, meetings, phone calls and retain correspondence and other documents which provide concrete answers to a series of questions:

- What documentation on the accommodation needs and disability has been received?
- What steps have you taken and information gathered to determine the accommodation needs?
- Are any performance issues or absences due to "disability"?
- What are the limitations on the employee's performance or functions caused by the disability?

[14] *Calgary District Hospital Group v. UNA, Local 121-R* (1994), 41 L.A.C. (4th) 319 (Alt. Arb. Bd.), *Greater Niagara General Hospital v. ONA* (1995), 50 LAC (4th) 34 (Ont. Arb. Bd.), *Canada Safeway v. RWDSU, Local 454*, [1998] 1 S.C.R. 1079 (S.C.C.) and *York County Hospital v. ONA* (1992), 26 L.A.C. (4th) 384 (Ont. Arb. Bd.)

- What difficulties are created for the employer by those limitations or otherwise by the absences themselves?
- In what ways could the employee's job be modified to suit those limitations?
- What are the implications for the employer of each or all of the possible modifications in terms of cost, productivity, timeliness, quality, employee morale, contravention of the collective agreement, risk of re-injury, or recurrence for the employee, health/safety risks to others?
- If job modification is not possible or if it would pose an unreasonable burden on the employer, what other possibilities for accommodation exist?
- What will be the effect on the employer of such accommodation?
- What will be the effect on the employee of modifying the existing job or of implementing the other possibilities?
- If accommodation is impossible or unreasonable, and the employee continues to be absent are there alternatives to termination?
- What is the concrete advantage to the employer of termination as opposed to preservation of the status quo?

b) — Accommodation Attempts

Recent decisions in the Supreme Court has reviewed and broadened the extent of the duty:

- Accommodation measures must be taken unless no further accommodation is possible without imposing undue hardship.
- Employers and unions must be sensitive to the various ways that individual capabilities may be accommodated.
- Workplace standards that unintentionally distinguish among employees on a protected human rights ground may be struck down or modified. Employers must build liberal concepts of equality into the workplace.
- Courts, labour arbitrators and human rights tribunals are to take a strict approach to exemptions from the duty to accommodate. Ex-

emptions are to be permitted only where they are reasonably necessary to the achievement of legitimate business related objectives.

- The employer must not rely solely on the information provided by the Workers' compensation board, CPP or other outside third party carrier's medical reports to determine if accommodation is appropriate.
- The employer is NOT required to create new positions. The employee in any position has to be able to perform the *essential duties* of the position. This is demonstrated in the *Holmes v. Attorney-General of Canada* (1997),[15] where the court stated that the undue hardship standard:

> *Does not require that an employer act as a placement officer or create a new position expressly for the disabled employee comprising new duties that were previously non-existent and that do not suit its need . . .. The employer's obligation is to make a genuine effort to accommodate an employee, efforts that are consistent with the type of work for which the worker was hired.*

c) — The Duty to Accommodate . . . and the Employment Contract

On July 17, 2008 the Supreme Court of Canada released another decision that helps define the scope of an employer's duty to accommodate, *Hydro-Québec v. Syndicat des employé-e-s de techniques professionnelles et de bureau d'Hydro-Québec, section locale 2000 (SCFP-FTQ).*[16]

In this case, an employee with 24 years of service at Hydro Quebec was dismissed for innocent absenteeism. The decision focused on the last 7.5 years of the employee's time with the company. During this time, she had been absent for 960 days due to a variety of physical and mental health issues. She had previously attempted to return to work after absences due to her health conditions and the employer had accommodated her by:

[15] *Holmes v. Canada (Attorney General)* (1997), 1997 CarswellNat 693, [1997] F.C.J. No. 577, 130 F.T.R. 251, 97 C.L.L.C. 230-022 (Fed. T.D.)

[16] *Hydro-Québec v. Syndicat des employé-e-s de techniques professionnelles et de bureau d'Hydro-Québec, section locale 2000 (SCFP-FTQ)*, 2008 SCC 43, [2008] 2 S.C.R. 561 (S.C.C.)

- Adjusting her work hours,
- Assigning her to a new position,
- Providing some workstation modifications.

Although these accommodations were successful in addressing the immediate problem at hand, the employee continued to accrue absences.

Justice Deschamps stated that, "*Because of the individualized nature of the duty to accommodate and the variety of circumstances that may arise, rigid rules must be avoided. If a business can, without undue hardship, offer the employee a variable work schedule or lighten his duties — or even authorize staff transfers- to ensure that the employee can do his or her work, it must do so to accommodate the employee.*"[17]

The employer in this case had made several attempts over 7.5 years to accommodate the employee but she remained unable to work on a regular basis and there was no indication that this would change in the future.

Therefore thc Court stated that "*the employer's duty to accommodate ends where the employee is no longer able to fulfill the basic obligations associated with the employment relationship in the foreseeable future.*"[18] The Supreme Court unanimously agreed that the company had not discriminated against the employee when it terminated her employment for innocent absenteeism.

Some key points to consider in accommodation of individuals with disabilities are:

- *Sensitive and considerate approach to accommodation and health issues*: The employer demonstrated a consideration for the employee's delicate health issues throughout the process.
- *Duration of attendance issues*: The duration of time the employer attempted to accommodate the employee (7.5 years). The employer gave this process consideration and did not rush to termination as an immediate option.

---

[17] *Ibid.*

[18] *Ibid.*

- *Accommodation attempts*: The employer had explored and attempted a variety of accommodation strategies in an attempt to bridge the gap between the employee's abilities and the job demands. It is important to consider all options with respect to accommodation in order to afford the employee the ability to attend and perform.[19]
- *Future prognosis for attendance*: The employer has sought an opinion as to whether the employee's ability to attend regularly would improve with treatment. If there is limited prognosis for recovery or ability to attend work in the future, the employer is not obligated to maintain employment.
- *Employment contract obligations*: The employee with accommodations is still expected to be able to complete his/her employment contract which would include attendance and performance of meaningful and productive work. An employer is not obligated to sustain an employee if they cannot fulfill the essential principles of the employment contract.
- Where an employer claims that accommodating a disabled employee poses an undue hardship due to safety concerns, it must identify each potential safety hazard and provide convincing evidence that the safety concerns outweigh the obligations owed to the disabled employee.

d) — Consistent Standards and Policies

Employers must prepare standards for job duties, physical demands analysis and policies that can be applied to all employees. The em-

[19] An employer may have to move an employee to a job more consistent with the employee's health status; *Calgary District Hospital Group v. U.N.A., Local 121-R* (1994), 41 L.A.C. (4th) 319 (Alta. Arb. Bd.). The employer may have to look for work comparable to the original job rather than giving the employee an inferior position; *York County Hospital v. O.N.A.* (1992), 26 L.A.C. (4th) 384 (Ont. Arb. Bd.). The employer may even need to create a new job by joining together all the light duties and then reassigning the heavy duties to other employees; *Greater Niagara General Hospital v. O.N.A.* (1995), 50 L.A.C. (4th) 34 (Ont. Arb. Bd.). In one decision, the employer's duty to accommodate included not only the duties and requirements associated with the current job but also the duties and requirements associated with a bundle of tasks within the ability of an employee with a disability; *Mount Sinai Hospital v. O.N.A.* (1996), 54 L.A.C. (4th) 261 (Ont. Arb. Bd.).

ployer can only defend bone fide occupational requirements with these standards and policies in place.

In the *Mills v. Via Rail Canada Inc.* (1999)[20] case the human rights tribunal ruled that Via Rail discriminated against the employee who had ongoing back problems because the employer applied inconsistent or makeshift standards to judge fitness to work. There were no standards for the jobs available and therefore the employer could not prove that the tasks were bone fide occupational requirements.

The Supreme Court of Canada has said that workplace standards, such as lifting requirements or work schedules, that unintentionally distinguish among employees on a protected human rights ground (i.e., disability, gender, religion, etc.) may be struck down or modified. Employers must build liberal conceptions of equality into workplace practices.

Discrimination can occur quite innocently in situations where an employer adopts a rule, a standard or a procedure, which, although neutral on its face and equally applicable to all employees, is nevertheless discriminatory and reflects upon an individual or group of employees because of some characteristic of that group such as its gender.

e) — Who Does the Duty to Accommodate Apply To?

The duty to accommodate is not limited to accommodating full-time or permanent employees. Employees who are temporary, probationary or part-time are also owed the duty, although the burden on the employer to establish undue hardship may not be as great, depending on the specific circumstances.

f) — Innocent Absenteeism and Disability

Although STD and LTD claims costs are declining as a percentage of payroll, in a survey completed by Watson Wyatt, the average participating organization is still spending more than $10.5 million a year in total absence claims. Almost $2.4 million of this relates to casual absences, a phenomenon that many respondents are just begin-

[20] *Mills v. Via Rail Canada Inc.* (1999), 35 C.H.R.R. D/127 (Can. Human Rights Trib.)

ning to track, but one that can have a large impact on organizational health and productivity.[21]

The concept of innocent absenteeism generally indicates excessive absence from the workplace due to factors beyond the employee's control. The employee cannot, generally, be found at fault for absences caused by illness, whether intermittent or chronic, or by injury. Because of the blameless nature of such absences, it has been established that incidents of innocent absenteeism cannot, in most instances, be addressed legitimately through the mechanics of discipline.

In saying this, however, it has also been established that the employer faced with an innocent absenteeism problem may, in some circumstances, protect its legitimate interests by terminating the employment relationship. The classical statement of the doctrine of termination for innocent absenteeism is the statement of Arbitrator Owen Shime in *Re U.A.W., Local 458 v. Massey-Ferguson Industries Ltd.* where he states:[22]

> *. . . in order to justify a discharge the company must establish: (a) undue absenteeism in the grievor's past record, and, (b) that the grievor is incapable of regular attendance into the future.*

In some cases, the record of absenteeism is so compelling that it establishes that the prognosis of regular attendance into the future is poor. In those cases, all the employer need show is the record of excessive absenteeism and then for the employee to show that he or she will be able to provide regular and consistent attendance to his or her duties in the immediate and foreseeable future.

You should be aware that arbitrators have upheld the employer's right to establish an innocent absenteeism control program. In fact, arbitrators have supported such policies in the vast majority of cases. Human resources professionals should consider carefully the development of attendance management programs and address any discriminatory features. When absence occurs it must be managed according to the policies but accommodation is necessary for individuals with disabilities.

---

[21] Watson Wyatt (2007) Staying at Work Report.

[22] *U.A.W., Local 458 v. Massey-Ferguson Industries Ltd.* (1972), 24 L.A.C. 344 at 348 (Ont. Arb. Bd.).

In order to successfully defend a discharge for innocent absenteeism, an employer should be prepared to demonstrate that thought and consideration was given to the employee's situation before discharge was affected. Each of the following factors may be relevant:

1. Attendance Record
   a. Level of absenteeism
   b. History of intermittent and frequent absences for different (albeit legitimate) reasons
   c. Level of hardship for the employer
2. Prognosis for future attendance
   a. Accurate medical information regarding future attendance
3. Warnings
   a. Documented series of counselling warnings
   b. Employee must understand that the consequence of inability to attend will be dismissal
4. Benefit Status
   a. If eligibility for benefits is effected, discharge may be precluded
5. Human Rights Considerations
   a. Can the disability be accommodated?
   b. Employer made reasonable attempts at accommodation
   c. Employee counselled to determine if assistance would improve the attendance
   d. Referral to EAP

A recent Supreme Court Decision has demonstrated that an employer can terminate after a lengthy period of absence if the collective agreement stipulates this agreement.

The Supreme Court of Canada has upheld the termination of a disabled employee who was dismissed after a long period of innocent absenteeism.[23] On January 26, 2007, the Court ruled 9-0 that the dismissal of the employee pursuant to a collective agreement that provided for the automatic dismissal of employees absent more than

[23] *Hydro-Québec* above, note 16.

three years due to illness or accident was a reasonable accommodation.[24]

The case, *McGill University Health Centre (Montreal General Hospital) v. Syndicat des employés de l'Hôpital général de Montréal* [RNF], involved the grievance of an employee with 15 years seniority who went on a leave of absence after a nervous breakdown. Following unsuccessful attempts to return to work on reduced hours, her employment was terminated some three years after she first went off sick. The union grieved the termination, asking that she be offered reasonable accommodation.

The arbitrator dismissed the grievance, pointing out that the employer had already accommodated the grievor by granting her rehabilitation periods more generous than those provided for in the collective agreement, and that she was still unfit for work at the end of the three-year period provided for in the agreement. After finding that the employer had accommodated the grievor, the arbitrator concluded that "the employer had treated the grievor in a way that was just and non-discriminatory in correctly applying an express rule set out in the collective agreement".[25]

An employer cannot terminate an employee who is absent from work because of his disability for extended periods of time due to a policy on absenteeism if:

- The employee can be accommodated in another position where they can productively perform the essential aspects of the job
- The employee's absence has been caused by a disability and he can provide persuasive medical prognosis that he has favourable prospects of returning to work in the foreseeable future.

If neither of these exist then termination is possible. So in the end the duty to accommodate continues to apply. This being said each decision in that duty should be carried out on a case by case basis with detailed analysis of all factors in the case.

---

[24] *McGill University Health Centre (Montreal General Hospital) v. Syndicat des employés de l'Hôpital général de Montréal*, 2007 SCC 4, [2007] 1 S.C.R. 161 (S.C.C.)

[25] Lynn Harnden of Emond Harnden (Harnden email 2007).

g) — The Roles in the Duty to Accommodate

Employer's Role:[26]

- To accommodate in good faith to the point of undue hardship;
- To cooperate with the union and employee on reasonable accommodation suggestions;
- To obtain expert assessment in complex accommodation situations.
- To participate in the accommodation process; employers have a right to inquire as to the reasons for absences or inability to perform the work duties;
- Employers may take reasonable steps to investigate and verify /disprove asserted non-medical reasons for absences or performance issues;
- The employer's right to medical substantiation will depend on contractual authority (expressed or implied) or statutory authority;
- A medical certificate is just one piece of information to be assessed by the employer; further inquiries may be necessary and appropriate;
- The duty to accommodate under human rights legislation enlarges the employee's duty to provide and the employer's right to inquire about medical information;[27]
- The employer is required to provide suitable modified work to assist with an employee's rehabilitation and return to work within the statutory obligations of the *Workplace Safety and Insurance Act* or the *Human Rights Code*;[28]

---

[26] Ontario Human Rights Commission. Policy And Guidelines On Disability And The Duty To Accommodate. Toronto, ON: The Commission; 23 Nov 2000. Available from: http://www.ohrc.on.ca/en/resources/Policies/PolicyDisAccom2/pdf. Accessed: 2008 Sep 16.

[27] www.ohrc.on.ca

[28] *Human Rights Code* R.S.O. 1990, c. H.19 and *Ontario Workplace Safety and Insurance Act, 1998.*

- Consent to release and disclose medical information should always be obtained;
- Confidentiality of accommodation information should be preserved. Limited to the Manager and disability management department in most situations;
- The employer is liable for the costs of medical services requested by the employer and medical documentation requested by the employer;
- It is important to note that if there is a connection between an employee's performance or absence and his/her disability, the employer is required to provide accommodation to the point of undue hardship rather than discipline.

Employee's Role:[29]

- To share information about accommodation needs;
- To actively cooperate in determining accommodation and attend assessments with experts as necessary to clarify accommodation needs;
- To offer a reasonable explanation for not accepting accommodation offers;
- To accept reasonable accommodation offers.

Unions Role:[30]

- To ensure the collective agreement does not inhibit reasonable accommodation processes;

---

[29] *Ibid.*

[30] The Supreme Court of Canada's decision in *Renaud v. Central Okanagan School District No. 23*, [1992] 2 S.C.R. 970 (S.C.C.) [hereinafter "*Renaud*"] sets out the obligations of unions.

CHAPTER 4: WORKERS' COMPENSATION ACTS

4.1 — Introduction

When an employee has a work related injury or illness the employer must understand the workers' compensation program in the province of the worker. Workers' compensation is a no-fault, government insurance program administered provincially by independent boards. Approximately 80 per cent of workers across Canada are covered by workers' compensation insurance. It provides "no fault" insurance protecting the employer from potential law suits. Workers' compensation is funded through premiums paid by employers and compensation levels are calculated as a percentage of net earnings and benefits are tax-free. Services and earnings differ from province to province. If an employer has employees in various provinces they must follow the province's workers' compensation policies in which the employee works. Therefore it is important to understand each of the province's processes and obligations.[1]

The employer is obliged to report a work-related injury to the Workers' Compensation Board (WCB)[2] by completing the appropriate "Employer's Report of Injury" form. The worker also has a responsibility to seek medical attention from their treating practitioner and to participate in the recommended treatment and to participate in the return to work process. The employer pays premiums or direct costs of the claims. Most of the province's programs incent early and safe return to work after an injury and therefore it is important to not only prevent an injury but also to offer suitable return to work options early in the process.

---

[1] See provincial legislation governing workers' compensation in the province of work activity http://www.awcbc.org/common/assets/benefits/rehab_return_to_work.pdf

[2] WCB is used to define the Board that is responsible for insuring workplace accidents. The name of this Board varies in each province.

The employer must understand the current system and stakeholders in this process in order to effectively manage work related injuries and illnesses. It is important to understand that although the WCB is operated by the provincial government that the employer pays for the premiums and the actions of the employer and its employees directly correlate to the cost of these premiums. Having an effective disability management program in place can significantly reduce the cost to the employer from direct premium rebates/surcharges to penalties for non compliance. The following information will use the Ontario *Workplace Safety and Insurance Act* as the premise for the steps. In each province these steps may vary and it is the employer's responsibility to understand the obligations within the province that the worker is performing the work. That means that if you are a national employer, the employer must report and follow the act within the province that the worker is performing the work not the province that the head office is located. Most organizations will have specific procedure to manage work related claims. If you are in a small organization this duty may fall to the human resources professional.

4.2 — Ontario *Workplace Safety and Insurance Act*

The Ontario work related injury will be used as an example. In Ontario the *Workplace Safety and Insurance Act*, S.O. 1997 covers all Work-related injuries and illnesses. This act came into effect on January 1998.

a) — Employer's Obligations

The employer must report the incident and claim to the workers' compensation board within 3 calendar days of learning of the injury/disease if it causes the worker to:

- Be absent from regular work;
- Require modified duties at regular pay or less than regular pay (for over 7 days)
- Earn less than regular pay at regular work and/or;
- Obtain outside health care.

An employer is required to cooperate with the other workplace party, their employee when an injury occurs. The employer's responsibilities are defined under Section 40(1):[3]

- Contacting the worker and maintaining communication throughout the absence;
- Identifying and arranging suitable employment;
- Sharing information related to the WSIB claim.

The employee has matching obligations to cooperate as defined under Section 40(2):[4]

- Contacting the employer and maintaining communication throughout the absence;
- Assisting the employer in identification of suitable employment;
- Giving the Board information regarding return to work.

4.3 — Entitlement

The following table provides the definitions for an accident as defined by each province's jurisdiction:

Alberta	"accident" means an accident that arises out of and occurs in the course of employment in an industry to which this Act applies and includes (i) a wilful and intentional act, not being the act of the worker who suffers the accident, (ii) a chance event occasioned by a physical or natural cause, (iii) disablement, and (iv) a disabling or potentially disabling condition caused by an occupational disease;

[3] www.wsib.on.ca Ontario *Workplace Safety and Insurance Act* S.O. 1997 section 40(1) .

[4] Ontario *Workplace Safety and Insurance Act.* S.O. 1997 section 40(2).

British Columbia	"accident" includes a wilful and intentional act, not being the act of the worker, and also includes a fortuitous event occasioned by a physical or natural cause;
Manitoba	"accident" means a chance event occasioned by a physical or natural cause; and includes (a) a wilful and intentional act that is not the act of the worker, (b) any (i) event arising out of, and in the course of, employment, or (ii) thing that is done and the doing of which arises out of, and in the course of, employment, and (c) an occupational disease. and as a result of which a worker is injured; (« accident »)
New Brunswick	"accident" includes a wilful and intentional act, not being the act of a worker, and also includes a chance event occasioned by a physical or natural cause, as well as a disablement caused by an occupational disease and any other disablement arising out of and in the course of employment, but does not include the disablement of mental stress or a disablement caused by mental stress, other than as an acute reaction to a traumatic event;
Newfoundland	Not defined
Northwest territories and Nunavut	Not defined
Nova Scotia	"accident" includes (i) a wilful and intentional act, not being the act of the worker claiming compensation,

	(ii) a chance event occasioned by a physical or natural cause, or (iii) disablement, including occupational disease, arising out of and in the course of employment, but does not include stress other than an acute reaction to a traumatic event;
Ontario	"accident" includes, (a) a wilful and intentional act, not being the act of the worker, (b) a chance event occasioned by a physical or natural cause, and (c) disablement arising out of and in the course of employment ("accident")
Prince Edward island	"accident" means, subject to subsection (1.1) a chance event occasioned by a physical or natural cause, and includes (i) a wilful and intentional act that is not the act of the worker, (ii) any (A) event arising out of, and in the course of, employment, or (B) thing that is done and the doing of which arises out of, and in the course of, employment, and (iii) an occupational disease, and as a result of which a worker is injured; (1.1) The definition "accident" in clause (1)(a) does not include stress other than an acute reaction to a traumatic event. (2) An accident that occurs while a person is actually engaged in rescuing or attempting to rescue or protect life or property in or about the industry in which the person is employed, shall be deemed to arise out of and in the course of the person's employment.

Quebec	"industrial accident" means a sudden and unforeseen event, attributable to any cause, which happens to a person, arising out of or in the course of his work and resulting in an employment injury to him;
Saskatchewan	Not defined
Yukon	Not defined

The eligibility definition includes any injury "arising out of and in the course of employment".[5] The employer has an opportunity to identify if they do not feel that the claim meets the definition initially by including a letter outlining any facts on this with the form 7.

Injuries and illnesses will be considered according to the Board's policies. Each jurisdiction will have different criteria for the entitlement and coverage. In Ontario Stress is excluded from the eligibility for WSIB claims with the exception of traumatic stress. There is a very specific definition[6] for this in the policies and it includes only events where there has been a death or risk of death. It is generally used by emergency personnel but is becoming more commonly referred to in other repetitive claims for individuals who work in the health care and service industries. In other jurisdictions the understanding of mental stress and workers' compensation eligibility definition is different.

Chronic pain policies exist in each jurisdiction to define the eligibility for coverage for chronic pain claims.[7] The following chart provides the definitions for injury in each jurisdiction:

5 Ontario *Workplace Safety and Insurance Act*, S.O. 1997.

6 http://www.wsib.on.ca/wsib/wopm.nsf/Public/150302

7 http://www.wsib.on.ca/wsib/wopm.nsf/public/150403

Alberta	N/A — see accident
British Columbia	N/A — See "Accident"
Manitoba	N/A — See "Accident"
New Brunswick	N/A — See "Accident"
Newfoundland	(1)(o) "injury" means (i) an injury as a result of a chance event occasioned by a physical or natural cause (ii) an injury as a result of a wilful and intentional act, not being the act of the worker, (iii) disablement, (iv) industrial disease, or (v) death as a result of an injury arising out of and in the course of employment and includes a recurrence of an injury and an aggravation of a pre-existing condition but does not include stress other than stress that is an acute reaction to a sudden and unexpected traumatic event (2) Notwithstanding paragraph (1)(o), stress that may be the result of an employer's decision or action relating to the employment of a worker including a decision to change the work to be performed or the working conditions, to discipline the worker or to terminate the worker's employment does not constitute an injury
Northwest territories/Nunavut	N/A
Nova Scotia	"injury" means personal injury, but does not include any type or class of personal injury excluded by regulation pursuant to Section 10;
Ontario	N/A — *See "Accident"*

Prince Edward Island	N/A — *See "Accident"*
Quebec	N/A — *See "Employment Injury"*
Saskatchewan	"injury" means: (i) the results of a wilful and intentional act, not being the act of the worker, (ii) the results of a chance event occasioned by a physical or natural cause; (ii.1) a disabling or potentially disabling condition caused by an occupational disease; or (iii) any disablement, arising out of and in the course of employment;
Yukon	"injury" means (a) an injury as a result of an event, or series of events, occasioned by a physical or natural cause, (b) an injury as a result of a wilful and intentional act, not being the act of the worker, (c) a disablement, but does not include the disablement of mental stress or disablement caused by mental stress, other than posttraumatic stress, (d) an occupational disease, which includes a disease from causes and conditions peculiar to or characteristic of a particular trade or occupation or peculiar to the particular employment; but does not include an ordinary disease of life, or (e) death as a result of an injury;

4.4 — WSIB Reporting Requirement

a) — Notification of Claim

i) — Employer Form 7[8]

The employer is responsible for completing a report of injury (form 7) within 3 days of the injury occurring. Completing this accurately and promptly will allow the WSIB to make decisions about claim eligibility. Note that the employer has a key opportunity to ensure that all information is submitted accurately to the WSIB to make a decision. The clearer the reporting initially, the more effective the decision can be made. It is advisable to include physical demands of jobs and offers of suitable modified work for this process as well as any additional information about the incident that may indicate more clearly the cause of the claim.

ii) — Health Care Practitioners Report Form 8[9]

A portion of the claim is the submission of a physician report to the WSIB regarding the injury. Many physicians are uncertain as to when it is appropriate to submit initial reporting forms to the WSIB (the "Board"), and under what circumstances the Board may request additional information related to a patient.

The Board has the ability to request any information it feels necessary in order to process claims under its insurance plan. Section 37(1) of the *Workplace Safety and Insurance Act* states:

> Every health care practitioner who provides health care to a worker claiming benefits under the insurance plan or who is consulted with respect to his or her health care shall promptly give the Board such information relating the worker as the Board may require.

This Section provides the Board with a broad authority to demand the delivery of information. If a physician treats an injured worker who wishes to make a claim under the insurance plan, he or she must promptly give the Board the information that it requests. The Board has indicated that after an initial visit relating to a claim, it will re-

8 http://www.wsib.on.ca/wsib/wsibsite.nsf/public/FormsEmployers

9 http://www.wsib.on.ca/wsib/wsibsite.nsf/public/FormsHealth

quest that the information of that visit to be sent by way of a "Physician's First Report" form (Form 8).[10]

After the initial visit, the Board may continue to request information regarding the treatment of the patient. In most circumstances, the patient's situation will dictate how the information is reported.

For example, if the physician who conducted the initial report continues to treat the patient, he or she will most likely be required to complete a "Physician's Progress Report" (Form 26) to update the Board with information regarding the treatment that has been provided, or if the claiming patient has been referred to a specialist, the specialist must complete a "Consultation Report" form.

There are, however, circumstances where the Board may request additional information, separate from the information provided on the reporting forms.

Most physicians who receive a request of this nature find it to be a nuisance. However, Section 37(1) of the Act provides the Board with a substantially broad power that allows it to demand "any information" relating to a claiming patient that it "may require."[11] Therefore, it is not unusual for the Board to demand a copy of the entire medical history of a patient.

The Board may opt to use this power in instances where it would like proof that the treatment provided is wholly work-related, and not treatment for an injury that was either aggravated by a workplace incident, or not at all related to the workplace.

Definition of a Worker:

The WCB premiums and obligations apply to all "workers". With the proliferation of contract and subcontracting relationships, an employer must understand who is a "worker". The following chart provides the definitions of a worker under each Jurisdiction:

---

[10] *Ibid.*

[11] Ontario *Workplace Safety and Insurance Act* S.O. 1997, Section 37(1).

Alberta	"worker" means a person who enters into or works under a contract of service or apprenticeship, written or oral, express or implied, whether by way of manual labour or otherwise, and includes (i) a learner, (ii) a person whose application to the Board under section 15 is approved, and (iii) any other person who, under this Act or under any direction or order of the Board, is deemed to be a worker, but does not include a person who ordinarily resides outside Canada and is employed by an employer who is based outside Canada and carries on business in Alberta on a temporary basis
British Columbia	"worker" includes (a) a person who has entered into or works under a contract of service or apprenticeship, written or oral, express or implied, whether by way of manual labour or otherwise; (b) a person who is a learner, although not under a contract of service or apprenticeship, who becomes subject to the hazards of an industry within the scope of Part 1 for the purpose of undergoing training or probationary work specified or stipulated by the employer as a preliminary to employment; (c) a member of a fire brigade or an ambulance driver or attendant working with or without remuneration, when serving (i) a municipality, a regional district, an urban area, an improvement district, a board of school trustees, a francophone education authority as defined in the *School Act*, a library board or a parks board, or

	(ii) a board or commission having the management or conduct of work or services on behalf of any of the bodies in subparagraph (i); (d) in respect of the industry of mining, a person while the person is actually engaged in taking or attending a course of training or instruction in mine rescue work under the direction or with the written approval of an employer in whose employment the person is employed as a worker in that industry, or while, with the knowledge and consent of an employer in that industry, either express or implied, he or she is actually engaged in rescuing or protecting or attempting to rescue or protect life or property in the case of an explosion or accident which endangers either life or property in a mine, and this irrespective of whether during the time of his or her being so engaged the person is entitled to receive wages from the employer, or from any employer, or is performing the work or service as a volunteer; (e) further, in respect of the industry of mining, a person while he is engaged as a member of the inspection committee, appointed or elected by the workers in the mine, to inspect the mine on behalf of the workers; (f) an independent operator admitted by the Board under section 2(2); and (g) a person deemed by the Board to be a worker under section 3(6).
Manitoba	"worker" includes (a) a person, whether or not under the age of 18 years, who enters into or works under a contract of service or apprenticeship, written or oral, expressed or implied, whether by way of manual labour or otherwise,

	(b) a learner, (c) a casual emergency worker as defined in subsection (4), (d) a person deemed to be a worker under subsection 60(2.1), (e) an employer who is admitted by the board as being within the scope of Part I under subsection 74(3), (f) an independent contractor who is admitted by the board as being within the scope of Part I under section 75, (g) a director of a corporation who is admitted by the board as being within the scope of Part I under subsection 74(3), (h) repealed, S.M. 2005, c. 17, s. 3, (i) a person or a member of a class of persons declared to be a worker under section 77, (j) a person who is employed for more than 24 hours a week by the same employer (i) in domestic service, (ii) as a sitter or companion to attend primarily to the needs of a child who is a member of the household, or (iii) as a companion to attend primarily to the needs of an aged, infirm or ill member of the household, (k) a person who is deemed to be a worker under section 75.1 (volunteer coverage), and (l) a person who is declared to be a worker under section 77.1 (work experience program).
New Brunswick	"worker" means a person who has entered into or works under a contract of service or apprenticeship, written or oral, express or implied, whether by way of manual labour or otherwise, and includes (a) a learner,

	(a.1) an emergency services worker within the meaning of any agreement made under the *Emergency Measures Act* between the Government of Canada and the Government of New Brunswick in which provision is made for compensation with respect to the injury or death of such workers, (b) a member of a municipal volunteer fire brigade, and (c) a person employed in a management capacity by the employer, including an executive officer of a corporation, where that executive officer is carried on the pay-roll.
Newfoundland	"worker" means a worker to whom this Act applies and who is a person who has entered into or works under a contract of service or apprenticeship, written or oral, express or implied, whether by way of manual labour or otherwise, and includes (i) in respect of the industry of fishing, whaling or sealing, a person who becomes a member of the crew of a boat, vessel or ship under an agreement to prosecute a fishing, whaling or sealing voyage in the capacity of a person receiving a share of the voyage or is described in the Shipping Articles as a person receiving a share of the voyage or agrees to accept in payment for his or her services a share or portion of the proceeds or profits of the venture, with or without other remuneration, or is employed on a boat, vessel or ship provided by the employer; (ii) a person who is a learner, although not under a contract of service or apprenticeship, who becomes subject to the hazards of an industry for the purpose of undergoing training or probationary work specified or stipulated by the employer as a preliminary to employment;

	(iii) a part-time or casual worker, and (iv) an executive officer, manager or director of an employer
Northwest Territories/Nunavut	"worker" means a person deemed to be or designated as a worker for the purposes of this Act under section 4, 5 or 6; « travailleur » 4. (1) The following persons are deemed to be workers for the purposes of this Act: (a) a person who enters into or works under a contract of service; (b) a person who, although not under a contract of service, is (i) undergoing training or probationary work as a preliminary to employment with an employer, (ii) engaged in, or training for, rescue or recovery services, ambulance services or firefighting services, or (iii) temporarily engaged in carrying out measures relating to emergencies or disasters under the *Civil Emergency Measures Act*; (c) a student who is participating in a work training or similar program provided by a school; (d) a patient who is participating in a work training or similar program provided by a health care facility; (e) a person who is committed to a correctional centre under the *Corrections Act* and working in a work release program outside the centre; (f) a person designated as a worker by the Commission under section 6; (g) a person deemed to be a worker by the regulations.

	(2) The Commission may determine that a person is a worker if the Commission considers that, in substance, the person has entered into or is working under a contract of service with another person, notwithstanding the appearance of a different arrangement between the two persons. 5. (1) a person whose remuneration comes primarily from harvesting wildlife is deemed to be a work is he/she: (a) lives in NT (b) is lawfully harvesting wildlife under a land claims agreement, treaty or aboriginal right or *Wildlife Act* (c) is not harvesting under a contract for services 2. Not withstanding any other provision of the Act. . . . 6. The commission may on application deem a worker of any other person that might not otherwise be considered a worker. . . .
Nova Scotia	"worker" means a worker within the scope of Part I, and includes: (i) a person who has entered into or works under a contract of service or apprenticeship, written or oral, express or implied, (ii) an officer, director or manager of an employer, where the person is actively engaged in the business and is carried on the payroll of the business at the person's actual earnings, (iii) a learner, (iv) a student admitted pursuant to Section 6, (v) a member of a municipal volunteer fire department admitted pursuant to Section 5,

(vi) in respect of the industry of fishing, a person who becomes a member of the crew of a vessel under any profit-sharing arrangement,

(vii) in respect of the industry of mining, a person while actually engaged in taking or attending a course of training or instruction in mine rescue work under the direction or with the approval, express or implied, of an employer in whose employment the person is employed as a worker in that industry,

(viii) in respect of any industry, a person while actually engaged in rescuing or protecting or attempting to rescue or protect life or property in the case of an explosion, a fire or other emergency, that endangers either life or property in or about the industry in which the person is employed,

(ix) any other person who, pursuant to Part I, the regulations or an order of the Board, is deemed to be a worker, and

(x) in relation to compensation payable to a dependant, a dependant,

but, subject to Section 4, does not include

(xi) a receiver, liquidator or other person appointed by a court or a judge with power to manage or carry on the business of an employer for winding-up or other purposes,

(xii) an employer, or

(xiii) a member of the family of an employer or a member of the family of a director of a corporation who

(A) is employed by the employer or the corporation, and

(B) lives with the employer or director as a member of the employer's or director's household.

Ontario	"worker" means a person who has entered into or is employed under a contract of service or apprenticeship and includes the following: (1) A learner. (2) A student. (3) An auxiliary member of a police force. (4) A member of a municipal volunteer ambulance brigade. (5) A member of a municipal volunteer fire brigade whose membership has been approved by the chief of the fire department or by a person authorized to do so by the entity responsible for the brigade. (6) A person summoned to assist in controlling or extinguishing a fire by an authority empowered to do so. (7) A person who assists in a search and rescue operation at the request of and under the direction of a member of the Ontario Provincial Police. (8) A person who assists in connection with an emergency that has been declared by the Lieutenant Governor in Council or the Premier under section 7.0.1 of the *Emergency Management and Civil Protection Act* or by the head of council of a municipality under section 4 of that Act (9) A person deemed to be a worker of an employer by a direction or order of the Board, (10) A person deemed to be a worker under section 12. (11) A pupil deemed to be a worker under the *Education Act.* ("travailleur")
Prince Edward Island	"worker" includes (i) a person who enters into or works under a contract of service or apprenticeship,

	(ii) a learner or student, (iii) a member of a municipal volunteer fire brigade, (iv) in respect of any industry, a person while he or she is actually engaged in rescuing or protecting or attempting to rescue or protect life or property, (v) an employer who is admitted by the Board as being within the scope of Part I under section 3, (vi) an independent contractor who is admitted by the Board as being within the scope of Part I under section 4, (vii) a director or officer of a corporation who is admitted by the Board as being within the scope of Part I under section 3;
Quebec	"worker" means a natural person who does work for an employer for remuneration under a contract of employment or of apprenticeship, except (1) a domestic; (2) a natural person engaged by an individual to care for a child or a sick, handicapped or aged person and who does not live in the dwelling of the individual; (3) a person who plays sports as his main source of income; (4) an executive officer of a legal person regardless of the work the executive officer does for the legal person.
Saskatchewan	"worker" means a person who has entered into or works under a contract of service or apprenticeship, written or oral, express or implied, whether by way of manual labour or otherwise, and includes: (i) a learner,

	(ii) a member of a municipal volunteer fire brigade; (iii) an executive officer of an employer, where that executive officer is carried on the pay-roll; and (iv) any other person not otherwise coming within this definition who, under this Act or under any direction or order of the board, is deemed to be a worker;
Yukon	"worker" means (a) a person who performs services for an employer under a contract of service or apprenticeship, unless the person is employed on a casual basis for purposes other than the employer's industry, (b) any person who, with the consent of the person charged with the management of a mine or of the person in charge of an authorized mine rescue crew, is doing mine rescue work after an accident, explosion, or other catastrophe, (c) a learner, (d) a director of an incorporated company carrying on in an industry in the Yukon, unless the board, on application by the director of an incorporated company, deems the director to not be a worker, (e) a member of the Legislative Assembly, (f) any person, sole proprietor or partner deemed by the board or by regulation to be a worker, but does not include (g) a person during any time the person is acting in a religious function as a duly ordained or appointed cleric, a member of a religious order or as a lay reader, and

	(h) a person who entered into or works under a contract of service or apprenticeship outside the Yukon, who ordinarily resides outside of the Yukon and is employed by an employer who is based outside of the Yukon and carries on business in the Yukon on a temporary basis. « *travailleur* » (2) Subject to subsection (3), when a person does any work in an industry for an employer engaged in that industry, the person who does the work shall, for the purposes of this *Act*, be deemed to be a worker of that employer except when the person doing the work is (a) an employer in an industry; (b) a director of a limited company who is deemed by the board not to be a worker; (c) a worker of another employer; or (d) a sole proprietor deemed by the board to be a worker. (3) The board of directors may designate classes of persons to whom subsection (2) does not apply

b) — Worker's Obligations[12]

Under the WSIA there are obligations that the worker must adhere to:

Section 22(1) — A worker shall file a claim as soon as possible after the accident that gives rise to the claim, but in no case shall he or she file a claim more than six months after the accident

Section 22(7) — When filing a claim, a worker must consent to the disclosure to his or her employer of information provided by a health professional under Subsection 37(3) concerning the worker's functional abilities. The disclosure is for the sole purpose of facilitating the worker's return to work.

[12]Ontario *Workplace Safety and Insurance Act* Section 22.

The Worker must under Section 40(2)[13]

- contact the employer and maintain communication throughout the lost time;
- assist in identifying suitable employment;
- Provide information to the WSIB and employer regarding the claim.

i) — Employee Form 6[14]

The employee is also responsible for completing a form 6 to report the injury. This will include the employee's account of the incident, symptoms and steps that the employee has taken since the injury. The employee or survivor must file a claim within 6 months after the accident.

The worker must consent to disclosure of functional abilities information through a consent located on Form 6 and Form 7. The Board may reduce or suspend benefits if the worker refuses to disclose this information. The employer should ensure that this consent is signed as quickly as possible to enable communication with the health care providers on functional abilities and planning of return to work. The Board process involves payment of two weeks of benefits without signature for disclosure of functional abilities.

The worker must give a copy of the claim to the employer and the employer must give a copy of the forms to the worker.

The WSIB may decide not to rule on a claim until all the reports are in but it may decide to rule based solely on the doctor and employee reports. It is the employer's responsibility to ensure that the board has as much information as quickly as possible to make this well-informed decision.

Each Board operates differently in how they decide entitlement. In Ontario there have been changes to the structure of the claims adjudication process and there are now three types of "case managers" or adjudicators that will be involved in the claim depending on its length and complexity. Level one is the Claims determination case manager; level two is the short term case manager and level three is the long

[13] Ontario *Workplace Safety and Insurance Act* S.O. 1997, section 40(2).

[14] Above, note 10.

term case manager. Maintaining contact and communication with the case manager will be an important part of managing the costs of the claim. Find out who your case manager is and ensure that you have regular contact. Provide them with as much information as you can about your jobs, modifications and return to work options. The case manager has the option to refer to a return to work specialist to promote early and safe return to work. Cooperation with this specialist will help you in planning return to work but make sure that you are in control of all return to work processes. Early return to work is the employer's responsibility, and beneficial to all parties.

If the employer does not agree with the decision then there is an appeal process. This unfortunately is like shutting the barn door after the horses are already out and may take more resources and time than ensuring the information is in initially.

The employer should begin to offer suitable and safe modified work at the time symptoms appear to avoid lost time which becomes the most costly part of any claim.

4.5 — Benefits Levels

In Ontario the levels of benefits are based on loss of earnings. There are no benefits based on loss of earning capacity (disability). The current wage replacement is 85 per cent pre-injury net average earnings less post injury net average earnings. All benefits are subject to cooperation in medical rehabilitation, return to work and LMRP.

The non economic loss NEL Process is one that provides for a benefit related to the level of disability of the employee and is determined once the employee reaches maximum medical recovery. Once the NEL is determined it is set for the extent of the claim. There is no automatic right to a second medical assessment unless there is a significant deterioration in the employee's disability.

a) — Employer Requested Health Examination[15]

If the accident employer requests it, a worker must undergo an examination by a health professional selected and paid for by the employer under Section 36(1). The worker may object to undergoing the

[15] http://www.owa.gov.on.ca/pdf_documents/17_EmployerRequestedHealthExams.pdf

examination, or to its nature and extent. If the worker objects, the employer has up to 14 days to ask for direction from the Board. This should be used only where there is limited or controversial information from the worker's own health care provider. It is always best to work directly with the worker's physician first in order to facilitate open communication and return to work planning.

4.6 — Health Care

Workers are entitled to receive payment for medical aid or health-care. This chart outlines the definition of Medical Aid or health care under each jurisdiction:

AB	"medical aid" includes medical and other services provided by a person licensed to practise the healing arts in Alberta, and nursing, hospitalization, drugs, dressing, x-ray treatment, special treatment, appliances, apparatuses, transportation and any other matters and things that the Board authorizes or provides;
British Columbia	Defined under health Care "health care", when used in Part 1, includes the things which the Board under this Act is empowered to provide for injured workers
Manitoba	"medical aid" includes (a) transportation to a hospital or other place where medical care can be given, (b) services provided by a hospital or other health care facility, (c) treatment or services provided by a health care provider, (d) diagnostic services, (e) drugs, medical supplies, orthotics and prosthetics, and

	(f) any other goods and services authorized by the board; (« aide médicale »)
New Brunswick	"medical aid" includes medical, surgical and dental aid, hospital and skilled nursing services, services of a registered chiropractor within his legal jurisdiction, artificial members and apparatus including the repair and replacement thereof, transportation, clothing allowances with respect to damage caused to clothing as a result of the use of an artificial apparatus or as a result of any accident, and such other treatment, services or attendance as are necessary as a result of any injury;
Newfoundland	"medical aid" means medical, surgical and dental aid, hospital and skilled nursing services and a prosthesis or apparatus and the repairing and replacement of them, transportation and other matters and things that the commission may authorize or provide;
Northwest territories/Nunavut	Medical aid includes (a) drugs, medical devices, medical care, dental care, surgery, psychiatric or psychological care, physical rehabilitation and any other health service provided by a health care provider or health care facility, (b) the transportation of an injured or diseased worker for the purpose of receiving medical aid, and (c) any other treatment to facilitate the recovery of an injured or diseased worker or to mitigate his or her disability
Nova Scotia	Medical aid includes:

	(i) any health care service, product or device that may be authorized by the Board and is provided to a worker as a result of a compensable injury, including those forms and reports required by the Board respecting the aid or services, and (ii) reasonable expenses, authorized by the Board, incurred by a worker in order to obtain medical aid
Ontario	"health care" means, (a) professional services provided by a health care practitioner, (b) services provided by or at hospitals and health facilities, (c) drugs, (d) the services of an attendant, (e) modifications to a person's home and vehicle and other measures to facilitate independent living as in the Board's opinion are appropriate, (f) assistive devices and prostheses, (g) extraordinary transportation costs to obtain health care, (h) such measures to improve the quality of life of severely impaired workers as, in the Board's opinion, are appropriate. (Section 32)
PEI	"medical aid" includes medical, surgical and dental aid, hospital and nursing services, chiropractic services provided by a registered chiropractor, occupation therapy and physiotherapy services provided by a licensed practitioner, x-ray and other treatment, drugs, dressings, appliances, apparatuses, transportation and other goods, services and things the Board may authorize in promoting the medical rehabilitation of an injured worker

Saskatchewan	"medical aid" means medical and surgical aid, hospital and skilled nursing services, chiropractic and other treatment and artificial members or apparatus;
Yukon	N/A

The Workers compensation Board will approve and pay for certain health care/medical aid for the injured worker. There are currently programs of care being developed within Ontario that are based on the evidence within the research and developed through a consensus based process with the health care providers. In Ontario these are the programs currently in place:

- Acute Low Back Pain;
- Asthma Program of Care;
- Chemical Sensitivity Program of Care;
- Upper Extremity Program of Care;
- Persistent Low Back Pain Program of Care (in pilot);
- Chronic Pain Program of Care (in progress 2008);
- Mild Brain Injury Program of Care;
- Lower Extremity Program of Care.

See www.wsib.on.ca for information on current Programs of Care.[16]

4.7 — Return to Work[17]

a) — Reemployment Obligations[18]

An employer is required to offer to reemploy a worker under Section 41 if:

- The employer regularly employs 20 or more employees;

[16] http://www.wsib.on.ca/wsib/wsibsite.nsf/public/HealthProgramsCare

[17] http://www.wsib.on.ca/wsib/wsibsite.nsf/Public.RTWWRPolicyHighlights

[18] Ontario *Workplace Safety and Insurance Act*, S.O. 1997 section 41.

- As a result of a work-related injury, the worker is unable to work, and;
- The worker is continuously employed with the accident employer for one year at the time of the injury.

Under Section 41 there is also an obligation to accommodate the work or the workplace for the worker to the extent that the accommodation does not cause undue hardship.

b) — Termination after Reemployment

When workers are terminated within 6 months of reemployment, the Board presumes that the employer has not fulfilled the reemployment obligation. The employer may rebut this presumption by establishing that the termination of the employee was not related to the injury.

When workers are terminated 6 months or more after reemployment, the presumption does not apply. In these cases the Board determines if the employer is in breach by reviewing the circumstances of the termination.

Download the *Return to Work Self Assessment Guide*[19] from WSIB to determine your current return to work program compliance.

c) — Work Integration Policies November 2010

In Ontario, there are policies defining return to work obligations and penalties and it is important for the employer to understand these policies. With an enhanced focus on return to work and a service model change within the board, employers are being asked to consider early and safe return to work as quickly as possible in the claim. The act continues to promote a self reliance model where the obligations are that of the employer and worker to participate on return to work but there are enhanced resources focused on return to work at the board level.

---

[19] http://www.wsib.on.ca/wsib/wsibsite.nsf/LookupFiles/Downloadable FileRTWSelf_AssessmentGuide/$File/RTWSelfAssessment.pdf

d) — Current WSIB Work Reintegration Principles[20]

This policy sets out general work reintegration principles such as:

- appropriate and early RTW that maintains worker's dignity and productivity and plays an important role in the worker's recovery and rehabilitation

Suitable work — is work that:

- is within the worker's functional abilities;
- the worker has, or is able to acquire, the necessary skills to perform;
- does not pose a health or safety risk to the worker or coworkers, and;
- If possible, restores the worker's earnings.

Available work — is work that exists with the accident employer at the pre-injury worksite, or at a comparable worksite arranged by the employer.

To determine whether a worksite is comparable to the pre-injury worksite the decision-maker considers whether:

- travel or assignment to different worksites is normal practice in the industry;
- travel or assignment to a worksite other than the injury site forms part of the employment contract;
- the worker normally accepts employment assignments in various geographic areas, and;
- Travelling to the proposed job is within the normal parameters of travel expected of a worker.

In Quebec Suitable Employment is defined within the Act as appropriate employment that allows a worker who has suffered an employment injury to use his remaining ability to work and his vocational qualifications, that he has a reasonable chance of obtaining and the working conditions of which do not endanger the health, safety or physical well-being of the worker, considering his injury.

In PEI Suitable work means work that a worker has the necessary skills to perform and is medically able to perform, and that does not

---

[20] WSIB Policy (19-02-01).

pose health or safety hazards to the worker or co-workers, as determined by the Board.

All other jurisdictions do not specifically define Suitable employment/work.

e) — What are the penalties for non-compliance in Return to Work?

Most workers and employers cooperate in the Return to Work (RTW) process. Those who do not cooperate may be penalized.

You may be penalized if the WSIB determines that you are not fulfilling your re-employment obligations:

- You can be fined up to the equivalent of the worker's net average earnings for the year before the injury, and;
- The WSIB may make payments to the worker, as if the worker were entitled to loss of earnings (LOE) benefits.

Workers may have their loss of earnings benefits reduced, suspended, or stopped if the WSIB determines that they are not co-operating in the RTW process.

4.8 — Work Transition Assessment[21]

The work transition assessment process is initiated between six and nine months from the date of injury when determining a suitable occupation for the worker. Every employer should exhaust all efforts internally to accommodate a worker back into the workplace before going to a work transition plan. The objective of the work transition plan is to restore the employee to their regular position within the labour market.

The Board will first complete a work transition assessment and then decide if a work transition plan is necessary. This will consider transferable skills first to determine if there is suitable work to meet the employee's skills, abilities and experience. If upgrading of skills is required then the plan is developed. In the past the average cost of a WSIB LMR assessment and program has been $300,000 and has been found to have limited success in finding employment for an in-

---

[21] WSIB Work Transition Plan (19-03-05)

dividual. The Board currently contracts out the Labour Market Re-entry Planning to outside vendors. It is up to the Board to decide which vendor they use in this process. In 2011, the WSIB will move the management of the work transition process back internally into the Board and only assessments and support services on job placements will be outsourced. The Board will consult with the worker and employer unless it is inappropriate to do so. It is important to understand the LMRP cost is paid for by the employer up to the maximum claim limit. Internal accommodation has been found to be much more effective and a less expensive option.

a) — Work Well Audits

A work well audit is a process that WSIB may use to determine if an organization is in compliance with all of the obligations under the *Workplace Safety and Insurance Act*. The WSIB will send out a notice to employers if they are in the high risk area (i.e. high level of claims) to perform a work well audit. A failure of the work well audit can lead to penalties to the organization.

Download the *Work well Audit Document*[22] to determine how you would score on your own work well audit. There are consultants that will assist you in preparing for a work well audit and ensuring your compliance with the Act.

b) — Payments by Employers[23]

Accurately Reporting Payroll

All employers registered with the WSIB have an obligation to report the value of each employee's gross insurable earnings (payroll). Accurately reporting payroll is the single most important account activity you have. It's also one way you can avoid additional charges being applied to your WSIB account.

---

22 http://www.wsib.on.ca/wsib/wsibsite.nsf/LookupFiles/DownloadableFile WorkwellAudit/$File/WorkwellAudit.pdf

23 http://www.csao.org/uploadfiles/magazine/vol14no2/wsib.htm

Insurable earnings are reported periodically during the year on a *Premium Remittance Form.*[24]. By submitting the form on time, you'll save unnecessary and costly penalties.

There are different types of premium assessments for employers dependent on their rate group, type of service and size. Most employers are rated as schedule one or schedule two employers.

The schedule one employers have assessments which are rate group and premium based according to rate group. The employer pays between $0.60 per $100 of payroll to over $3.00 per $100 of payroll depending on the risk of that rate group. At the end of the year the employer may be eligible for rebates or surcharges depending on how the employer faired according to the rest of the rate group. You are considered under the NEER program.

If you are a schedule two employer you pay all the costs of the claims plus additional administrative charges. If you are an employer in construction you are rated under the CAD program and will pay premiums based on number of claims.

If you are a smaller employer you may be rated under the MAPP program. It is important to understand how you pay your WCB as this will help you to determine the best cost management process for your claims.

Paying Premiums on Time

Another way to avoid penalty charges is to make premium payments on time. When a premium payment is received past the due date, or is not received at all, you are subject to a *monthly late payment charge*. The WSIB Interest Rate is equal to the Bank of Canada Rate plus 6 per cent.

Prevent Claims and Facilitate Early and Safe Return to Work

The proper prevention of claims is always the best cost management approach to work related claims but in most situations the next most effective management is providing a solid early and safe return

---

[24] http://www.wsib.on.ca/wsib/wsibsite.nsf/LookupFiles/DownloadableFile PremiumRemittanceFormInstructions0976A/$File/0976A.pdf

to work process to reduce lost time. This will be the focus of several chapters within this book.

4.9 — Human Resources Professional Role

The Human Resources Professional may be responsible for the management of work related claims. If this is the case it is important to understand the strategies to improve claims management through the use of the following activities:

- develop an early and safe return to work policy and process;
- ensure early reporting of incidents and injuries;
- facilitate early and safe return to work through modified work offerings;
- early communication with workers;
- education of managers on safety principles and the importance of early and safe return to work;
- communicate regularly with workers;
- develop a relationship with the adjudication team to provide proactive management of claims;
- consider assistance for complex claims management and appeals;
- collect data on injuries and incidents in order to develop a proactive prevention strategy for workplace injuries;
- develop a process that involves all workplace parties in work related claims management and return to work;
- Do not rely on the Board to manage your return to work or offers of suitable work . . . if you wait for that assistance you will end up paying larger premiums. The control of this cost is in the company's hands.

CHAPTER 5: ACCESSIBILITY FOR INDIVIDUALS WITH DISABILITIES

5.1 — Introduction

Human Resources Professionals must consider the accessibility of the workplace for individuals with disabilities. Barriers occur within our workplaces which prevent individuals with disabilities from accessing employment. These barriers occur in the built environment but also occur in policy, printed materials, and communication strategies. The Human Resources Professional should work to remove the barriers that are present and help individuals access the workplace. This will lead to the ability to access talents and skills that the company requires.

5.2 — Accessibility of the Built Environment

"Universal access" is the term applied to environments built based on "universal design". The term universal design does not imply that everything built must be fully usable by everybody, but simply that design solutions will attempt to address the needs of the widest possible range of the population in a reasonable manner. Universal design objectives are not pursued to the point that the viability of a project or the programs for which it is intended would be threatened.

In performance terms, a "universally accessible environment" is one in which those who wish to use it are able to do so without difficulty. Striving to meet this ideal will create environments that perform better for all users. This is understood to include wheelchair users, ambulant mobility impaired, hard of hearing and deaf persons, blind, visually impaired and people with low vision, and people with perceptual or cognitive differences. Universal design by its very nature unfortunately may lead to ignoring an individual's needs. As everyone with a disability has different requirements it is important to understand that even with universal design there will still be the requirement for individual accommodation but having universal design principles incorporated in your workplace will reduce barriers for a large percentage of the population.

For example, we have come to expect the presence of ramps, the presence of larger washroom stalls with grab bars and lever door handles. These are ways that universal design opens up access and eliminates barriers in our workplaces.

The Canadian Human Rights Commission has developed a report outlining International Best Practices in Universal Design: A Global Review (August 2007)[1]. The toolkit includes some checklists that can be used to examine the accessibility of your business. While these are suggested areas to consider, the checklists do not replace the standards that will be incorporated into the *Building Code* through the accessible built environment standards. It is also important to understand that these do not replace the need for individual accommodation as every individual with a disability will have specific accessibility needs.

5.3 — Accessibility for Ontarians with Disabilities Act, 2005

The Ontario government using representative committees is developing a set of standards under the *Accessibility for Ontarians with Disabilities Act, 2005* (AODA)[2] which have the goal of improving the accessibility of businesses in Ontario by the year 2025. The AODA builds on the strong foundation of the Ontario *Human Rights Code* (the Code) that protects the human rights of all Ontarians.

The AODA's regulations establish the accessibility standards. An accessibility standard ("the standard") applies only to a person or organization that does at least one of the following activities:

- provides goods, services or facilities;
- employs people in Ontario;

---

1 International Best Practices in Universal Design: A Global Review (August 2007) Canadian Human Rights Commission. This report can be ordered or downloaded at www.chrc.ca

2 *Accessibility for Ontarians with Disabilities Act* S.O. 2005 Chapter 11 http://www.e-laws.gov.on.ca/html/regs/english/elaws_regs_070429_e.htm

- offers accommodation;
- owns or occupies a building, a structure or a premises;
- plays a part in a business or other activity that the regulations may identify.

In preparing annual accessibility plans, organizations must consider the following:

- Accessibility plans must address a broad range of disability issues, taking into account the full definition of disability under the AODA and the Ontario *Human Rights Code*.
- The plans must examine all aspects of an organization's operations, including its bylaws, practices, facilities, programs and services.
- Organizations must take into consideration their roles as service providers and employers.
- The plans must identify steps to be taken over time to remove identified barriers and prevent any new ones.
- Organizations are accountable to their communities for accessibility improvements. They are required to consult with people with disabilities and to make accessibility plans available to the public to ensure accountability at the local level.
- It is important that organizations consider integrating accessibility planning into their business planning cycles to ensure a thoughtful, effective and efficient process and meaningful outcomes.

5.4 — Accessibility Directorate of Ontario[3]

The Accessibility Directorate of Ontario is the organization within the Ontario government that is responsible for day-to-day administration of the AODA. The functions of the Accessibility Directorate include:

- giving advice to the minister;

---

3 http://www.mcss.gov.on.ca/en/mcss/programs/accessibility/index.aspx

- providing support to the Accessibility Standards Advisory Council and to standards development committees;
- coordinating consultations;
- conducting research;
- providing information to the public.

The AODA Committees have developed 5 key sets of standards:

- customer service (Now regulation 429/07);
- information and communication (awaiting ministry approval at the time of this publishing);
- transportation (awaiting ministry approval at the time of this publishing);
- employment (awaiting ministry approval at the time of this publishing);
- built environment (awaiting ministry approval at the time of this publishing);

Each of these standards was developed by a committee appointed by the minister with representation from all sectors and includes at least 50 per cent representation from individuals with disabilities. As each of the standards is approved they will become regulations that each business in Ontario must consider.

The Accessibility Standards for Customer Service became law on January 1, 2008.[4]

All businesses or organizations that provide goods or services to the public or to other third parties in Ontario are legally required to comply with the requirements of the standard. There are tools and a compliance guide online that can help the organization with ensuring that all steps are taken for due diligence to this regulation.

5.5 — The Steps to Accessibility

As an organization in Canada, you need to ensure you have policies and procedures to manage disability in your workplace that are con-

---

4 http://www.mcss.gov.on.ca/en/mcss/programs/accessibility/Complying Standards/toolsToHelpYouComply.aspx

sistent and fair for all employees and customers. An accessibility consultant helps you to maintain your due diligence in policy and procedure development. They will work with your management team to develop a consistent and fair process that can help you to rest assured that you can be legally compliant in your day to day practice with the *Customer Service Regulation* under AODA, 2005 and with ensuring that your place of business is accessible to those employees and customers with disabilities.

5.6 — Policy and Procedure Development

Develop an accessibility committee to review the current policy and template created to assist managers in responding to customer service requests. The following steps will help you develop policies for legal diligence:

1. Review of the current policy
2. Obtain an outline of the guidelines and processes with respect to accessibility including the current Accessibility Plan and Customer Service Policy and Procedures.
3. Meet with the accessibility committee to understand the accessibility strategy, policy and procedures and vision for accessibility at the your organization
4. Review of all related policies and procedures, current equipment and devices, current staff training processes
5. Develop procedures for providing accessible customer service.
6. Develop supporting tools and toolkit for managers
7. Develop communication package for staff to address customer service standards
8. Provide a process document that includes tools and resources and how to access resources for any customer service request
9. Develop a communication package for managers that will include the policy, outline the resources and steps to access resources.

5.7 — Training of Board, Staff, Volunteers and Contractors

Review the accessibility regulations to determine the best approach for training staff with respect to accessibility in customer service:

1. Review of the training program.
2. Adjustment of materials for various work groups.
3. Schedule logistics for the training.
4. Evaluation and adjustment of the training program as required.
5. Develop a process for the training tracking.
6. Roll out of training for staff.
7. Develop a training process for volunteers and contractors.
8. Review wording for the contracts to outsourced services to ensure inclusion of training requirements.
9. Training program evaluation.

5.8 — Marketing and Communications

Work with the communications team and accessibility committees to:

1. Develop a package for staff on customer service standards, templates, toolkits and responsibilities.
2. Develop logistics for rollout of communications packages.
3. Analyze the rollout and tracking of staff communication process.
4. Develop communications for customers regarding feedback provision and resources available for accessibility.
5. Evaluation of communications/marketing process.
6. Ensure accessibility of communications materials.

5.9 — Coordination of Resources

Ensure that there is access to resources to manage customer service needs for individuals with disabilities:

1. Identification of key responsibilities within the organization for management of the Customer Service Process for Individuals with disabilities.
2. Review and document resources available to manage customer service demands.
3. Develop a flow for the process to access resources.
4. Ensure mechanisms to evaluate access to resources and additional resources required.
5. Determine needs for external resources to manage customer service needs.

5.10 — Feedback Database

Work with the accessibility committee to develop a feedback database that will allow for ease of capture of customer service requests and feedback. Once the data base is in place the analysis of requests and documentation of requests should be implemented.

1. Identification of customer service feedback systems and database to track feedback.
2. Develop feedback protocol and content.
3. Develop documentation of customer service feedback process and response from the organization.
4. Develop reporting of feedback and subsequent responsibilities for improvement in response.

5.11 — Role of Accessibility Consultants

There are consultants that will specialize in assisting organizations in accessibility need identification and ensuring that your organization is compliant with all existing regulations. This is an area where an outside consultant is beneficial due to the complexity and the financial impact of the decisions associated with this process.

The Accessibility Consultant can be found through a web search, communication with colleagues or government websites.

The consultant may provide the following support services:

Accessibility Audit: Comprehensive assessment of the corporation's current accessibility and provision of recommendations to improve universal design. The accessibility consultant works with the design team to set short and long term accessibility goals and standards.

Accessibility Assessment: Assessment of the individual and needs in order to determine appropriate accessibility strategies to facilitate customer service. Provision of legal and business assessment of duty to accommodate the individual with the disability.

Accessibility Standards Development: Review of current organizational status with respect to standards and regulations. Development of protocol for building or renovations so that areas are built with accessibility considered.

5.12 — Human Resource Professionals' Role

The Human Resources Professional will be faced with the challenge of assisting individuals with disabilities in accessing the employment setting. It is advisable that as many barriers to access be reduced through the development of the following:

- accessible built environment standards;
- workstation purchasing guidelines;
- policy development that focuses on reducing barriers;
- accommodation policy creation;
- management of budgets that allow for use of assistive technology and services that improve access such as interpreters, computer technology, workstation changes;
- creation of an environment for inclusion;
- development of culture and diversity awareness programs;
- training programs for all employees on diversity and access;
- management programs on understanding ways to reduce employment barriers;

- creation of recruitment programs through connection with specialty organizations such as Ontario Hearing Society, March of Dimes, or JOIN (a consortium of associations focused on employment for persons with disabilities.)[5]

5 http://www.joininfo.ca.

Chapter 6: Recruitment Practices for Individuals with Disabilities

6.1 — Introduction

When developing a recruitment program within your organization it is important to consider the best strategy to ensure that you are able to access candidates with the skills and talents for your organization. Individuals with disabilities will help to fill that need but there are specific legal obligations in the recruitment process. The Canadian Human Rights Commission website has a guide for hiring individuals with disabilities[1] which is helpful in ensuring that your application process and interviewing is in legal compliance.

The recruiter must consider all steps in accessing employment from the posting to the hiring stages.

6.2 — The Posting

The posting should not include any requirements that are not part of performance of the essential duties of the job. In order to ensure that you are compliant you can also include that your company is an equal opportunity employer.

6.3 — Application Process

How are the applications received? Consider having the ability for applicants to apply through various methods including online, paper applications, or providing individual assistance to complete the application. This will allow you to access individuals with various types of disabilities.

---

1 Note refers to website but there is no website in note "A Place for All: A Guide to Creating an Inclusive Workplace" Minister of Public Works and Government Services 2006 Cat. No. HR21-62/2006. www.chrc-ccdp.ca.

6.4 — The Interview

An employment interview is conducted to learn more about the suitability of people under consideration for a particular job. However, sometimes the information sought during interviews is not relevant to the job being filled and may let discriminatory elements affect the selection process.

For example:

- an applicant's place of birth seldom has anything to do with ability;
- height and weight requirements are not always accurate measures of physical strength and may act to screen out women or some racial or ethnic groups that tend to be smaller in stature.

A skilled interviewer can properly assess a candidate without drawing out a lot of unnecessary information. Although no employer can anticipate every possible interview situation, he or she should be sensitive to the kinds of situations that can lead to a human rights complaint.

a) — Interview Notes

Usually, interviewers will have copies of résumés or applications available at the interview for easy reference or to use as the basis of interview questions. When many applicants are being interviewed, interviewers often make notes on the résumés to help differentiate candidates.

Even though these notes may be solely for the use of the interviewer, they must not identify or differentiate candidates according to the prohibited grounds (for example, "uses a wheelchair" "blind" "will need a lot of accommodation!").

Avoid asking:

- for a list of all disabilities, limitations or health problems;
- whether the applicant drinks or uses drugs;
- whether the applicant has ever received psychiatric care or been hospitalized for emotional problems;
- whether the applicant has received worker's compensation.

The employer should:

- disclose any information on medically related requirements or standards early in the application process;
- convey to the prospective employee an outline of the physical/cognitive demands of the work activities so as to best provide the applicant with a clear understanding of the demands of the job and what accommodations he/she may require;
- ask whether the applicant has any condition that could affect his or her ability to do the job, preferably during a pre-employment medical examination.

A disability is only relevant to job ability if it:

- threatens the safety or property of others or prevents the applicant from safe and adequate job performance even when reasonable efforts are made to accommodate the disability.

Employers are obligated to offer candidates with disabilities an accommodation of their needs if required for any part of the interview or test screening process. The Supreme Court in City of Montreal (2000)[2] said that an employer may violate human rights legislation, not only when an employee or job applicant has an actual disability, but also when she/he has a perceived disability or once suffered from a disability that she/he no longer has.

If the applicant's disability becomes an issue at the interview, e.g. where the applicant chooses to talk about his/her disability, an employer may make inquiries about the applicant's accommodation needs. Inquiries should be limited to the applicant's ability to perform the essential duties of the job. Questions should not be unnecessary, such as "How did you end up in a wheelchair?" or "Have you been blind all your life?" They should be asked with the aim of ascertaining the applicant's ability to perform essential duties and any accommodations required to perform the job duties.

Any questions beyond this scope should be made with great caution and care as it may lead to a complaint on the ground of disability should the applicant not be successful. Additionally, if an employer fails to canvass possible accommodation measures where disability has become an issue at an interview, this also could potentially lead

---

2 *Quebec (Commission des droits de la personne et des droits de la jeunesse) v. Montreal (City)*, 2000 SC 27, [2007] 1 S.C.R. 665 (S.C.C.).

to a complaint on the ground of disability should the applicant not be successful. Any other disability issues should not be raised until a conditional offer of employment is made.

DO ASK:

Questions directly related to the applicant's ability to perform the essential duties of the job.

Is there any setting or equipment that will facilitate the interview process for you?

- This question is acceptable, as an employer may always ask applicants whether they will need reasonable accommodation for the hiring process. The question will probably make most sense after a brief description of what the hiring process involves (e.g., an interview, timed written test, or job demonstration).

Is there any specific technology that you currently use or have used in your previous jobs that assisted you in your work performance?

- This question, placed in the proper context, is acceptable under any one of three scenarios: (1) an applicant voluntarily discloses a hidden disability; (2) an applicant voluntarily discloses that he will need a reasonable accommodation to perform the job; or (3) an employer reasonably believes that an applicant will need a reasonable accommodation because of an obvious disability. An employer may ask the applicant whether she will need reasonable accommodation and what types of reasonable accommodation would be needed to perform the job functions. This question is permissible because the interviewer can explain that despite the query about past and present technology, the question is intended to identify reasonable accommodations that may be necessary in the future.

Other than technology, what supports did you have in previous jobs? If none, are there any you would benefit from?

- This question appears to be another way of asking whether an applicant needs reasonable accommodation and what types of accommodations are needed to perform the job. To the extent that the interviewer frames it as such, it is permissible under any of the three scenarios described in response to the previous question. However, if directed to an applicant who does not voluntarily disclose a hidden disability or whose disability is not obvious, it may be unlawful, depending on how it is phrased.

DON'T ASK:

- whether the applicant is currently under a physician's care name of family doctor
- whether the applicant is receiving counselling or therapy

It is not unusual for an employer to ask about, or for a job applicant or an employee to volunteer information about her/his specific medical condition. However, an employer or supervisor may be placed in a vulnerable position if he or she directly receives any information about the particular medical condition of an applicant or employee. This information leaves the way open for an allegation to be made that subsequent decisions relating to the hiring of the applicant, or the promotion or termination of the employee were based on that information.

b) — Possible Interview Accommodations

- Provide sign language interpreters to facilitate verbal and visual interaction and communication;
- Change the venue if necessary to promote ease of access — certain venues are more accessible than others;
- Consider accessibility of common spaces such as washrooms or meeting areas;
- Widen hallways and entrances to workspaces and common areas if necessary to promote ease of access and movement;
- Install access ramps where necessary to promote ease of access and movement;

Tests/examinations:

- Allow candidates extra time to complete, if required, to relieve some pressure

Medical exams should be conducted after selection and only if an employee's condition is related to job duties. Offers of employment can be made conditional on successful completion of a medical exam. Pre-placement examinations should be created in a way that they are directly correlated with the physical and cognitive demands of the job. Many organizations will complete functional assessments (pre-placement — after an offer has been made) but these should be carefully developed with an assessor who can understand the job demands and any accommodation that may be available. If the applicant is not successful in the pre-placement assessment the organization continues to have a duty to accommodate the applicant's needs and consider the process of accommodation.

6.5 — Placement

The individual who accepts a position is not obligated to disclose a disability at any point in the employment cycle until that individual requires accommodation. Therefore you may find that the individual does not disclose the need for accommodation until after the offer of employment and this individual begins to attempt to perform the duties. At the point that accommodation is requested the employer must begin the duty to accommodate process.

6.6 — Employment contract

The employment contract cannot discriminate against the employee in its wording and its specific requirements. Therefore it is important to ensure that the employment contract contains only the essential elements and clearly outlines the employment requirements. It is also important to understand that even an employment contract that dictates hours of work, or productivity levels are subject to accommodation under the human rights code. For example, a policy that states that employees cannot lose more than 3 days during probationary period of work or the employment contract is terminated. If those absences are directly related to a disability, the employer must consider accommodation to undue hardship (see chapter 3 on Human Rights and Accommodation).

6.7 — Orientation and On-boarding

Job training, orientation and on-boarding is an important process that can make or break the success of the employee at the workplace. Accommodation for how on-boarding is completed must be considered including providing alternate training strategies for an individual with visual impairments or learning disabilities. Consider orientation tools, environment and process when determining accommodation needs. Individuals working with specific organizations in the community may have access to funded interviewing and orientation supports. For example the Canadian Hearing Society supports access to an ASL interpreter for interviews and some training. Make sure to ask the new employee if they are working with an outside agency that may provide this support.

6.8 — Human Resources Professional Role

The role of the Human Resources Professional for the organization is recruiting new employees with the talents and shields to keep the company productive include tapping into resources. The HR Professional should:

- develop a network of community resources to partner with when recruiting persons with disabilities;
- develop recruitment processes that eliminate barriers; and
- develop policies and procedures for recruitment that eliminate possible discriminatory risks.

CHAPTER 7: PREVENTING DISABILITY IN THE WORKPLACE

7.1 — Introduction

Every employer has an obligation to prevent workplace injuries but should also consider prevention of all illnesses and injuries that may lead to disability. A full health and wellness strategy is one of the best financial investments for an organization.

7.2 — The Organizational Impact of Health

Many studies have been completed that demonstrate the impact of health on an organization's ability to produce. Although health measures can be difficult to capture in day to day business accounting there has been improvement in our understanding of the costs.

Presenteeism is one of the issues that is becoming more noticeable in a company's productivity. This term is defined as "the impact on productivity of physical or emotional issues". For example an individual in distress about their family, health issues or who is in pain will perform with less productivity than an individual who is not distressed. Studies have shown that the impact on productivity, quality and safety risks is high in individuals who are distressed, smoke, are inactive or obese.

What are the issues and trends that workforces are dealing with across Canada that impact employee health?[1]

- The boomers continue to age . . .. the millennium generation approaches: with this change there are at least three groups of workers with different work ideals;

---

[1] Emile Tompa, Claire de Oliveira, Roman Dolinschi, Emma Irvin, "A Systematic Review of Disability Management Interventions with Economic Evaluations" (2008) J Occup Rehabil 18:16–26.

- Manufacturing operations downsize while the service industry expands;
- Mechanical risks appear to be decreasing while psychosocial risks are increasing;
- Small businesses (less than 20 employees) make up 96 per cent of employers in Canada;
- The work week averages 62–65 hours and is increasing;
- Part time and contract employment is most available, leading to a need to accumulate jobs to gain a full income;
- Employers are concerned about rising mental health claims (58 per cent), aging workforce (54 per cent), and employee engagement (48 per cent);
- Only 5 per cent of firms are prepared to deal with the mental health stigma in the workplace.

How do these trends impact employee health and company bottom line?[2]

- There is a coexistence of OLD risks (heavy workloads, repetitive work, painful postures, noise, etc.) with NEW risks (information overload, computer work, stress, violence in the workplace, environmental hazards, etc.);
- There is a lessening of work related accidents but an increase in number of deaths;
- By 2020 it is predicted that the primary cause of death will be depression;

2 These concepts are supported in: A Dupruis, A DeBruin, "The Relevance of the Notion of Work Life Balance" to "Non- standard Workers" 2004 Albany and Palmerston North Labour Market Dynamics Research Programme; C Cooper, S Cartwright, "Healthy Mind: Healthy Organization - A Proactive Approach to Occup- ational Stress" Human Relations, April 1994 Vol. 47 no. 4, at 455-471; Watson Wyatt, Staying @ Work Report 2005; WG Wilson, DM DeJay et al, "Work Characteristics and Employee Health and Well-being: Test of a Model of Healthy Work Organization" Journal of Occupational and Organizational Psychology, Vol. 177 o. 4 Dec 2004 at 565-588.

- Annual days lost per employee has increased from 7.3 days in 1997 to 8.1 days in 2007;
- Presenteeism costs are estimated at 75 per cent of all health costs;
- There is an increase of psychological distress at work (16.3 days per employee per year are working in high distress, 8.3 in low distress);
- Between 7 per cent and 9 per cent of employees claim to be victims of harassment at work;
- The face time with supervisors has reduced (less than 1 per cent of supervisor interaction is face to face) in a time when supervisor and employee relationship is needed;
- Only 35 per cent of organizations have mental health return to work programs;
- A high level executive that earns $100,000 per year will cost at least $150,000 to replace when they leave.

In an age where risk is now an underlying part of our work environment and society, an organization may not see immediate illnesses. But make no mistake these issues are impacting organization's bottom line today and will impact businesses' ability to stay competitive in the future.

The immediate results of these risks:

- Reduced productivity;
- Increased errors;
- Increased accidents;
- Reduced sales;
- Poor customer service;
- Reduced presenteeism;

The long term results of these risks:

- Illnesses such as heart attacks, diabetes, depression, anxiety disorders;
- Loss of customers;
- Loss of long term employees;

- High turnover rates;
- Legal costs of harassment and disability cases;
- Strained labour and management relationships;
- Increased long term disability and health benefits costs;

7.3 — Roles

a) — What can a front line employee do to manage these issues?[3]

- Increase understanding of their role in the organization and how the job that they do meets overall organizational goals;
- Manage energy and productivity;
- Take responsibility for managing personal health issues;
- Use time and organization strategies to manage workloads;
- Develop support systems at work and at home to manage personal and work stressors;
- Utilize health programs provided by the employer to maximize health.

b) — What can a supervisor do to manage these issues?

- Increase face to face time with employees;
- Increase manager presence;
- Reintroduce team meetings;
- Increase relationship building activities and TRUST building activities with employees, not just communication;
- Measure workload demands;
- Ensure appropriate resources to enable the team to meet the workload;

[3] C Cooper, I Robertson, "Creating Healthy Workplaces: The Supervisor's Role" International Review of Industrial and Organizational Psychology, 2004, Volume 19, Chapter 3.

- Address issues of stigma, harassment, and develop team resiliency.

c) — What can a CEO and Board do to manage these issues?[4]

- Move thinking about human impacts of management decisions to corporate level;
- Gain expertise in Human Resource Management, change processes, and mobilization;
- Enhance quality of Human Resource Management;
- Provide management training on how to detect mental health issues in the workplace
- Assess workloads
- Develop a high level of TRUST with employees to see stronger employee performance

d) — Management Don'ts[5]

A National Post article[6] highlighted the impact of the trends in global business that impact employee mental health and productivity. The following list was provided as a list of management behaviours that lead to higher mental health risks in an organization:

- Imposing unreasonable demands on subordinates and withholding information needed to carry out their jobs;
- Refusing to give employees reasonable discretion over day to day functions
- Failing to credit employee contributions and achievements
- Creating a treadmill effect — too much to do, too little time
- Rejecting out of hand employee's concerns about workload

---

4 Graham S Lowe, "Healthy Workplaces and Productivity: A discussion paper prepared for the Economic Analysis & Evaluation Division" April 2003, Health Canada. (Lowe, 2005)

5 Global Business and Economic Roundtable on Addiction and Mental Health, 2005

6 *Ibid.*

- Tolerating or fostering unclear company policies and job ambiguity
- Promoting an "email only" culture of communication

e) — What can Human Resources Professionals do to manage these issues?

- Provide programs and resources for managers to manage employee mental and physical health;
- Offer targeted programming to meet needs of the employee population;
- Assist management in moving thinking of human management principles into corporate decision making;
- Use a Balanced Scorecard approach to measure the human resource impact that directly affects bottom line and profit;[7]
- Provide education to corporations, leaders, managers and employees on mental health stigma, health and return to work management strategies;
- Provide return to work initiatives for mental health return to work;
- Provide management tools for improving health of employees;
- Guide corporations through healthy workplace strategy visioning to make health a part of doing business;
- Provide targeted programs for managing employee health risks.

7.4 — Accident prevention processes and practices

The Human Resources Professional has access to data about injuries and illnesses. Analysis of this data will allow the company to work with the health and safety representatives in the organization to develop strategies to reduce future injuries or illnesses. The company should understand the legal framework of occupational health and

[7] Balanced Scorecard http://www.balancedscorecard.org/

safety act and how to ensure due diligence in managing workplace health and safety. In smaller organizations the human resources professional may be the employee responsible for managing the workplace health and safety programs. The company should implement behaviour-based programs that will facilitate the health and safety of the workforce.

- Define injury/illness trends and collective injury/illness data specific to the workforce;
- Perform a worksite hazard analysis;
- Examine the workplace culture for any issues with respect to psychological harm;[8]
- Investigate all incidents and accidents for root causes;
- Develop a participative approach to all preventative programs;[9]
- Determine ways to prevent further similar accidents including hazard prevention and controls
    - Engineering controls
    - Work practice controls
    - Personal protective equipment
    - Administrative controls
    - Medical management
    - Training and education
- Implement changes to prevent accidents;
- Implement health and wellness strategies and programs to prevent illness and injury
    - Perform health risk assessments
    - Review benefit usage
    - Develop a health strategy
    - Implement a healthy workplace culture

---

[8] See www.guardingmindsatwork.ca

[9] See www.iwh.on.ca Blueprint for Participative Approach to Ergonomics.

- Implement specific workplace programs to address issues
- Evaluate the effectiveness of the changes.

7.5 — Health and Safety Regulations

Health and safety legislation and regulations set the minimum standard for safety in the workplace. There is an important connection between health and safety and disability management. The Human Resources Professional must consider possible causes of work related impairments so that they can facilitate a safe and early return to work without further jeopardizing the health and safety of the worker. In addition, they should be recommending strategies to decrease the risk of all workers through preventive health and safety programs such as ergonomic interventions.

The Human Resources Professional must be familiar with the health and safety legislation that governs their workplace. For federal workplaces, the Canada *Labour Code* Part II applies. For workplaces under provincial jurisdiction, each province sets out its own health and safety legislation. In addition, the Human Resources Professional must work closely with health and safety professionals in his or her organization to collaboratively work towards the safety of all workers.

a) — The Canada *Labour Code*[10]

The Canada *Labour Code* — Part II governs health and safety in organizations under federal jurisdiction such as federal government workplaces and crown corporations. For all other workplaces, each province has its own health and safety legislation.

b) — Provincial Occupational Health and Safety Acts

Occupational Health and Safety Acts apply to all organizations provincially regulated and operating in that province or territory. It covers health and safety regulations that must be followed by all employers. The main premise of the legislation is that the employer takes "every reasonable precaution to ensure the safety of its employees".

---

[10] Canada *Labour Code*, R.S.C., 1985, c. L-2.

Province	**Act**	**Website**
Alberta	*Occupational Health and Safety Act*	http://employment.alberta.ca/documents/WHS/WHS-PUB_li009.pdf
British Columbia	http://www2.worksafebc.com/publications/OHSRegulation/Home.asp	http://www2.worksafebc.com/publications/OHSRegulation/Home.asp
Manitoba	The *Workplace Health and Safety Act*	http://web2.gov.mb.ca/laws/statutes/ccsm/w210e.php
Nova Scotia	The *Occupational health and Safety Act*	http://nslegislature.ca/legc/index.htm
New Brunswick	The *Occupational Health and Safety Act*	http://www.gnb.ca/0062/acts/acts-e.asp#GlossO
Newfoundland	The *Occupational Health and Safety Act*	http://assembly.nl.ca/Legislation/sr/statutes/o03.htm
North West Territories	The *Safety Act*	http://www.justice.gov.nt.ca/Legislation/SearchResults.asp?Option=Title& DBTable=Leg&Parameter=S&Page=1
Nunavut	The *Safety Act*	http://www.canlii.org/en/nu/
Ontario	The Occupational Health and Safety	http://www.e-laws.gov.on.ca/navigation?file=browseStatutes&lang=en
Prince Edward Island	The *Occupational Health and Safety Act*	http://www.wcb.pe.ca/index.php3?number=62171&lang=E

Province	Act	Website
Quebec	The *Act respecting Occupational health and Safety*	http://www.canlii.org/en/qc/laws/stat/rsq-c-s-2.1/latest/rsq-c-s-2.1.html or http://www.publicationsduquebec.gouv.qc.ca/accueil.en.html
Saskatche-wan	The *Occupational Health and Safety Act, 1993*	http://www.publications.gov.sk.ca/details.cfm?p=743
Yukon	The *Occupational Health and Safety Act*	http://www.gov.yk.ca/legislation/legislation/page_o.html
Federal	Canada *Labour Code* (Part II — Occupational Health and Safety) *Government Employees Compensation Act* (see Accident prevention activities and safety program)	http://laws.justice.gc.ca/en/index.html http://www.hrsdc.gc.ca/eng/labour/health_safety/overview.shtml

c) — Occupational Health and Safety Act

The occupational health and safety act has the mandate that employers take "every reasonable precaution" to keep workers safe. There are very specific regulations that must be followed. The ministry of labour has the mandate to inspect and enforce this regulation. There is a focus on prevention with the Ministry of Labour and the workers' compensation boards. In Ontario there is a new mandate to inspect high risk workplaces at least four times per year. As well there are specific mandates for reduction of musculoskeletal disorders and new legislation to address violence in the workplace.

d) — Evolution of the Internal Responsibility System

The following chart outlines the evolution of the internal responsibility system which is the premise of all health and safety programs.

An Internal responsibility system places the responsibility for health and safety in the workplace one every worker within the organization.

The key premise of the IRS is that labour and management can work together to deliver effective solutions to many health and safety problems that arise in the workplaces (1975 Ham Commission)

1975	The Ham Commission Report recommends joint committees
1976	Bill 139 establishes the *Employee's Health and Safety Act*. The Minister can order joint committees
1978	Bill 70 establishes the *Occupational Health and Safety Act*. Mandatory joint committees in many workplaces
1987	Bill 79 adds Workplace Hazardous Materials Information System to the *Occupational Health and Safety Act*
1990	Bill 208[11] amends the *Occupational Health and Safety Act*, broadening the requirement for joint committees. Establishes certified members and the right to stop work. It also created the Workplace Health and Safety Agency and expanded the scope of the IRS, adding directors' and officers' liability.

The Ontario OHSA[12] came into effect in 1979. The legislation is founded on the principle of an Internal Responsibility System (IRS) within each organization where every employee is responsible for the health and safety of all employees.

There are rights involved in a properly functioning IRS:

- Openness and the Right to Know;
- The Right to Refuse unsafe work;
- The Right to participate.

[11] http://www.worksmartontario.gov.on. ca/scripts/default.asp?contentID=5-1-1-1

[12] Ontario *Health and Safety Act*, R.S.O. 1990, c. O.1 last amendment: 2009, c.33, Sched. 20, s. 3.

There are several parties involved in the IRS:

- The health and safety committee — auditor of the IRS;
- The ERS — government inspector or officer as an external auditor and watchdog;
- The OHS professional — champion and resource to the IRS and the management system;
- Safe workplace Associations, safety councils, consultants;
- In each legislation and regulations the workplace parties' duties are well defined.

e) — A Health and Safety Checklist

In order to ensure the company has done all things within the company's power to ensure the safety of the employees the following questions can be reviewed with each manager/supervisor:[13]

- Do you understand the nature of the work that your employees are doing?
- Do you fully understand the hazards and risks associated with the work you're directing?
- Does each member of the management team understand for whom you are responsible as a supervisor (contractors' employees people moving through the area)?
- Are you clear about the boundaries of the physical area for which you are in charge?
- Are you familiar with the regulations that apply to the kind of work that you perform?
- Do you know which employer rules, procedures; policies, etc. apply to your area and the work you complete?
- Do you understand what authority and responsibility for health and safety has been delegated to you by your own manager?

---

[13] F.E. Bird and G.L. Germain, *Loss Control Management. Practical Loss Control Leadership* (Rev. ed.). (Loganville, Georgia: Det Norske Veritas Inc., 1996).

- Do you know how frequently and in what manner you will have to account to your manager of delegated authority and responsibility for health and safety?
- Do you routinely inspect the workplace you are in charge of (not waiting for the committee to do it for you) getting to the root causes of problems you find?
- Do you investigate close calls, incidents and loss events as opposed to paying attention only to the high severity accidents; again seeking the root cause of the problem?
- Do you ensure that new people are trained before they begin?
- Is refresher training done frequently enough and on your own initiative?
- Do you reinforce training with safety talks of various kinds, particularly safety talks at the worksite (such as tailgate or toolbox talks)?
- Do you go see i.e. job observation as opposed to waiting for your people to call?
- Are you encouraging people to bring problems to you and to not cover up mistakes?
- Are you sensitive to events that increase risk, such as novelty and high-energy activities and allocate your efforts at risk reduction accordingly?
- Do you do task analysis, job planning and similar analyses so as to avoid learning by trial and error with new equipment, processes and materials?
- Do you attempt to eliminate obstacles to the use of protective devices?
- Are your realistic when setting tasks and allocating resources so that people do meet targets safely?
- Do you enforce standards and rules through discipline where necessary and almost always as a last resort after education, persuasion and obstacle removal?

- When you delegate work, are you clear about the health and safety delegation clear expectations about health and safety performance?
- Do you hold your people accountable for delegated work involving health and safety on a regular basis?
- Do you take actions when you learn of hazards not covered by your existing activities and procedures (i.e. not resting on your proactive laurels but always vigilant)?
- Are you a creative problem solver when it comes to novel health and safety concerns not just a rule follower of rule enforcer?
- Do you take health and safety problems that are outside your jurisdiction or beyond your ability to solve to senior people?

7.6 — Job Hazard Analysis[14]

A Job Hazard Analysis is a process used to review job methods and uncover hazards:

- That may have been overlooked in the layout or design of the equipment, tools, processes or work area;
- That may have developed after production started, or;
- That may have resulted from changes in work procedures or personnel.

a) — Steps in performing a job hazard analysis

- Select the job to be analyzed;
- Break the job down into successive steps or activities and observe how these actions are performed;
- Identify the hazards and potential accidents. (This is the critical step because only an identified problem can be corrected or eliminated);

[14] National Safety Council's "Accident Prevention Manual for Industrial Operations — Administration and Programs", Ninth edition. "Job Hazard Analysis," U.S. Department of Labour — OSHA Publication No. 3071. "Job Safety Analysis" — Safety Manual No. 5, U.S. Department of Interior, Mining Enforcement and Safety Administration.

- Develop safe job procedures to eliminate the hazards and prevent potential accidents.

b) — Methods of Conducting Job Hazard Analyses

There are two basic methods for conducting the Job Hazard Analysis:

- Direct observation
- Group discussion

A fast and efficient method of conducting a JHA is through direct observations of job performance. In many instances, however, this method may not be practical or desirable. For instance, new jobs and those that are done infrequently do not lend themselves to direct observation. When this is the case, the JHA can be made through discussions with persons familiar with the job. Individuals often involved in the process include, but are not limited to, first-line supervisors, safety specialists, engineers, experienced employees and outside contractors.

c) — Identifying the Hazards and Potential Accidents

The purpose is to identify all hazards, both *physical* and *environmental.* To do this, ask yourself these questions about each step:

- Is there a danger of striking against, being struck by, or otherwise making harmful contact with an object?
- Can the employee be caught in, on, by or between objects?
- Is there a potential for a slip, trip or fall? If so, will it be on the same elevation or to a different elevation?
- Can he/she strain himself/herself by pushing, pulling, lifting, bending or twisting? (use MSD checklists for risk analysis)[15]
- Is the environment hazardous to one's safety or health?

d) — Develop Solutions

- Find a new way to do the job;

---

[15] MSD Prevention www.wsib.on.ca or www.worksafebc.ca

- Change the physical conditions that create the hazard;
- Try to eliminate remaining hazards by changing work methods or procedures;
- Try to reduce the necessity of doing a job, or at least the frequency at which it must be performed.

e) — Selecting Jobs to be Analyzed

When selecting jobs to be analyzed, most people start with the worst first. You should be guided by the following factors:

- *Frequency of Accidents* (including "near misses"): A job that repeatedly produces accidents is a candidate for a JHA. The greater the number of incidents associated with a job, the greater its priority claim for a JHA.
- *Production of Disabling Injuries*: Every job that resulted in a serious or disabling injury should be given a JHA.
- *Severity Potential*: Some jobs may not have a history of accidents but may have the potential for severe injury.
- *New or Revised Jobs*: Jobs created by changes in equipment or in processes obviously have no history of accidents, but their accident potential may not be fully appreciated. Analysis should not be delayed until accidents or near-misses occur.
- *Multiple Employee Exposure*: Jobs that expose more than one individual to potential hazards should also be analyzed.

f) — Job Observation

- Review the job standards and processes as documented;
- Select the right person to observe;
- Brief him/her on the purpose of the job safety analysis;
- Observe the person performing the job and try to break it down into basic steps;
- Record each step.
- Check the breakdown with the person involved.

It is important to select an experienced, capable and cooperative person who is willing to share ideas. There may be a need to observe several employees performing the same job to understand different approaches and body mechanics. If the employee has never participated in a job hazard analysis, explain to him/her the purpose — to make a job safe by identifying and eliminating or controlling hazards — and show him/her a completed job safety analysis.

g) — Writing Instructions

Once the JHA is completed it is important to document new written instructions for the job and include this in the training of all employees.

- Involve the health and safety committee in writing the instructions;
- Ask for feedback from the employees that do the job;
- Start each instruction with an action word;
- Each instruction should be observable;
- Each instruction should be measurable;
- Test the instructions with employees who perform the work.

When evaluating a given procedure, ask the following question. *"What should the employee do — or not do — to eliminate this particular hazard or prevent this potential accident?"* The answer must be specific and concrete to be beneficial. General precautions such as "be careful", "use caution" or "be alert" are useless. Answers should state what to do and *how* to do it.

This recommendation, "Make certain the wrench does not slip or cause loss of balance" is incomplete. It does not tell *how* to prevent the wrench from slipping. Here is a more complete recommendation. "Set the wrench properly and securely. Test its grip by exerting a slight pressure on it. Brace yourself against something immovable, or take a stance with feet wide apart before exerting full pressure. This prevents loss of balance if the wrench slips."

Job Hazard Analyses can be very beneficial if they are performed correctly. They not only result in a safer job, but also increase productivity and eliminate waste. Take the time to do them correctly; and more importantly, use them.

Where job hazards are identified it may be beneficial to consult with a specialist in ergonomics or health and safety to complete a full risk analysis on high risk jobs that lead to musculoskeletal disorders or high demand jobs.

7.7 — Fines and Convictions

Under the External Responsibility System supervisors, directors and officers are regularly fined under the *Occupational Health and Safety Act*. The main purpose of any conviction under the OHSA is to deter any further health and safety risks and to provide deterrence and a process by which the employer improves their health and safety performance. Many of the arbitrators under the OHSA will provide fines or even jail terms where there is a history of the employer receiving convictions.

The Ministry of Labour Inspectors[16] uphold and enforce the Act. They inspect the workplace and investigate potentially hazardous situations, accidents and work refusals. The inspector may issue an order where there is contravention of the Act and may provide advice and mediation where there are disputes between workplace parties. Due diligence is the primary defence against a conviction under the OHSA. Inspectors are automatically involved in all critical incidents and work stoppages but they may also inspect your workplace at any time. The organization must provide access to all workplace areas, paperwork and policies during an inspection.

The Inspectors have a success rate of 80 per cent on all convictions. There is a full process for proactive due diligence and even reactive due diligence that will allow an employer to ensure the health and safety of his workers prior to convictions.

In 2005 an additional 200 inspectors were added to the Ontario Ministry of Labour to focus on the HIGH RISK employers. Those employers with the worst experience in the bottom of the rate group will have inspections. These inspectors have also been given additional powers to provide TICKETING under the OHSA.

---

[16]http://www.labour.gov.on.ca/english/

Log on to the Ministry of Labour's[17] website in your jurisdiction for information on the changes to the inspection process and potential ticketing process.

a) — Occupational Health and Safety Changes in 2009

Musculoskeletal Disorder (MSD) Prevention Program

In March 2009 the Ontario Ministry of Labour indicated that they would begin inspecting workplaces for musculoskeletal injury prevention programs. The expectation is that every workplace would take every reasonable precaution to prevent MSD in the workplace. The employer will need to demonstrate their compliance with this through policy and procedures, prevention strategies, investigations of incidents and education programs for employees. The number of working days lost to "stress" might be high, but almost twice as many workers are affected by musculoskeletal disorders (MSDs) such as back pain, arm or neck strains or diseases of the joints. Indeed MSDs are, by some margin, the most commonly reported cause of work-related ill health.

What this data masks, however, is the proportion of people who have both MSDs and a stress-related illness. There is a growing body of evidence which tells us that having chronic low back pain, or a progressive condition such as rheumatoid arthritis, increases the risk of depression or anxiety.[18] Moreover, the chances of a speedy return to work after an MSD-related absence are enhanced if people have positive mental health[19]

There is now a growing body of research which shows that early intervention, treatment, condition management and vocational rehabilitation can significantly reduce the damage which MSDs do to

---

[17] http://www.labour.gov.on.ca/english/

[18] C Dickens (2002) "Depression in Rheumatoid Arthritis: A Systematic Review of the Literature with Meta-analysis" Psychomatic Medicine, 64, 52-60.

[19] JM Disorbio, D Bruns, GBarolat (2006) "Assessment and Treatment of Chroci Pain" Practical Pain Management, March 1-10.

physical and mental health, to labour market participation, to labour productivity and to the social and family lives of patients.[20]

To calculate the cost of MSDs (or any illness) the following factors must be estimated:

- *Direct costs* (including medical expenditure, such as the cost of prevention, detection, treatment, rehabilitation, long term care and ongoing medical and private expenditure).
- *Indirect costs* (including lost work output attributable to a reduced capacity for activity, such as lost productivity, lost earnings, lost opportunities for family members, lost earnings of family members and lost tax revenue).
- *Intangible costs* (including psychosocial burden resulting in reduced quality of life, such as job stress, economic stress, family stress and suffering)[21].

These costs vary considerably depending on the condition, on the severity of the symptoms, and whether these cause short or long term absence or disability. Moreover, they vary depending on the particular methods used to calculate the costs.

The MSD Prevention Program should include:

- Policies and Procedures to manage MSD;
- Training of Managers and Employees in MSD Prevention;
- Risk Assessment of Hazardous positions;
- Use a participatory approach through ergonomic committees;
- Implementation processes for MSD Prevention Strategies;
- Examination of Work Processes that increase risk including physical, psychological, cultural, corporate productivity measures, job satisfaction etc.;
- Evaluate the program effectiveness.

---

[20] Dame Carol Black, "Working For a Healthier Tomorrow: Dame Carol Black's Review of the Health of Britain's Working Age Population" 17 March 2008, Produced by the cross-government Health, Work and Well-being Programme.

[21] World Health Organizational, International Classification of Impairments, Disabilities and Handicaps, "A Manual of Classification relating to the consequences of disease" Geneva:WHO, 1980, 47.

b) — *Occupational Health and Safety Amendment Act* (Violence and Harassment in the Workplace), 2009 — Bill 168

New legislation was introduced on April 20, 2009 in Ontario that would require employers to develop policies to address workplace violence and harassment and to assess the risk of violence in its workplace. The changes were passed and every employer in Ontario with over 5 employees must comply as of June 15, 2010. The act includes a new duty to address domestic violence in the workplace.

Definitions

Workplace harassment — means engaging in a course of vexatious comment or conduct against a worker in a workplace that is known or ought reasonably to be known to be unwelcome.

Workplace Violence — means

a) The exercise of physical force by a person against a worker in a workplace that causes or could causes physical injury to the worker.

b) An attempt to exercise physical force against a worker in a workplace that could cause physical injury to the worker.

c) A threat of violence.

What Employers Need to Know

The Ministry of Labour currently takes the position that section 25(2)(h) of the Act requires employers to "take every precaution reasonable in the circumstance for the protection of a worker" and that includes assessing the risk of workplace violence. It is prudent for an employer at the very least to have a policy addressing workplace violence and to assess the risk of violence in its workplace.

- Develop a threat management team to assist with risk assessments, policy development and determining strategies to manage violence and harassment in the workplace;
- Perform a workplace risk assessment on all jobs (see sample workplace risk assessment survey in toolkit);
- Draft a policy that addresses workplace violence;
- Define a process for dealing with critical violent incidents;

- Define acts of violence, including threats of violent action against personnel and company property;
- Declare that the company will not tolerate violent or aggressive behaviour;
- Describe disciplinary action that will be taken for offenders in strict terms;
- Tell all employees that they are responsible for reporting violent acts or what appears to be the possibility of a violent act to their supervisor;
- Ask employees not to intervene but to call their manager or 911;
- Tell employees what to do in extreme situations, e.g. gun-wielding, hostage taking;
- Describe how victims will be protected in the future;
- Deliver an education program on preventing workplace violence;
- If appropriate, have the policy reviewed by your legal advisor;
- Schedule regular reviews of the policy to ensure it is relevant. Communicate the policy to all employees, including senior personnel;
- Ensure all new employees receive a copy of the policy;
- Have all employees acknowledge in writing or by e-mail that they have received and read the policy and/or amendments;
- Post the policy and/or amendments prominently in a place where all employees will see it and have regular access to it;
- Have the appropriate company officer distribute a copy of the policy to all managers and supervisors with instructions about what is expected of them in carrying out the policy;
- Provide training or education where necessary;
- Announce the policy and provide highlights for employees;
- Ask managers to schedule an annual discussion about this policy with their staff.

c) — Workplace Wellness Programs

Where, then, should senior managers focus their attention: the individual worker, the organization, or society as a whole? The answer is "all of the above," but in a thoughtful and coordinated fashion. The approach advocated here is to develop and institutionalize an integrated model of worker health, safety and productivity as an overall business strategy.

Focusing for a moment on the organization as a whole, it is more the norm than the exception that health, safety and productivity issues are addressed separately and discreetly by different functions within the organization: employee benefits, employee assistance, risk management, occupational medicine, safety, organizational development, operations, human resources, employee relations, labor relations or other departments.

Fragmented, department-specific strategies attempt to manage individual and organizational risks, although oftentimes these risks are common to several functions simultaneously within the organization and might be better managed through cooperative or integrated activities.

Arguments in favor of integration and coordination of functions include the following:

- Cost efficiency and lack of duplication can be achieved when resources and experiences are shared across departments and functions;
- To achieve efficiencies, organizations need to develop and apply common metrics so that a uniform story can be told using data and measures that are commonly understood and accepted; and
- A health, safety, and productivity approach will lead to reduced competition for senior management attention and scarce resources.

While these arguments may make sense at face value, there are also some significant barriers and blockages that can be voiced against a health, safety and productivity management model. They include the following:

- There is often turf protection by program managers and a consequent lack of interest in sharing resources, knowledge and experience with others viewed as internal competitors;

- Managers may complain that they "lack the time" to devote to "non-essential" tasks and processes — managers may view integration efforts as "busy time" that distracts employees from their "real" jobs;
- Managers may declare that different departments and organizations function under different sets of rules. Some departments may be subject to federal or provincial regulations, others may be in charge of implementing organized labor contracts, and yet others may be responding to specific senior management directives;
- There may be momentum to continue doing things as they have always been done, because "they work" and there is a reluctance to "fix something that isn't broken." In addition, employees may argue that even if they wanted to they could not integrate and coordinate their activities because of "hard coded" reporting relationships and a lack of authority to introduce new structures. Further, they may argue that senior management needs to authorize a re-organization for such activity to take place; and
- Similarly, opposition forces may argue that there is no evidence that an alternative model or models that emphasize integration are better than existing structures and work practices. Furthermore, they may assert that the idea may appear to work in theory, but it would cost more than it would save and thus not produce a short term ROI.

d) — Why Develop a integrated health, safety, and productivity management program:

- Poor employee health is responsible for unnecessary and avoidable health, safety and productivity losses;
- Employee health can be improved through well-founded, evidence-based, well implemented, and measurable health, safety and productivity management interventions;
- Providing health benefits alone is not enough — employers need to take an active role in delivering health education, awareness building, risk reduction and counseling programs that support health, safety and productivity enhancement efforts;

- Administration of health benefits, health promotion, workers' compensation, non-occupational disability, occupational health and safety, behavioral health, organizational development, and other relevant functions can and should be coordinated in order to maximize the impact of a "package" of human resources programs;
- Improvements in employee health will not only reduce medical care costs but also enhance worker safety, productivity and organizational competitiveness; and
- Successful health, safety, and productivity management programs can save more money than they cost and thus achieve a significant and positive ROI for the organization.

A workplace wellness program will allow every organization to demonstrate its commitment to employees and their health concerns. In order to develop a workplace wellness program the organization will need to understand the current employee health risks and potential strategies to address those risks.

- Implement health and wellness strategies and programs to prevent illness and injury[22]
    - Perform health risk assessments
    - Review benefit usage
    - Perform a wellness culture audit[23]
    - Develop a health strategy
    - Implement a healthy workplace culture
    - Implement specific workplace programs to address issues

Once the data is analyzed within the organization for retrospective (health costs already used) and prospective (future risks based on lifestyle and health behaviours) risks, a strategy should be developed to meet the needs of the employees. This strategy is best developed

---

[22] 2006 Wellness Councils Of America at www.welcoa.org

[23] Graham S. Lowe, PhD, "Healthy Workplaces and Productivity: A Discussion Paper Prepared for the Economic Analysis and Evaluation Division" April 2003, Health Canada.

and monitored by a wellness committee made up of management and employee representatives.

In order to have an integrated health management program the company should consider including the following areas:

Care Management

- Acute/chronic disease management sometimes referred to as tertiary prevention which includes efforts to prevent complications of existing disease (e.g., disease management programs directed at chronic diseases such as diabetes, congestive heart failure, and depression);
- Work related injury, disability and illness management; and
- Medical or large case management.

Health Promotion and Disease Prevention (Health Management)

- Primary prevention efforts to prevent poor health among the currently healthy through behavioral risk factor reduction and lifestyle modification programs (e.g., programs that increase physical activity, support healthy diets, prevent obesity, prevent smoking, manage stress, prevent falls, encourage moderate alcohol consumption, maintain social connections and support structures, and assure appropriate immunizations);
- Secondary prevention efforts directed at early detection of disease (e.g., screening for cancer, hypertension, high blood glucose, hypercholesterolemia, unhealthy body weight; receiving counseling on quitting smoking); and
- Self care, consumerism, demand management programs.

There are three levels of health promotion and wellness programs that should be initiated.

- Educational and Awareness Programs:
    - pamphlets, lunch and learn sessions, health fairs
- Health Engagement Programs
    - gym membership support, weight watchers on site, smokers cessation programs, walking programs, flu vaccinations on site

- Workplace Culture Programs
    - bike racks, walking trails, showers at work, policies on healthy eating, cafeteria selections, health staff

Workplace Environment

- Occupational & environmental medicine;
- Ergonomics and job design;
- Employee safety;
- Medical surveillance programs; and
- Return to work and job accommodation.

Corporate Culture and Organizational Health

- Clarity about and communication of socially responsible organizational values;
- Focus on workplace stress reduction and work-life balance; and
- Organizational efforts to improve work climate, morale, employee attitudes, including periodic assessment of these organizational dynamics.

e) — Main Components for Integrating Health Management

1. Alignment between health, safety and productivity management and the overall business strategy of the organization.
2. Interdisciplinary team focus.
3. Champion or a team of champions.
4. Senior management and business operations as key members of the team.
5. Prevention, health promotion, and wellness staff are heavily engaged in the process.
6. Emphasis on quality of life improvement, not just cost cutting.
7. Data, measurement, reporting, evaluation, and return on investment studies become increasingly important over time.
8. Communication is constant and directed throughout the organization.
9. Constant need to improve by learning from others.
10. Have fun.

7.8 — Human Resources Professional Role

In most organizations there will be resources for managing the occupational health and safety act requirements but in smaller organizations this may be the role of the human resources professional. It is important to fully understand the regulations under this law as there are specific requirements for certification, meetings, minutes, and response to concerns. The human resources professional should be the champion for the internal responsibility system and strategy for improving employee health. The key components in the human resources role are:

- Ensure legislative compliance according to the organizations' line of business, size and employee activities;
- Develop a strategy to incorporate both occupational and non occupational prevention strategies;
- Develop strategies that will improve management and employee commitment to health and injury prevention;
- Analyze the organization trends both retrospectively and the risks prospectively by carrying out a risk analysis;
- Gather data on injury and illness incidents and report to senior management regularly the costs and impact on the company;
- Reward employee involvement in health and safety initiatives;
- Develop policies for new health issues such as violence in the workplace, musculoskeletal disorder prevention and mental health company culture programs;
- Facilitate improved internal responsibility mechanisms through proactively dealing with issues from the health and safety committee.

CHAPTER 8: HOW TO DEVELOP A DISABILITY MANAGEMENT PROGRAM

8.1 — Getting Senior Management Commitment

In order for your disability management program to be effective you must ensure that senior management is committed to the process and the duty to accommodate. In many cases this can be well below the senior management's corporate radar and you must bring it to their recognition. The following are strategies to improve commitment and awareness:

- Outline the costs of disability in your workplace;
- Detail the direct and indirect costs including loss of productivity and how that ties to loss of sales or production;
- Develop a plan to address disability management;
- Outline the key benefits to the organization and how it fits with the organizations strategic planning and mission.

For example: the cost of disability is 8 per cent of payroll and indirectly costs the company 14 per cent. By implementing a disability management program you can improve the costs by 10 per cent in the first year and continue that trend. Depending on the profit margin the number of sales to cover that 10 per cent of payroll is $100,000

8.2 — Strategic Planning Approaches to Managing Disability

Linking strategic planning with the Disability Management program is often over-looked in most organizations. By incorporating the organization's strategic plan it will demonstrate how Disability Management programs support the organization's mission, vision values and long-term strategic goals. It provides for irrefutable evidence that the program is an important business strategy that will help the organization attain its stated objectives and provides a framework for shared ownership of program initiatives. This will result in many benefits to the organization's Disability Management program.

Benefits include:

- Organizational-wide support for the program at all levels;
- Increased program compliance;
- Program awareness;
- Marketing strategy.

The business case for an integrated approach will need to involve a formal review of costs and benefits associated with both an integrated and a non-integrated approach to return to work and disability management. This will involve reviewing internal data but also any research or studies that have been completed external to the organization. The ability to search out credible research and to integrate research into presentations to senior management and labour executives can also be an effective strategy in the promotion of an integrated approach.

The National Institute of Disability Management and Research (NIDMAR)[1] indicates that a solid disability management program from the best practices literature review, the market research and the focus groups all support the following principles:

a. Occupational and non occupational illnesses and injuries should be treated equally

b. Early intervention in the illness or injury even prior to an absence is important to provide solutions to improve health and productivity and reduce lost time

c. Comprehensive case management should be involved in ALL cases including ensuring that the following is implemented in each and every case:

i. A multidisciplinary approach (i.e. all stakeholders understanding their roles and responsibilities including employee, manager, union, human resources, health professionals, family physician, etc.

[1] National Institute of Disability Management and Research (1995). Disability Management in the Workplace: A Guide to Establishing a Joint Workplace Program. Port Alberni, BC: NIDMAR.

ii. Implementation of evidence based treatment and return to work processes

iii. Focus on functional abilities while monitoring precautions and limitations with health professionals

iv. Proactively addressing timelines i.e. use of duration guidelines, ensuring proactive receipt of functional information from professionals, return to work transitional programs that are goal oriented and time limited based on evidence

v. Rights based approach understanding the legal responsibilities of all parties including employment standards under (OHR Act, ES Act, OHS Act, WSI Act, Collective Agreements, etc.)

d. Consistent approaches to accommodation and return to work process for all individuals in every department

e. Consistent communication between all stakeholders involved in the process (i.e. employee, manager, disability management professional, union, HR, MD)

f. Ensuring all parties have clear education and training on roles and responsibilities and are held accountable for those responsibilities

g. Tracking and measurement of the process for quantitative and qualitative evaluation

h. Collaboration between management and union to work towards the goal of improving employee health and productivity.

a) — Mission statement

A mission statement outlines the values and beliefs of the workplace and the commitment of the joint committee as well as the overall goal of the company in terms of disability management and return to work. The core purpose of the program should be clearly stated in the mission statement and should focus on the promotion and preservation of the employability of workers with disabilities, through effective disability management processes.

A Sample Mission Statement:

COMPANY ABC is committed to the provision of reasonable accommodation for all employees who are ill or injured and require support to return to full function. We believe that employees are the most valuable investment of the company and support of early stay at work and return to work processes benefit both the company and the employee. We will endeavour to work with the employee to find reasonable accommodations within the workplace and work with the employee and the health care provider to support recovery at the workplace. We understand that commitment to this process is crucial to the business and to the ill/injured employee and their family. We will work together with employees to protect their employability and productivity.

b) — Goals and Objectives

Goal statements will outline the objectives that the program hopes to achieve, such as the development of written policies and procedures for return to work. The goal statements should outline objectives that are specific, measurable, achievable and realistic for the workplace.

Goals of the disability management program. It is recommended that organizations set specific goals for the program to be monitored and measured on a yearly basis. This will ensure that the program is meeting the needs of the organization and is outcome based. *Suggested goals* are:

a. 100 per cent of employees that are off work will have DMP contact and coordination of return to work

b. 100 per cent of employees will contact the DMP by day 3 of the absence.

c. 100 per cent of employees will be offered suitable and meaningful accommodation upon return to work

d. There will be a reduction in gaps between STD and LTD

e. There will be reduction in the number of employees moving to LTD by x per cent

f. There will be a reduction in lag time in reporting of WSIB claims

g. There will be a reduction in lost time WSIB injuries by 50 per cent

h. Transitional programs will be offered for under 8–12 weeks in 75 per cent of cases

i. There will be 100 per cent communication with employee and manager every 2 weeks from DMP during employee absence and during return to work (specify information content required)

j. There will be 100 per cent communication on roles and responsibilities during the initial communication with employees and managers from DMP

k. There will be 100 per cent training to all managers on duty to accommodate and return to work program

Sample Short Term Objectives & Indicators:

Objective:	*Meet the requirements of the jurisdiction with respect to applicable human rights, WSIA and employment standards acts*
Indicators:	• Return to work policies, protocols and procedures are consistently and fairly implemented • Program evaluations and action plans are made to address gaps • Return to work request guidelines are in place and accessible • Accessibility standards are adhered to
Objective:	*Review 100 per cent of individual return to work requests of existing employees and respond appropriately in a timely, dignified, and confidential manner*
Indicators:	• The return to work initiative maximizes employee integration and participation in the workplace

	• Communication with the absent employee, manager and medical community 100 per cent of time within 3 days of absence • Minimal delay in the return to work process for the employee
Objective:	*All employees understand their return to work rights & responsibilities within the return to work process*
Indicators:	• Prompt communication of return to work need to the employer • The employee co-operates in the return to work process
Objective:	*Company commitment to and understanding of return to work as a multiparty process*
Indicators:	• The roles of all parties are defined and flow of processing return to work requests is completed and communicated • Return to work policies and procedures and supporting tools are implemented • Return to work request communication packages are accessible
Objective:	*All parties have the knowledge and behaviours to support return to work*
	• Training specific to each party's role within the workplace and in successful return to work activity

Indicators:	• Each part knows how to provide the necessary support to facilitate successful return to work activity • Current modified work programs are analyzed and adjusted • Communication with carriers to support return to work is maintained
Objective:	*Eliminate potential injury and illness risks*
Indicators:	• Policies and programs are reviewed that support injury and illness reduction • Ergonomic analysis of workstations are in place • Physical cognitive and visual demands are completed of all jobs • Health and wellness programs are implemented

8.3 — The Service Delivery Process for Large and Small Work Sites

The specific disability management structure and service delivery processes will differ based on the size of the organization. Smaller organizations, such as those work sites with one location will only require a one-tier system. Larger organizations, those companies with multiple work sites and locations function more effectively with a two-tiered disability management committee structure. The two-tier committee structure is described as follows:[2]

1. *Corporate level*: An autonomous steering committee or administrative committee comprised of a balance of senior management and senior union representatives that can oversee the program at the divisional level. This corporate level joint committee can provide a broader perspective to the local joint steering committee and identify ways in which diverse work sites within a large organization can use resources to assist return to work efforts.
2. *Joint-Steering Committee*: Established at the local or divisional level and has balanced representation from both union and management. This divisional joint committee is responsible for the day-to day implementation, co-ordination, promotion and evaluation of the program. They could also resolve serious disputes that arise at the workplace during return to work initiatives.
3. *Individual Programs*: Within the management of disability in the workplace there will be variable programs to manage stay at work and attendance programs, prevention programs, health management programs, return to work, accessibility and accommodation. In order to best manage disability in any workplace these programs should be integrated and comprehensive to avoid gaps.

8.4 — Steps to Implement a Disability Management Program

Step #1

- In collaboration with the union and management, develop and implement a comprehensive disability management program with the right skill sets, the right services and supportive policies and procedures.

Rationale

The organization should examine closely the goals and objectives of the proposed program and what should be accomplished. It is im-

---

[2] Don Shrey, et al, *"Disability Management Best Practices and Joint Labour — Management Collaboration"* 2006, Int. Journal of disability Management Research 1:1 at 52–63.

portant to set the goals and objectives to understand what this program should accomplish. It is important to use the market research to develop a model, which is ultimately leading to reduction in costs through improved employee health.

The policy on Disability Management Program short-term disability absences needs to include wording, which is consistent with the implementation of this disability management program. It is also important to educate the employees of the organization on the program and to develop strategies that will improve the perception and the delivery of the program.

The communication strategy will also be important in order to ensure that the program is consistently used and delivered.

Step # 2

- Education of employees and managers on the Disability Management Program process

Rationale

It is important to focus on the health management process that will help employees. There is a need to ensure that all employees understand the process and have readily available tools to refer to access the program. This may include provision of fridge magnets, process algorithms and manager and employee packages either in paper or online format.

A priority should be set to train all managers in the policies related to health and disability management and enforcement of those policies should be a part of the manager's performance criteria.

The Disability Management Program steering committee should develop a strategy to maintain regular communication on the program through use of newsletters and communicating through management meetings the successes of the process.

The Disability Management Program team should also develop readily available packages on work related and non work related injuries to standardize the process.

Promotional training should be considered when launching the program and all orientation programs should be revisited to ensure that accurate procedures are communicated to new employees and new managers.

The company can use a number of programs available for the employees with integration of messaging and access to the services. The following is recommended to improve communication of services:

- Computer portal with an area specifically for health services;
- Pocket/desk cards with core programs and access information to place at the desk or in the brief case;
- Regular awareness bulletin boards;
- Presentations in staff meetings about services;
- Training sessions for management team about services and access information;
- Training sessions for all staff including managers on disability management process and roles and responsibilities.

Step # 3

- When developing the disability management program ensure that the focus remains on health management and return to work as opposed to adjudication and absence management

Rationale

Most organizations in Canada currently have an increasing percentage of absences related to short term and casual absences. having absences managed through Disability Management Program leads to a negative image of the Disability Management Program. There is a need to understand the data on absence and to implement appropriate management driven programs to manage absences, which are not related to disabilities.

The company should consider development of consistent and fair policies with respect to absence management. This would then allow interventions to be provided for health issues, for return to work planning, and for culpable absenteeism issues. The manager should be able to access timely absence reports from this system and then be able to accurately manage the absence. The employee population should be provided with education on absence costs and effect on the company and any new policies on managing absence so that they can have a personal understanding of the importance of attendance and the consequences of culpable absenteeism. The managers should be provided with a structured policy on absence management and training on how to manage these absences and the resources available for involving the health services in the absence process.

Step # 4

- Review policies and procedures of the Disability Management Program to clarify roles and responsibilities of stakeholders in the program through a labour management collaborative steering committee

Step #5

- Identify roles and responsibilities with respect to casual absence and disability related absences

Step # 6

- Launch the Disability Management Program in a way that will promote the positive health and productivity aspects of the program

Step # 7

- Establish an auditing program for the Disability Management Program provided in order to ensure solid objectives are met and that processes are followed consistently according to SDHU's policy and philosophy

Rationale:

Regular and consistent provision of data on absences both related to disability and casual absences will allow the manager to better manage the employee. It is also important that the data collected is consistent from year to year as this will ensure that the trends noted are accurate.

The company should set measurement and baseline data gathering standards and reporting standards so that the cost of health and disability for the company can be easily reported to senior management. Human Resources should be responsible for the management of this data and this should be reported to senior management with recommendations on a quarterly basis. The reporting should occur on a regular basis in a readable format for all managers in order to maintain the focus on absence and disability management. It is also important to tie actions and responsibilities to all reports provided in order to ensure that the information is properly used to address lowering the costs of disability and absence at the company.

It is important to tie the reporting data to performance measures for managers along with productivity, as this will ensure that the data is attended to in a meaningful way. Other companies have developed performance measures for disability health and safety that are tied to manager performance reviews. This leads to a workplace culture that is focused not just on productivity but productivity, which comes from a safe and healthy population. Longer term productivity results will be realized.

8.5 — Developing Policy and Procedures

a) — Promote Equitable Access to Services

Equitable access to services in Disability Management and Return to work involves adopting an *integrated approach* in which all workers, regardless of their occupation or cause of disability (whether work related or not) will have equal access to disability management and return to work services to assist them in maintaining their employment or employability.

In many companies throughout Canada, workers with work related or occupational injuries or illnesses are given a priority for accommodation and return to work, and this is generally related to the costs and financial penalties associated with lost time incidents under most Workers' Compensation legislation. It is often overlooked that the cost of non work related illnesses can far exceed that of work related injuries. Any insurance programs and premium costs are paid for by the employer and should be considered as part of that cost benefit analysis.[3]

b) — Human Resources Professional Role

To promote equitable access to services include:

---

[3] See chapter 15 Evaluation of Disability Programs.

- Development of written policies and procedures, with active participation of management and labour, that mandates an integrated approach;
- Data collection and analysis to demonstrate the costs (both human and financial) of a non-integrated approach and the potential cost benefits of an integrated approach;
- Early intervention for all workers who are absent from work due to work related and non-work related causes. Early intervention should be clearly defined in written policies and procedures and communicated to all workers / managers;
- A coordinated case management and / or return to work approach for all workers based on criteria for case management involvement outlined in the written policies / procedures.

c) — Sample Policy and Procedures

Injured/Ill Worker's Early and Safe Return to Work Policy

Return to Work Definition: Return to work is the process or strategy of safely returning employees to the workplace on a timely basis as the employee's capabilities allow and can be matched with suitable work.

Philosophy

The Management of [company name] is committed to cooperating with all of their employees who have been injured on or away from the workplace and will do everything they can for an early and safe return to work. At [company name], we will provide a modified work program to any of our injured/ill employees until he/she is able to return to their pre-accident job, wherever possible.

Roles and Responsibilities

Employer will:

- Contact injured /ill worker as soon as they are aware of the injury/illness and stay in regular contact throughout any absence that may be necessary;
- Cooperate in providing suitable work;

- Give WCB/carrier information as required;
- Provide workers with Work Fitness Form to take to the treating practitioners for completion;
- Educate workers about the return to work program;
- Set specific time frames for the return to work;
- Review worker's progress regularly;
- Pay full wages and benefits for the day or shift on which the injury occurred if it is work related;
- Make certain that workers understand their obligations to cooperate;
- Set clear procedures to follow in reporting injuries. (Establish an Accident/Injury Reporting Policy.)

Worker will:

- Contact supervisor immediately of any injury or absence;
- Stay in regular contact;
- Help identify and cooperate in suitable work arrangements;
- Give WCB/carrier information as required;
- Return to work within 24 hours with the completed form to develop with the employer an early and safe return to work as able. Where this is not possible the employee will inform the supervisor of any restrictions so that return to work planning can occur;
- Choose a doctor or qualified practitioner. Note: A change in doctor cannot be made without permission of WCB.

Company will:

- Assess each individual's situation according to the health practitioner's report of restrictions and recommendations and will provide modified work to suit the degree of injury;
- Assist in the employee's active recovery and encourage the worker to return to work to their pre-accident job, where it can be done safely;

- Identify jobs that are suitable for accommodating injured workers on a temporary basis in order to facilitate the early and safe return to work program and limit any loss of their earnings.

Accommodations

A change or modification to the job or workplace so that the work is within the injured or ill person's functional capabilities and the risk of injury is reduced. It is the company's philosophy to adjust and modify the worker's own job position first and follow the hierarchy of accommodation. All accommodations will be individualized and developed according to the capabilities and restrictions of the worker and the specific job demands and processes.

Types of Accommodations:

- Reduce hours;
- Graduate RTW hours;
- Change of position — provision of a stool if needed or sit stand workstations;
- Ergonomic adjustment to the work areas;
- Lifting equipment to assist with lifting;
- Alteration of height of equipment, tools and parts;
- Re-assign duties;
- Restructure the job;
- More frequent rest breaks;
- Work platform vs. ladders;
- Ladders for climbing scaffolds;
- Mini stretch breaks (10–15 minutes);
- Chair with back support vs. Picnic table;
- Anti-vibration tools (e.g. anti-vibration jackhammer/screwdrivers);
- Make heavy tools available at waist height;
- Light shop work, general clean-up, inventory;

- Development of training or job standards;
- Performance of job hazard analysis on jobs;
- Painting trailers, containers (light work with brush);
- Washing trucks;
- Pickup or delivery of plans.

Chapter 9: Roles and Responsibilities in Managing Disability

9.1 — The Roles and Functions of Stakeholders Involved in Disability Management

There are various stakeholders that may be involved in the Disability Management Program. It is important for the Human Resources Professional to understand the roles and responsibilities of these various stakeholders so as to support their initiatives and participation in the return to work processes. The roles and functions of professional that may be involved in the Disability Management program processes are described.

a) — Return to Work Coordinator/Disability Management Professional

There are internationally accepted Standards of Practice for the Certified Disability Management Professional (CDMP) or Certified Return to Work Coordinator (CRTWC).[1] To review the full extent of those standards visit www.nidmar.ca

The Disability Management Professional generally assumes overall responsibility for the administrative aspects for the Disability Management program while the RTW Co-coordinator position is responsible for the return to work activities. General roles and responsibilities of these professionals include:

- Coordinate and communicate with all involved parties such as union, supervisors, rehabilitation specialists, insurance providers,

---

1 www.nidmar.ca National Institute of Disability Management and Research (1999). Ethical standards and professional conduct. Occupational Standards in Disability Management. Port Alberni, BC: NIDMAR. National Institute of Disability Management and Research (2000). Code of Practice for Disability Management. Port Alberni, BC: NIDMAR.

health care providers, health and safety specialists, Ergonomist, family physicians and medical specialists;

- Ensuring that ill/injured workers are identified as soon as possible to ensure proper rehabilitation and early and safe return to work;
- Develop the return to work plan with input from each individual injured worker and other stakeholders;
- Monitor the progress of each case;
- Document all activities in each case;
- Report trends to the health and safety specialists, joint labour management committee and/or joint health and safety committees;
- Assist workers with application for medical benefits or obtaining medical assistance/treatment;
- Provide information to worker and family;
- Develop strategic alliances with community and internal groups to assist with the program;
- Facilitate regular, open communication between all;
- Develop and maintain an atmosphere of trust, support and respect;
- Arrange work site accommodations, assistive devices, job restructuring;
- Ensure disabled individuals are aware of their rights, obligations and the effect of specific decisions on their right to benefits;
- Maintain current and accurate database information;
- Report to relevant persons — workers progress;
- Develop resource network / library;
- Work collaboratively with joint committee;
- Make appropriate referrals;
- Acts as primary contact to outside agencies.

b) — Primary Care Physician

Traditionally, GPs have not necessarily seen their role as being concerned with work. They may have been trained to enquire about a patient's occupation as part of their general medical history, they may see, treat and refer for occupational injuries and they may be aware of the negative health effects of certain jobs, but now they are being encouraged to take a more active role in a dialogue between employer and employee.

An article in Journal of Occupational and Environmental Medicine[2] reports a study in which researchers examined the impact of five major characteristics of primary treating physicians (PTPs) on RTW. The five characteristics were behaviours displayed by the PTP as reported by the injured worker. Workers were asked whether the doctor:

- understood the physical and mental demands of the injured worker's job well or very well;
- discussed the need for work restrictions or changes in the injured worker's job;
- discussed how to avoid reinjury;
- treated them with courtesy and respect;
- explained their medical condition and treatment in an understandable way.

The researchers concluded: "Our findings indicate that the PTP's interpersonal behaviours have a significant positive association with return to work and degree of recovery. Our results confirm the importance of these elements of physician behaviour on important outcomes among injured workers and are consistent with the findings from several other studies."

i) — Physician Role in Timely Return to Work

The Canadian Medical Association (CMA) developed a Policy for Physicians Role in Return to Work. This policy outlines the role of

---

2 Gerald F. Kominski, PhD, Nadereh Pourat, PhD, Dylan H. Roby, PhD, & Meghan E. Cameron, "Return to Work and Degree of Recovery Among Injured Workers in California's Workers' Compensation System" 2008, J Occup Environ Med. 50 at 296-30.

the physician in communication with the employer and facilitation of return to work as the employee is able.[3]

In 1994 the OMA[4] suggested a role for the attending physician in the timely return to work process and gave specific recommendations. There has since been a significant change in the landscape affecting timely return to work. There is now a focus on ability rather than disability and there has been an increased demand for medical information and advice from physicians and other health care providers concerning patient functionality, restricted work and modifications to the workplace to help accommodate the disabled patient.

The clinical role of the patient's personal family physician (attending physician) is still patient centred and remains to:

1. provide medical treatment in order to achieve optimum functionality and discuss with the patient anticipated recovery and healing times early in the course of treatment;
2. support and encourage the patient to participate in a Timely Return to Work program;
3. provide medical report(s) as per Canadian Physicians and Surgeons of Ontario (CPSO) requirements;
4. accept overall responsibility for the patient's medical care;
5. request and help co-ordinate appropriate auxiliary treatment and rehabilitation services; and
6. protect the patient's medical confidentiality.

In Ontario, the attending or treating physician has several distinct considerations when dealing with an injured or ill patient where they require time off work and possibly a Timely Return to Work program:[5]

- The patient may have a WSIB claim, in which case treatment and TRTW service provision would fall under *The Workplace Safety and Insurance Act*. The reader is referred to the WSIB policy "In-

---

3 "The Physician's Role In Helping Patients Return To Work After an Illness or Injury (UPDATE 2000)" The Canadian Medical Association (CMA) policy 2000.

4 "The Role of the Primary Care Physician in Timely Return to Work", December 2008, OMA Ontario Medical Association (OMA).

5 *Ibid.*

jury/Illness and Return to Work/Function" (see www.wsib.on.ca);

- The attending or treating physician has an obligation to provide medically necessary services to the patient during the course of the clinical investigations and treatment of the specific illness or injury that is preventing the patient from attending work or causing the patient to seek accommodation in the work place. These clinically medically necessary services must be billed to the provincial health plan (OHIP) under the "*Health Insurance Act*";
- The attending or treating physician has an obligation to provide accurate and timely objective medical information for the entitlement of eligibility for insurance benefits as per CPSO requirements. The provision of such a report is an uninsured service and may be charged to the requesting third party or to the patient;
- The attending or treating physician should provide accurate and timely objective medical information for the purposes of TRTW. This information should highlight duration of illness, expectations for recovery and work capability, where known. The provision of such a report is an uninsured service and may be charged to the requesting third party or to the patient; and
- The attending physician needs to consider whether s/he will play a role as TRTW coordinator when requested by the employer/employee or the other third party.

ii) — CPSO Obligations

In the case of third party insurance benefits, physicians are commonly requested to provide objective medical information. This is most readily done from documented and reproducible clinical findings from examination of the patient/employee. A treating physician is under an obligation to provide a medical report when requested by, or on behalf of, a patient. The CPSO Third Party Reports Policy (#8-02) requires physicians to provide medical reports to third parties "within 60 days [of request], unless other arrangements are made. If additional time is required to prepare an appropriate report, due to complexity or other appropriate reasons, this should be discussed with the third party".

Physicians are required to report information they have within their knowledge or within their medical chart. Hence, if a third party other than WSIB, for example, sends a request for a functional ability assessment (FAF form) to a physician and the physician knows the answers, s/he is obliged to provide the information. If s/he does not know the answers to some questions, s/he can reply "I do not know", and is not obliged to perform tests or provide a service to find the answer.[6]

The role of the primary care physician is to:

- Ascertain a worker's functional abilities;
- Review the physical demands analysis with the worker to look at job task options;
- Refer and arrange for diagnostics and medical treatment of ill or injured workers;
- Complete the functional assessment form;
- Suggest ways to modify specific tasks to put less strain on existing injuries;
- Collaborate with other health care specialists like Ergonomist, health & safety specialists and rehabilitation specialists etc.;
- Utilize evidence-based treatments and therapeutic agents to actively treat injured workers.

c) — Occupational Health Nurse[7]

The Occupation Health Nurse is a Regulated Health Professional whose primary responsibilities include the medical case management of ill/injured workers. The Occupational Health Nurse is often the first-line contact with the ill/injured worker.

Their responsibilities include:

- Initiate and maintain contact with the ill/injured worker;
- Establish rehabilitative and recovery goals with key stakeholders;
- Administer first aid, medications and treatments;

---

6 Excerpt from OMA "Role of the Physician in Timely Return to Work", 2008.

7 Canadian Occupational Health Nurse Certification, www.oohna.on.ca

- Communicate and liaise with treating practitioners, insurers and other stakeholders;
- Medical case management of each ill/injured worker;
- Wellness promotion.

d) — Insurance Providers[8]

Insurers such as WCB, insurance carriers — short-term disability, long-term disability, and motor vehicle insurers also have key responsibilities. These responsibilities include:

- Objectively determine entitlement and loss of earnings benefits;
- Supply benefits, arrange and provide for rehab service and treatment, provide assistive devices;
- Monitor the worker's treatment, recovery, progress, and the return to work process;
- Provide necessary information to the workplace disability management team to assist with decision making;
- Help to resolve difficulties and disputes;
- Levy penalties for non-co-operation;
- Attend return to work meetings as required;
- Decide whether return to work initiatives have been successful, and determine whether other approaches are required;
- Encourage and support return to work initiatives;
- Arrange medical opinions and assessments as required;
- Communicate with worker, employer, and treating practitioners.

e) — Occupational Therapist[9]

The Occupational Therapist is a Regulated Health Professional whose primary responsibilities include worker treatment and functional assessments. These include:

---

[8] Canadian Life and Health Insurance Association, CLHIA.

[9] Canadian Association of Occupational Therapists, www.caot.ca.

- Work site ergonomic evaluations;
- Work site modifications;
- Recommending appropriate assistive devices;
- Performing physical/cognitive demands analysis' of job descriptions;
- Teaching/coaching workers to perform modified tasks;
- Developing return to work plans with the health care provider, employee and employer.

f) — Ergonomist[10]

An Ergonomist is a skilled professional who assesses and problem-solves human factors issues involving the relationship between people and their working environment as it affects efficiency, safety and ease of action.

g) — Physiotherapist[11]

The Physiotherapist is a Regulated Health Professional. Generally, physiotherapists may be involved in both treating and assessing. Their responsibilities include:

- Treatment of soft tissue injuries;
- Assessment of a worker's functional abilities;
- Working collaboratively with and support the return to work program (e.g. work hardening).

h) — Health and Safety Professionals[12]

The Health and Safety Professional plays a very important role in supporting and assisting with the Disability Management program. Their responsibilities include:

- Monitor incident/accident trends;
- Develop and implement proactive health and safety programs;

---

[10] Association of Canadian Ergonomists, www.ace-ergocanada.ca.

[11] Canadian Physiotherapy Association.

[12] Board of Canadian Registered Safety Professionals.

- Ensure that the safety program meets legislative requirements;
- Co-ordinate the health and safety program;
- Hazard assessment, identification, analysis and control to decrease risk of workplace incidents/accidents;
- Work site modifications.

i) — Human Resources Professionals[13]

Human Resource professionals play a key role in the Disability Management program development and implementation. In addition, they play a very important role in supporting the day-to-day management of the program. Their responsibilities include:

- Job coaching/matching/counselling;
- Developing protocols to support the implementation of the program;
- Assisting with the management of worker performance issues;
- Coaching supervisors and middle management to support program objectives;
- Enforcement of program policies and procedures;
- Completing job descriptions and outlining the bona fide occupational requirements;
- Interpreting and negotiating collective agreement;
- Communicating roles and responsibilities of various stakeholders;
- Ensuring program meets/exceeds legislative compliance.

j) — Union/Worker Representatives

The union/worker representative's fundamental responsibility is to protect the employability of workers and ensure that the return to work program does not violate the worker's rights and the collective agreement. They must also visibly support and promote the program. Other responsibilities include:

---

[13] HRPA, www.hrpa.ca

- Participating on the joint labour-management committee;
- Building disability management program provisions into the collective agreement;
- Advocating for the right's of the injured/ill workers;
- Assisting in identifying tasks that could be modified;
- Supporting the Return to Work Coordinator and Disability Management Professionals and other;
- Supporting the health and safety program and reinforcing safe work practices;
- Communicating program benefits to injured workers and co-workers;
- Assisting in marketing and promoting the RTW program;
- Attending the return to work meetings with the worker.

9.2 — The Scope of a Human Resource Professional's Caseload

1. Recruitment and Hiring of individuals with disabilities.
2. Orientation and on-boarding processes.
3. Managing stay at work processes including early identification of issues that should be accommodated for and performance management.
4. Attendance management.
5. Early identification of cases and early intervention.
6. Management of WCB or insurer reporting for benefits management.
7. Management of employees off work and temporary accommodation.
8. Co-ordination and implementation of return to work processes.
9. Evaluation of permanent accommodations.
10. Ensuring corporate adherence to duty to accommodate statutes.

CHAPTER 10: COMMUNICATIONS

10.1 — Marketing Your Disability Management Program

Not only has evidence shown that work is good for you but returning to modified work can help recovery.[1] A critical part of any successful RTW program is communicating the program to everyone in the workplace. Ideally, everyone should know about the program before an injury or illness occurs. The concepts of early and safe return to work and return to work as part of recovery may be part of a cultural shift in your workplace and therefore require communication and information being readily available prior to implementing the program.

Internally, this means that all management, supervisors, workers and unions (if applicable) need to know that the program exists, the benefits of the program and their role in making it a success. There are many ways to inform everyone in the workplace about the program. Consider using e-mail, the company intranet, memos or newsletters, bulletin boards, and meetings with managers, workers and unions.

Developing and distributing an information package and/or providing education sessions to everyone in the company can be effective ways to market the program. An information package can include the following information:

- Benefits of the program for both the employer and workers;
- The RTW process including what the worker can expect during the process and who to contact during an absence. A diagram or workflow showing the steps in the process is also useful;

1 Dame Carol Black, "Working For a Healthier Tomorrow Dame Carol Black's Review of the health of Britain's working age population" 17th March 2008 Produced by the cross-government Health, Work and Well-being Programme. G Waddell & AK Burton, *Is work good for your health and well-being*? (Dept for Work & Pensions, TSO, UK 2006).

- Assistance that can be provided during the worker's absence and upon their return to work;
- The roles and responsibilities of everyone in the process;
- Required documentation for RTW.

It is also a good idea to train supervisors in the areas of work disability prevention and RTW planning including ergonomics and accommodations. Studies have found that supervisors are important to the success of RTW due to their proximity to the worker and their ability to manage the immediate RTW work environment[2]. Providing supervisors with the skills required to have positive relationships with their workers is important for a successful RTW outcome.

Externally, the program needs to be communicated to the health care community. They should know that the company has a RTW program and will work with them throughout the worker's recovery to provide work that fits their abilities.

An information package for the health care community could include:

- Benefits of the program;
- Letter to health professionals including return to work and modification options;
- A Functional Abilities Form;
- A Physical/cognitive Demands Information Form;
- Sample return to work process;
- Standard restrictions for jobs in the workplace.

The Board and any other insurer should also know if the company has a RTW program. They should also have the names of key contacts in the company for RTW.

Communication and education should be done as soon as the program is developed. Everyone should know what they need to do if someone in the workplace becomes disabled — before it happens. Education is especially important for managers or supervisors as they

---

[2] E MacEachen, J Clarke, RL Franche & Irvin E. "The process of return to work after injury: findings of a systematic review of qualitative studies." Scandinavian Journal of Work, Environmental & Health (2006) 32(4) at 257–269.

play an important role in helping the worker who is injured or ill return to work.

Included in the toolkit are information sheets for employees, health care professionals, sample letters and forms that can be used for return to work.

Information Sheet for Employees with Injuries or Illnesses[3]

In order to help you stay healthy and recover well, here are some points to assist you with the return to work planning process.

Recovery from many medical conditions is more rapid and complete when people are able to stay active and keep life as normal as possible. This also usually slows or reverses the progress of chronic conditions. The ability to function normally will probably come back step-by-step rather than all at once. You and your physician can help to make this process easier. You should ask your physician for an activity prescription that describes specifically:

- What activities or tasks you need to avoid because of risks of further injury or delay in healing;
- What you should and can safely do now both at home and at work; and
- How that will change over time.

In developing an activity prescription, you and your doctor should consider:

- Demands of the job. What specific activities do you need to do at work?
- Risk. Any specific medical harm that might come from doing particular tasks or functions;

[3]Adapted from JOEM letters to editor submitted 2009; "Preventing needless work disability by helping people stay employed", Sept 2006, Amer Coll of Occup & Env Med.; Amer Acad Orth Surg position statement at http://www.aaos.org/about/papers/position/1150.asp; G Waddell & AK Burton, "Is work good for your health and well-being?" (2006) Dept for Work & Pensions, TSO, UK.; C D'Arcy & CM Siddique, "Unemployment and health: an analysis of "Canada Health Survey" (1985) Data. Int J Health Serv 15 at 609–635; J Talmage & M Melhorn, *Physicians Guide to Return to Work* (AMA Press, 2005); Canadian Medical Association, Policy on Physicians Role in Return to Work; Ontario Medical Association, Policy on Physicians Role in Return to Work.

Information Sheet for Employees with Injuries or Illnesses[3]

- Capacity. Temporary or permanent changes to your previous ability to perform specific things such as lift, walk, reach, grasp, see well in the dark, make important decisions, etc.;
- Tolerance. Your ability to cope with or endure discomfort, fatigue, and other sensations.

If you are temporarily unable to do some parts of your usual job, talk to your employer to see whether adjustments can be made, or if there is something else productive you can do at work — as long as the tasks are medically safe and within your current ability. Most jobs can be modified simply to allow you to have the capacity to do the work i.e. getting help temporarily for lifting, rotating jobs, building in rest breaks, implement ergonomic changes. It is healthy to return to your own job duties as quickly as possible even with slight modifications.

In addition, you can:

- Ask your physician for a referral to an occupational therapist, physical therapist, occupational medicine specialist physician, or other expert to analyze your workplace situation and suggest modifications;
- Either informally ask your employer to work with you to find a solution, or make a formal request for a reasonable accommodation under the Ontario *Human Rights Act* if your impairment meets that law's definition of disability or your collective agreement (if applicable). Many times a simple and very low-cost change is all that is required.

If you are unable to return to your own job:

- Ask your employer to consider other jobs that you have the skills and abilities to perform that is available in your workplace.

It's ALL about Your Health . . . Information for Employees on MSD and RTW[4]

- Focus on capacity not incapacity. It's natural to be anxious or even guilty about the parts of your job which you may find difficult to perform because of your MSD;
- You still have much to contribute and you should play to your strengths. Your specialist knowledge and experience doesn't disappear just because you are suffering pain, discomfort or mobility problems, you can still contribute in many ways. Work with your managers and your colleagues to find out how you can maximize your impact at work within the constraints of your condition. Be open with them and they should respond better;
- Talk to your manager soon. Your line manager, despite what he or she might tell you, is not a mind-reader. If your MSD is causing you difficulty or you anticipate a period when you will need to adjust your working time, talk to your manager so that you can both plan what to do about it. The earlier the better as managers don't like last minute surprises, but they can usually find a solution to most problems if they have some notice. You might also find it useful to talk to your Union representative, your HR manager or someone in occupational health;
- Don't delay;
- Play an active part in the management of your condition. Your MSD is bound to get you down sometimes and you will feel like it's controlling your life at home and at work. But you don't need to be a passive victim of pain or immobility. Find out more about your condition, watch for patterns in pain or fatigue and learn how you can minimize its impact on your functioning and your mood. This can sometimes be very hard to do, but persevere; people who play an active part in the management of their condition tend to get back to work more quickly;

[4] Adapted from Stephen Bevan, Eleanor Passmore & Michelle Mahdon, "Fit For Work? Musculoskeletal Disorders and Labour Market Participation" (The Work Foundation, September 2007).

It's ALL about Your Health . . . Information for Employees on MSD and RTW[4]

- Know your rights. As both a patient and as a worker you should know what support and advice you are entitled to. If you are a Trade Union member, you Union should be able to guide you on much of this;
- Family involvement in job retention and rehabilitation. Your family and friends are important sources of support. They may not realize that staying in or returning work is both possible and desirable. You need to help them to help you by getting them involved in your rehabilitation at work. Even small adjustments to working time or travel to work arrangements can make the world of difference.

10.2 — Information Sheet for Treating Health Professionals

The following is a sample letter that can be used to request information from a physician:

Return to Work — Letter to Health Care Practitioner

Dear Health Care Practitioner:

We need your help.

[Company Name] has adopted the philosophy of returning an injured/ill worker to meaningful, productive work of value, where possible, when an occupational or non-occupational injury occurs in order to protect their earning ability and minimize the disruption to their personal lives.

COMPANY has developed a Return to Work Program which is committed to providing suitable work consistent with the functional capabilities of the injured /ill worker in consultation with WSIB/carrier and yourself. The injured/ill worker will gradually be phased back into their regular job, if possible, with modified work within their capabilities (as assessed by you).

What we need from you:

1. Please complete the attached Workplace Safety & Insurance Board's Functional Abilities Form for Timely Return to Work OR Work Fitness Form and give the injured/ill worker both the

canary copy (which the worker will return to us) and the pink copy (which belongs to the worker). This will assist you, as well as the injured/ill worker and us, in planning for his/her rehabilitation.

2. Please list any specific physical precautions that we should consider.

Our goal, with your cooperation, is to return the injured/ill worker to his/her pre-injury position as soon as possible. This program was developed to benefit all concerned and we appreciate your cooperation.

If you have any questions concerning the above, please contact us.

Sincerely,
[Name]
[Title]
[Phone Number]

Physician Information Sheet on MSD and RTW[5]

- Identify where job retention or early return to work is good for the patient. It is easy to assume that work is unambiguously bad for your patient, especially if you suspect that aspects of their job make their symptoms worse. Consider carefully whether, with some adjustments you can recommend, staying at work on lighter duties or with adjusted hours might still be a better option than a prolonged absence from work;
- Think beyond the physical symptoms. Bring to bear your understanding of the biopsychosocial model and the limitations of the biomedical model in your diagnosis of the patient and — most importantly — your assessment of the role that their job might play in helping them stay active and avoid isolation;

5 Adapted from Stephen Bevan, Eleanor Passmore & Michelle Mahdon, "Fit For Work? Musculoskeletal Disorders and Labour Market Participation" (The Work Foundation, September 2007); G Waddell & AK Burton, "Is work good for your health and well-being?" (2006) Dept for Work & Pensions, TSO, UK.

Physician Information Sheet on MSD and RTW[5]

- As a GP you are ideally placed to identify the early presentation of many MSDs. Where appropriate, you should seek to refer patients to specialist teams as early as practicable, to enable management of the condition to begin;
- Avoid catastrophizing. A patient can hold a very negative view of the impact and likely progression of their condition if the way that clinicians present it focuses on incapacity rather than capacity;
- Encourage self-management. Try to ensure that the patient can adopt strategies to manage aspects of their own condition, especially if they are staying in or returning to work. A feeling of empowerment and control will help their mood and ensure that they can keep on top of important aspects of their incapacity while at work;
- Early intervention. The evidence suggests that long periods away from work are usually bad for MSD patients. The longer they are away from work, the more difficult it is to return. Early action, preferably in partnership with the patient and their employer, can help achieve a balance between the individual's need for respite and their need to work;
- Recommend an ergonomic assessment of work, work processes and work station to ensure that any adjustments and supports are in place to support safe return to work.

Physician Information Sheet on Mental Health and RTW

- Identify where job retention or early return to work is good for the patient. It is easy to assume that work is unambiguously bad for your patient, especially if you suspect that aspects of their job make their symptoms worse. Consider carefully whether, with some adjustments you can recommend, staying at work on lighter duties or with adjusted hours might still be a better option than a prolonged absence from work;
- Bring to bear your understanding of the biopsychosocial model and the limitations of the biomedical model in your diagnosis of the patient and — most importantly — your assessment of the role that their job and continuity of employment might play in helping them stay active and avoid isolation;
- As a GP you are ideally placed to identify the early presentation of many Mental Health conditions. Where appropriate, you should seek to refer patients to specialist teams as early as practicable, to enable management of the condition to begin;
- Avoid catastrophizing. A patient can hold a very negative view of the impact and likely progression of their condition if the way that clinicians present it focuses on incapacity rather than capacity. Assist the employee in finding solutions and coping strategies for the work and home activities. Suggest a self referral to the employee assistance program(EAP) at the workplace;
- Encourage self-management. Try to ensure that the patient can adopt strategies to manage aspects of their own condition, especially if they are staying in or returning to work. A feeling of empowerment and control will help their mood and ensure that they can keep on top of important aspects of their incapacity while at work;
- Early intervention. The evidence suggests that long periods away from work are usually bad for individuals with mental health conditions. The longer they are away from work, the more difficult it is to return. Early action, preferably in partnership with the patient and their employer, can help achieve a balance between the individual's need for respite and their need to work;

Physician Information Sheet on Mental Health and RTW
• Recommend counseling to proactively address coping strategies at work. Suggest an occupational therapist that may assist with assessment and management of work, work processes and work station to ensure that any adjustments and supports are in place to support safe return to work.

10.3 — Training Program for Managers

What is clear is that the role of line managers in early intervention is crucial, both in work retention and rehabilitation. A 2007 survey by the Engineering Employers Federation revealed that 40 per cent of companies that train line managers to tackle sickness absence reported a decrease in absence, compared to 26 per cent who saw a decrease where no management training was carried out[6]. This was supported in the systematic review completed by RL Franche, et al.[7]

Many line managers feel ill-equipped to manage injury or illness absences. They may find aspects of mental health or chronic disability awkward and embarrassing to talk about or confront and feel concerned about challenging or asking for more information about a physician's sick notes, making home visits or telephoning staff at home for fear of being accused of harassment or falling afoul of the law and landing themselves and their organization in a legal arbitration or human rights complaint. They are also unknowledgeable about or uncomfortable with the idea of rehabilitation and return to work principles.

Managers need to have the skills to deal with a worker that is ill or injured. The Human resources professional should develop a comprehensive training program for supervisors, lead hands, and coaches within the workplace to include:

- manager checklist for reporting injury/illness;

6 European Agency for Safety and Health at Work (EU-OSHA) 2007 Psycho-social Working Conditions Survey.

7 E MacEachen, J Clarke, RL Franche & E Irvin. "The process of return to work after injury: findings of a systematic review of qualitative studies." (2006) 32(4) Scandinavian Journal of Work, Environmental & Health at 257–269.

- manager checklist on what to ask/not ask when employee reports injury/illness;
- tips to manage attendance;
- tips on accommodations and job task analysis;
- strategies to use when having a difficult conversation;
- picking up cues that an employee may have difficulty functioning at the workplace;
- ways to reintegrate employees at the workplace;
- steps to set up and manage a return to work program;
- sample return to work forms and plans;
- understanding of stakeholder roles in return to work;
- understanding of the laws and policies for return to work and duty to accommodate;
- resources to help.

The toolkit contains a full manager training toolkit with checklists and outlines of strategies on return to work.

Sample Manager's Checklist

Name of Employee

____

EE #:

____

The Early and Safe Return to Work Package is to be provided to every employee reporting a work related injury or illness requiring medical attention and/or resulting in lost time (days away from work or restricted duties). Please indicate below that you:

❑ Have completed *Loss Control Report* (Use questions on reverse side of page when completing the *Loss Control Report* to ensure all required information is gathered)

- ❑ Have completed *Witness Report(s)* if required — witness gets yellow copy
- ❑ Had employee sign the *Worker Claim/Consent Form*
- ❑ Printed employee's name on the top of the *Functional Abilities Form.* Advised the employee to return the *Functional Abilities Form* today or at the start of the next shift
- ❑ Advised employee to return the completed *Worker's Report of Injury/Disease Form 6*
- ❑ Gave the employee the written offer of modified duties

I have completed all of the above steps

__________________________________ Supervisor's Signature

__________________________________ Date

Employee receives the *Employee Package Folder*

- ✓ Fit for Work/FAF Form
- ✓ White & Pink copy of the Worker Claim/Consent Form
- ✓ Written job offer of modified duties

I have received the above forms and my supervisor has offered me modified duties.

______________________________________ Employee's Signature

______________________________________ Date

Forward the following documents to the Human Resources Department:

- Signed copy of *Manager's Checklist*
- Yellow copy of *Worker's Claim/Consent Form*
- *Witness Report(s)*
- Completed *Functional Abilities Form/Fitness for Work* when returned
- Completed *Worker's Report of Injury/Disease Form 6* when returned

A Guide to Completing the Loss Control Report

The following list of questions will assist you in completing Section B and D of the Loss Control Report for an employee who has reported a gradual onset of pain due to their job duties.

Employee Name: ________________ Date: ____________ EE #: ________________

1. When did you first begin to notice the pain?

____

2. Has the pain changed since then and if yes, how?

____

3. What job were you doing when you first had the pain? List M# of the machines involved.

____

4. What specific activity or part of your job causes the pain to occur? List M# of the machines involved.

____

5. Is the pain constant or does it occur at a particular time of day?

____

6. What relieves the pain?

____

7. Had you previously had similar problems? Did they resolve on their own or did you see a doctor?

____

8. Did you make complaints to anyone at work? What did you tell them? (Have each employee complete a Witness Report).

____

A Guide to Completing the Loss Control Report

9. When was your last visit to the doctor? Did you discuss this problem with your doctor during this visit?

---

10. Have there been any changes to your job during this period of time?

---

11. What rotation schedule is being followed in your work area?

---

12. Have there been any changes outside of your work during this period of time? Hobbies/sports/general health/etc?

---

13. Additional information:

Chapter 11: Step by Step Return to Work

11.1 — Return to Work

Return-to-work programs are a way for employers to get their injured/ill employees back to work as safely and as early as possible and at the fullest duty possible. Return-to-work programs also reduce absenteeism and the cost of workers' compensation and insurance plans.

Employers should institutionalize their aggressive return-to-work policies and emphasize their commitment of providing an income to their employees. Conversely, employers should expect that their employees make a commitment to return to the workplace and abide by any work restrictions. By returning an injured/ill employee to a modified work environment, employers "shut their benefits systems down, close their exposure to the Human Rights Complaints, and reduce the potential for litigation".[1]

a) — Principles of Return to Work[2]

- A safe and timely return to work is in the best interest of the ill and injured worker and the organization;
- Early intervention is critical;
- A positive approach to disability is necessary;

---

1 Dianne E Dyck Dianne, *Disability Management: Theory, Strategy and Industry Practice*, Second Edition (Toronto: Butterworths Canada, 2002); RL Franche et al. "Workplace-based return-to-work interventions: A systematic review of the quantitative literature" (2005) 15:4 J Occup Rehabil. at 607–631; Institute for Work and Health; Seven Principles of Return to Work (2007).

2 D Leckie & MK Grewal, *Disability Claims Management*, Second Edition (Toronto: Butterworths Canada, 2002).

- Provide Meaningful and goal oriented work that matches the employees capabilities;
- Appropriate compensation for the work completed;
- Resolve cross jurisdictional boundaries before return to work;
- Return to work plans must recognize the employee's diminished capabilities and not compromise recovery;
- Ensure general workplace safety is not compromised;
- Return to work is not a disciplinary tool;
- Follow the hierarchy of return to work.

b) — Hierarchy of Return to Work

The best outcome comes from following the hierarchy of return to work. There is maximum opportunity that the employee will return to his own job with this hierarchy.

1. The original job at the original worksite (with no accommodations or temporary accommodations)
2. The original job at the original worksite (with permanent accommodations)
3. A similar job within his or her original department or work unit
4. A new job within the organization (identify transferable work skills)
5. A new job in another organization or to self employment with retraining as necessary.

11.2 — Steps for Employers

- *Always begin return to work planning with the employee.* Communicate with the employee your sincere and genuine concern for the health of the employee. Communicate roles and responsibilities of the return to work program and offer suitable return to work options. The employee has the best understanding of the job and the current health situation and will be able to problem solve on strategies to return to work. Ask what they feel they can/can't and may be able to do;

- *Encouraging an early return to work.* The longer an employee is out of work due to treatment, the more he/she will worry about losing the job. And the longer a person is away from the job, the more mentally detached he or she will become;
- *Considering a gradual return to work.* Allowing part-time and flex-time work, as well as a temporary change in job duties, may help reduce stress, leave time for additional medical counselling and allow workers to gradually get back to a normal routine. However, there should be a clear understanding between the employer and the employee as to the details of the return-to-work arrangement, including the expected length of time for special accommodations, work duties and supervision;
- Incorporating other possible *stress-reducing accommodations* for returning employees, such as altering the pace of work; lowering the noise level; providing water and/or ice to combat a dry mouth caused by medication;
- *Offer temporary modified duty work that fits within the injured employee's work restrictions.* Employers should avoid telling the physician that the injured employee is not welcome to return to work unless he or she is at 100 per cent. Because the employer is already paying out 100 per cent in disability benefits, the employer is that much ahead of the game if accommodations are made that would get the employee back at any percentage of ability. By offering temporary modified duty work, the employer is "getting the employee back to work at a functioning level to where they are providing a service to the company and keeping the company's benefit dollars down";
- *Communicate with the health care professional.* Instead of getting a list of work restrictions for the injured employee, the employer should find out what activities the employee can engage in. Once the employer determines what the injured employee can perform, within the parameters of the medically prescribed work restrictions, then the employer can assign the employee to tasks in the company. Some companies have institutionalized 30-, 60-, and 90-day limits for participation in a modified duty program. Any limitation should be based on what the employer believes is

an acceptable time period and the worker's capabilities /recovery needs;

- As long as the employee remains on the worksite, the employer is able to
    - work with the employee and the claims administrator to maintain medical management;
    - observe the employee's functional behaviour during the course of the workday;
    - maintain the close link between work and pay in the employee's mind; "occupational bond"; and
    - maintain close communication to hopefully avoid the expensive and adversarial process of claims management;
- *Develop close relationships with physicians.* Quite often both employers and physicians will focus on the aspects of the job which an employee cannot currently perform, rather than on those which they can. Communication between the employer and the health care provider on possible accommodations can open doors to what an employee can do. Any changes to the modified duty program should be communicated with the injured worker's physician. The personal relationships that employers maintain with outside physicians are critical to the success of any modified duty program. A physician who is familiar with the employer and the employer's policies will know that the injured employee will work in a safe work environment and not be asked to violate any of the work restrictions.

Document, document, document. An employee who is participating in a modified duty program must follow all the prescribed work restrictions as well as all the other rules and guidelines established by the employer. As long as the injured employee is working for you, and you are accommodating the employee's work restrictions, any work-related problems that arise become personnel issues. Modified work duty employees who face personnel issues are dealt with on the same across-the-board basis as other employees. Of course, the employer must be able to document that it did not engage in any discriminatory activity against the injured employee.

11.3 — 10 Return to Work Principles

The following principles of return to work are based on the latest evidence with respect to workplace based interventions and their effect on return to work.

1. Senior Management Commitment to accommodation
2. Treating occupational and non occupational conditions the same in return to work
3. Early reporting of difficulties at the workplace
4. Early Contact and Offer of Modified Work
5. Offer of return to work as close to regular duties as functional capabilities permit
6. Supervisor support for accommodations
7. Communication between health professionals and the workplace
8. Ergonomic workplace visits
9. Regular monitoring of accommodations
10. Full assessment of permanent accommodations within legal guidelines to ensure that accommodations meet all legal and business requirements

The Return to Work Process Flowchart

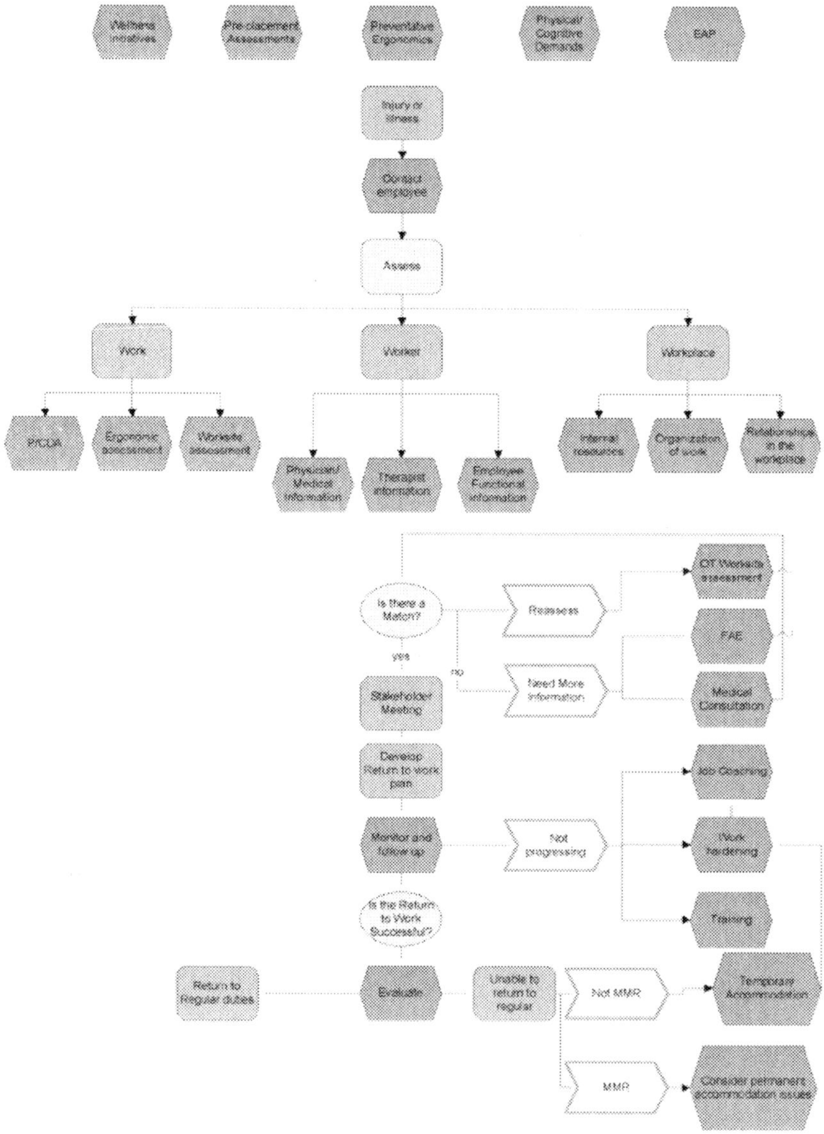

11.4 — Roles and Responsibilities in the Return to Work Process

Employee

1. To be at work
2. To advise Manager of any absence
3. To specify the reason for any absences
4. To seek proper medical attention
5. To cooperate with the employer to ensure timely and successful return to work
6. To make suggestions for appropriate accommodation of needs for timely return to work
7. To maintain contact with the Manager during extended absences

Employer

1. To promote and maintain a work environment which protects overall health, safety, and wellness of all employees
2. To ensure that high quality services are provided to company in an efficient and cost effective manner
3. To demonstrate commitment to attendance management by ensuring:
   - That all Managers maintain their own good attendance;
   - That all Managers act consistently in dealing with attendance issues at all levels of the organization;
   - That there is a fair and equitable application of the Attendance Management Program;
   - That all employees receive orientation to the Attendance Management Program.

Manager

On behalf of the employer, as the individual closest to the employees, the Manager is in the best position to know who is absent, how often, and what assistance may be required. The following are the responsibilities of the Manager:

1. Managing the attendance of all employees within their area of supervision

2. Providing feedback on a regular basis to each individual employee and to the group of employees as a whole

3. Communicating levels of acceptance and expectations for attendance at work

4. Ensuring consistent and timely application of the Attendance Management Program

5. Providing employees with the assistance they require

6. Implementing an appropriate plan of action

7. Ensuring confidentiality of all individual employee information

Union Representative

The following are the normally accepted responsibilities of the union.

1. Providing ongoing support and assistance for the employee

2. Encouraging the employee to cooperate with the employer in ensuring timely and successful return to work

3. Ensuring that the employees understand their responsibilities within the collective agreement

4. Ensuring there are negotiated benefits for the employees

5. Ensuring confidentiality of employee information

Company Support

Throughout the various phases of the Attendance Management Program, staff from the Disability Management will work with the Manager, the employee and the union on any issues that may arise. Advice and direction will be provided regarding the various resources and contacts that may be required. The following are the responsibilities of these departments:

1. Providing advice to Managers on such topics as modified work, job accommodation, EAP availability, and other resources

2. Ensuring confidentiality

3. Training Managers and orienting employees on wellness issues and programs

4. Administering the appropriate provisions under the collective agreements as they pertain to the Attendance Management Program

5. Assisting Managers and employees with the coordination and implementation of a comprehensive return to work plan of action

6. Providing Managers with employee attendance statements

7. Reviewing attendance management practices and available programs to ensure that system needs are met.

11.5 — Elements of a Return to Work Program

A successful return-to-work program requires a combination of several elements:

1. *A written return-to-work policy.* The policy should outline the company's philosophy on and dedication to returning employees to productive employment. The policy should be included in the employee handbook or orientation materials. It should spell out how the program works, such as what benefits are available, how to report an injury, and how to contact the employer's physician network (if the employee chooses to use it). It should also be coordinated with any other human resources policies to ensure that all benefits are coordinated.

2. *Job descriptions.* The purpose of detailed job descriptions is to give the employee's physician an idea whether the employee is able to safely return-to-work with his or her medical restrictions. The job tasks should be separated into "essential" and "nonessential" duties. Some employers complement the written descriptions with videotape to ensure accuracy and complete understanding. A well constructed physical/cognitive demands analysis will help with a clear job match.

3. *Communicate with the physician community.* By cultivating a relationship with the physicians, the employer can give the physicians a better understanding of the business and the requirements of the job, in addition to ensuring that the goal of returning employees to work is shared by every member of the return-to-work team.

4. *Set up a return-to-work team.* A return-to-work coordinator should oversee the program, but they should be supported by all members of the return-to-work team, which may include the treating physician, the supervisor, the injured employee, the union representative, the human resources contact, and the safety person. The coordinator's responsibilities may include maintaining records, communicating with the insurance claims person, preparing all necessary forms, reporting the injury, overseeing all claims management activities (e.g. investigation, light duty, drug testing), obtaining job descriptions for the treating physician and conducting progress reviews to ensure the success of the program. The supervisor would be involved in individual cases when one of his or her employees is involved. Among other things, they might take the employee to the doctor, participate in the accident investigation and suggest a worksite modification to ease the transition back to work.

5. *Train the supervisors and employees.* The program should be communicated to all employees and supervisors so everyone knows what to expect when an injury occurs. This serves several purposes including reducing litigation and minimizing other employees' perceptions of preferential treatment. The number one issue for employees in most complex cases is that their employer neglected to explain what they could expect from the workers' compensation system/insurer. Means of communication may include everything from company newsletters to an intranet site devoted to company benefits like workers' comp.

6. *Promote an empathetic attitude.* Before an injury, an employee typically has personal and professional relationships at work that give them a sense of self-worth and identity. When they are injured, these relationships and feelings of self worth begin to erode. It's a downward spiral that often causes employees to lose their drive to return-to-work. Employers must counter these negative "psychosocial" factors by showing compassion and concern for the worker's well-being. This can be accomplished in several ways, including frequent communication with the employee to check in with them and inform them of new developments at work. In short, keep them in the loop. The employer can also send a get-well card and show an interest in the employee's re-

covery that goes beyond simply wondering when they will be able to resume their responsibilities.

7. *Offer transitional duty.* The employer should offer transitional duty that will return the worker to productive work as soon as he or she is medically able to perform such work. Generally, three types of transitional duty may be offered: light duty involves a less demanding job; modified duty involves the same job but scaled down to meet the employee's medical restrictions; and work hardening involves part-time work that is gradually brought up to full-time. The transitional duty, in whichever form, should have a time line; 60 to 90 days is a good target. The employer and employee should also set goals for the transitional duty period. Above all, the work should focus on the employee's abilities and provide some meaningful employment, as opposed to the proverbial job of counting widgets.

8. *Evaluate the results of the program.* Once an employee completes the return-to-work program, the employer should sit down with the employee and determine how the program worked, paying particular attention to areas for improvement. The employer should also track certain program indicators such as days away from work, medical costs of disability, length of transitional duty, etc. These benchmarks will help the employer measure the success of the program.[3]

11.6 — Return to Work Support Tools

Tools

- Development of company policies and procedures for return to work with accountability and communication with all employees;
- Training programs for all employees on Return to Work and accommodation;

[3] These concepts are supported in the following: DE Shrey, "Effective Worksite-Based Disability Programs" *Sourcebook of Occupational Rehabilitation* by Phyllis M. King (Ed.) (New York, NY: Plenum Press, 1998) at 389–409; Emile Tompa, Claire de Oliveira, Roman Dolinschi & Emma Irvin, "A Systematic Review of Disability Management Interventions with Economic Evaluations" (2008)18:16 J Occup Rehabil at 26.

- Early communication and offers for accommodation and modified work;
- Accommodation of job, schedule, etc. to assist employee who has identified issue;
- Team meeting with all parties earlier in process to determine action plans;
- Offer access to resources to assist in improving the attendance, such as EAP, disability management, altered scheduling, co-worker support, etc.;
- Request further specific functional information related to work activities from the health professional (i.e. doctor, physiotherapist, occupational therapist, etc.);
- Request a Functional Abilities Form to be completed by the physiotherapist;
- Request a formal Functional Abilities Assessment;
- Request an Independent Medical Examination;
- Assessment by a occupational therapist to develop an accommodation plan;
- Hire a Disability management case manager to assist with management of case on an ongoing basis;
- Formalize the documentation through letters to the employee outlining conversation, concerns, expectations and potential consequences if expectations are not met.

11.7 — Disability Management & Return to Work Tips for Managers

As a front line manager you are well aware of the challenges faced when employees are away from the workplace due to illness or a work related injury. The direct and indirect costs associated with such absences can be high and a proactive approach can assist your organization in fostering a healthy work environment that encourages employees to return to work as soon as possible.

Here are a few tips that can assist you in managing absences:

- Prevention is always the priority — are there current workplace practices/issues that can be addressed in a collaborative fashion that may prevent absences or injuries?
- Timely and proactive communication is the foundation to managing absences whether for short term illness or longer term work related injuries. Without appropriate communication an employee may feel increasingly out of touch and undervalued. Have you been able to contact the employee since the beginning of their absence?
- A cooperative approach enhances mutual success. Are you able to work with the employee to plan for and make appropriate adjustments to help facilitate a successful return to work?
- If the employee has been away due to a work related illness or injury claim ensure that you are fully aware of the restrictions or modifications required to ensure a safe and sustainable return to work. Are there any specific return to work barriers that the employee faces?
- Communicate with the other team members (within privacy guidelines) about the return to work plan and how they may be impacted. This promotes cooperation and addresses potential concerns. What do the other team members think about the absence and how may they be able to assist in a successful return to work for their co-worker?
- Follow-up in a timely and sensitive manner once the employee has returned to the workplace. Successful return to work programs requires continuous monitoring and addressing of any barriers that may arise. Schedule a follow-up date with the employee who has recently returned to work.
- As a manager you need to listen well and remain objective. Dissatisfaction or tension between employees often leads to absences. Be a problem solver and foster a healthy work environment every day. Are there performance issues that need to be addressed in your area?
- Become familiar with your Disability Management Program within the company where all stakeholders i.e. employees, man-

agers, human resources and union understand their roles and responsibilities.

CHAPTER 12: COMMUNICATION IN MANAGING DISABILITY

12.1 — Introduction

Communication is the key to success for any return to work process. Early and sincere communication about the employee's health and capabilities and offer of accommodation has been demonstrated to be one of the most important parts of a disability management program. The communication skills of the manager and the human resources professional provide a foundation even before an injury or illness occurs. Consider management communication skills training if you wish to improve any part of your program.

12.2 — Contact Tips

When an employee is off work due to illness or injury it is important to maintain contact. The purpose of this contact is to ensure that the employee understands that they are important to company and that they have the support for return to work.

Things to consider when making contact:

1. Who should make contact? The Human Resources Manager should work with the manager to ensure that the most appropriate contact should be made by the company. In most cases early on, the contact should be coming from the manager but as the absence progresses towards LTD the contact may be more appropriate from a Human Resources Professional. It is HR's responsibility to ensure that the contact is occurring by whomever is assigned to the task.
2. When should the contact occur? The contact should occur early in the absence (within the first day of absence). If the individual is hospitalized, contact with a family member may be most appropriate to find out if the individual is feeling up to a contact from his/her manager.

3. What should the contact contain? The main purpose of the call is to offer support and indicate to the employee that you are willing and able to modify their work to support return to work. (See What to Ask and What not to Ask tips).

4. How often should the contact occur? If the absence extends, the manager should maintain contact at least every two weeks. In some situations the contact may be done weekly (if there is regular progress in the individual's health) or in other situations where the individual has been off work and receiving LTD monthly contact is appropriate. When there is an event or change happening at the company, this is an opportunity to communicate with the employee (i.e. social gathering, new training, promotions, etc).

5. What should be documented? It is important to maintain a record of your contact with the employee and any attempts to contact the employee during their absence. All contacts and attempts should be logged to demonstrate the company's due diligence in maintaining contact. Key points of the contact are also important i.e. proposed RTW dates, modifications suggested, questions asked and answered.

6. Other Considerations — It is important to realize that every employee's needs are individual.

a. When contacting an individual at home make sure that you consider the best time of day for them, set up expectations for the next call (i.e. when would be best to call next? what time of day? what number?).

b. The contact should be voice contact and not just email.

c. In situations where the individual suggests that they feel "harassed" by the call, suggest that the call be made by Human Resources Professional or ask what would be a more appropriate schedule for the employee?

d. In situations where you or the manager are unsure of how to approach the "delicate matter" the manager/HR can contact your employee assistance program to discuss the most appropriate approach for the call.

e. Contact your medical advisor for questions about frequency and appropriateness of call if there are complex medical issues involved in the absence. (Remember you are not discussing the medical issues with the employee, you are discussing employer support).

a) — What can an Employer Ask?

NOTE: How a question is asked is just as important as what is asked. Ensure that any question is asked with respect and sincere need for resolving the absences and providing support for the employee.

DO ASK

- Reason for absences;
- Is the absence work related or not work related (If work related, ensure that a WCB claim has been filed)?
- If there is any way to improve the absences;
- If there is any support that the company can offer to improve the absence;
- If there is need for accommodation of functional disabilities;
- The length that the employee expects the absence or accommodation may be required
  - A medical note from the physician outlining the employee's abilities and length of time the employee is expected to require accommodation;
- Duties within the workplace he/she can do. Focus on his/her abilities.

DON'T ASK

- For a diagnosis of the employee's medical condition;
- For any personal information that will not be used in determining solutions to the absence.

12.3 — Communication with Workers

Communication with the worker and the approach to the communication is important. Here is an example of two different approaches to communication. The first scenario focuses on the illness and injury, the second scenario focuses on the worker role.

If you had a physical problem (insert your choice...but let's make it a back case for now), and were quickly referred to a medical practitioner by your supervisor and employer, you could have two different kinds of medical experiences in the "first minute" you were seen at the "clinic".

Scenario 1: (practitioner knows a patient is in the room and is a "back case"). He/she goes in . . . hello, I'm xxx. I hear you hurt your back. How did you hurt it? What type of pain do you have? How much pain? On a scale of 1–10, give me a number of how much pain . . . and here is a pain chart so you can draw x's or lightning bolts etc. to show me where the pain is and how it feels". I'll give you something for the pain.

The outcome of this is . . . the worker is immediately "a patient". He is a "back case". The medical practitioner thinks the pain is of high importance. Thus the worker should concentrate on his pain and think of it in all sorts of different ways. He won't be better until his pain is all gone, because that is the most important thing to his medical expert. Work is not in the picture.

Scenario 2: (same set up). The medical professional goes into the room. "Hello, I am xxx. I understand you work at the tire company. I see you are a press tender. Yes, I know of that job. You do important work, and it takes great coordination. How long have you worked there? And, you are now having difficulty lifting and bending because of your back problem. How does it interfere with lifting, can you sit, how is reaching? Our goal is to work with you to get you better from your xxx and to improve your lifting and bending so you can return to the tire company very soon and to your home activities."

The outcome of this is . . . the worker still is a worker. He is even attended by someone who knows and appreciates his job. Yes, he does work hard and he is glad it is acknowledged. His provider understands his FUNCTIONAL difficulties and will help him get over it so he can continue his role as a worker . . . and in his life activities also. Functional progress will be the goal.

No matter how good the practitioner, if the patient feels ill and a sick person, he/she will focus on those symptoms (and the focus on pain can lead to the pain patient). Work is an afterthought, or if it is discussed, it is in a general context.

Most workers leave their job to see the practitioner with the worker image intact and most of us believe we will be better very soon and be back to normal. The provider who does excellent care and keeps the worker proud of his/her work and has the return to function (his/her regular job) can avoid this medicalization and still give the needed care.

a) — Points to Remember in Communication

- The individual is a worker — focus on return to work early, discuss return to work at the first opportunity after the injury and illness;
- Focus on what the individual can do at work. (Use the "Can Do, Can't Do, Maybe Do checklist");
- Acknowledge safety and restrictions and ensure the modified work adheres to this;
- Offer support and coping strategies and suggestions at the workplace;
- Focus on the individual as a valued employee doing meaningful and productive work;
- Refer to case management those cases with "Red or Yellow flags";
- Deal with issues regarding relationships or communication at work;
- Use this handy chart to outline the employee's perception of what they feel that they are able to do at the workplace for a foundation to determine the questions that you may need to ask a health care professional or the building blocks of a modified return to work program.

My Job Tasks I Can Do	My Job Tasks I May Be Able to Do	My Job Tasks I Can't Do
i.e. computer keyboarding	filing	lift boxes of supplies

My Job Tasks I Can Do	My Job Tasks I May Be Able to Do	My Job Tasks I Can't Do

Once the employee has defined what they are able to do and what they are unable to do, the manager will have a better sense of whether a return to work can begin immediately or if there is more clarification required.

b) — Communication Strategies: Using Motivational Interviewing (MI)

It is advisable to become skilled in Motivational Interviewing when managing return to work programs as you are looking to develop behavioural change and buy in from the employee and the other stakeholders. The following section outlines the principles of motivational interviewing (MI) and how you can apply those skills to return to work discussions.

i) — Using OARS to Move Your Motivational Boat Forward

Motivational Interviewing (MI)[1] is not a "bag of tricks" to get someone to do something they don't want to do. Rather, MI is a "way of being" with people. OARS [Open-ended questions; Affirmations; Reflective listening; Summaries] help engender the MI spirit of collaboration and build a solid foundation of human resources professional-worker communication. Motivational enhancement strategies are less likely to be effective without this foundation.

Empathy is a key part of cultivating the MI spirit of collaboration and OARS. Empathy is the professional's sensitive ability and willingness to understand (and experience) the worker's thoughts, feelings, and struggles from the worker's point of view. Simple phrases, such as "So you are pretty frustrated with trying to return to work," or "Many of the workers also have difficulty fitting work and medical

[1] http://www.motivationalinterview.org/clinical/whatismi.html; S Rollnick & WR Miller, (1995). "What is motivational interviewing?"(1995) 23 Behavioural and Cognitive Psychotherapy at 325–334.

appointments into their lives," can help build solid relationships with workers.

ii) — Open-ended Questions

Open-ended questions can't be answered with a "yes" or "no." Rather, they invite workers to tell their stories. Human Resources Professionals who use open-ended questions receive less biased data from workers because open-ended questions allow workers to give spontaneous and unguided responses, which help build rapport and trust. These responses enable HR Professionals to find out information they otherwise would not have thought to ask about but that is nevertheless pertinent to the situation. Open ended questions usually begin with the phrase, "Tell me about . . . (how your return to work plan is going?)" or, "To what extent . . . (have you been able to take breaks as we had discussed?)" vs. closed-ended questions, which usually begin with "Did you . . . (perform your work duties as discussed?) Closed-ended questions focus on the human resources professional's agenda and thus place the worker in a passive and less engaged role.

iii) — Affirmations

Statements of appreciation and understanding are important for building and maintaining rapport. Human Resource Professionals can affirm workers by acknowledging their efforts to make changes, no matter how large or small. Some examples are, "You took a big step by coming here today"; or, "That is great that you were able to return to work for 2 weeks"; or, "You've overcome a lot."

iv) — Reflective Listening

Reflective listening involves taking a guess at what the worker means and reflecting it back in a short statement. The purpose of reflective listening is to keep the worker thinking and talking about change. Reflective listening can be used (1) to understand the workers' perspectives and let them know you are listening; (2) to emphasize the workers' positive statements about changing so they hear their positive statements about changing twice — once from themselves and once from the Human Resources Professional; and (3) to diffuse resistance. Several types of reflections are useful; all of these should be crafted as statements rather than as questions, which allows the worker to elaborate on their ideas.

1. *Repeating*. This is the simplest form of reflection, often used to diffuse resistance.

Worker: "I don't want to return to work."

HR: "You don't want to return to work."

2. *Rephrasing*. Slightly alter what the worker says in order to provide the worker with a different point of view. This can help move the worker forward.

Worker: "I really want to return to work."

Hr: "Returning to work is important to you."

3. *Empathic Reflection*. Provide understanding for the worker's situation.

Worker: "What do you know about returning to work? You have done my job."

HR: "It's hard to imagine how I could possibly understand."

4. *Reframing*. Much as a painting can look completely different depending upon the frame put around it, reframing helps workers think about their situation differently.

Worker: "I've tried to RTW and failed so many times."

HR: "You are persistent, even in the face of discouragement. This must be really important to you."

5. *Feeling Reflection*. Reflect the emotional undertones of the conversation.

Worker: "I've been considering returning to work for some time now because I know it is important for my health."

HR: "You're worried about your health."

6. *Amplified Reflection*. Reflect what the client has said in an exaggerated way. This encourages the client to argue less, and can elicit the other side of the client's ambivalence.

Worker: "Staying away from work isn't that bad."

HR: "There's no reason for you to be concerned about your work." (Note: it is important to have a genuine, not sarcastic, tone of voice).

7. *Double-sided Reflection.* Acknowledge both sides of the worker's ambivalence.

Worker: "Being off work allows me to rest."

HR: "On the one hand, being off work allows you to rest. On the other hand, you said previously that it also causes you stress because you have reduced finances and are getting out of shape."

v) — Summaries

A summary is longer than a reflection. Use summaries in order to transition to another topic, or to highlight both sides of the worker's ambivalence. Example: "You have several reasons for wanting return to work consistently; you say that your husband will stop nagging you about it and you will be able to pay your bills more consistently. On the other hand, you say the schedule is a hassle, and you are in pain. Is that about right?" Use summaries at the end to recap major points.

c) — How to Handle Worker Resistance

Resistance comes in many forms. Workers may argue with you, or more covertly, ignore you, or "yes" you to death. Upon encountering resistance, it is important to respond in a manner that defuses it rather than fuels it. In MI, resistance is viewed as a problem of communication between the worker and practitioner, rather than one that lies within the worker alone. Human Resource Professionals can ask themselves several key questions when they encounter resistance:

- Does my communication style match the worker's readiness to change? Am I pushing the worker to do more than he or she is ready for?
- Am I dismissing the worker's feelings and concerns?
- Am I undermining the worker's sense of personal autonomy to make a decision about their care?
- Am I acting as expert and telling the worker what changes him or she needs to make and how to make them?

Reduce resistance by:

- Using reflective listening;
- Using empathic statements;

- Focusing on building the relationship rather than on worker change;
- Engaging workers by first discussing issues that are important to them;
- Exploring concerns about why they don't want to talk about the behaviour; and
- Emphasizing that the issue of whether or not to change is their decision.

d) — Core Questions in Discussion for RTW[2]

- How are you feeling about return to work?
- What are you looking forward to? — — incorporate these things early in return to work plan
- What do you think will present a challenge? — what can you do about these — do not avoid them
- What was a challenge before you were off?
- In what areas would you want further training?
- How do you think others might perceive you here?
- What would you like to do about that?
- How would you like to be reintroduced to the group?
- Have you thought about what you will say about your absence?
- What do you think will be the most stressful part of your work day?
- Where do you feel your strengths will lie?
- Which tasks give you energy?
- What tasks zap your energy?

---

[2] Code of practice for disability management: describing effective benchmarks for the creation of workplace-based disability management programs. National Institute of Disability Management and Research, 2000; "Facilitation Skills for the Return to Work Expert" Gowan Consulting; Mental Health and Accommodations.

- Is there anything your supervisor can do differently in terms of how they communicate, give feedback or instructions?
- Can you give me some direction about how to approach you if we become concerned that you are unwell again?

12.4 — The Employer's Right to Information

An employee has an obligation to provide information to demonstrate a satisfactory reason for any absence. The employer has a corresponding right to inquire about the reason for the absence.

a) — Medical Excuses for Being Absent

It is the right of the organization to request documentation for sick days. Most organizations have built in a "sick note" requirement after consecutive days of absence (varies between 3–7 days). It is recommended that instead of a "sick note" that the employer develop a policy that includes a "fit for work note" or a "functional abilities form". Most sick notes have become a barrier to return to work, a burden on health care professionals, and nondescript in helping with return to work planning. This process can delay return to work and direct communication with the manager on stay at work/return to work options.

b) — Non-Medical Excuses for Being Absent

It is generally open to you to investigate and challenge the non-medical excuses offered to you through any lawful means to whatever extent you deem appropriate. Note that this approach has an employee relations cost attached to it.

c) — Adequacy of Medical Information

The employer is not automatically bound to accept the assertions of the employee or for that matter his doctor when medical justification for absence is asserted. Where the facts raise a reasonable question concerning the adequacy or sufficiency of a certificate, the employer can generally and usually should request more medical information or clarification.

d) — Request for Health Examinations

There are some statutory rights to medical examination at the request of the employer.[3]

- Section 23 — *Workplace Safety and Insurance Act*;
- In some industries *Occupational Health and Safety Act* provides authority for a requirement of medical examination;
- In some collective agreements there is the right for the employer to request an independent medical examination.

e) — Is there a difference in what we are able to ask with physical vs. mental health disabilities?

The other piece that continues to be debated in the judicial system is how much an employer can and should inquire for medical information when in the accommodation process? On numerous occasions where a mental health illness was the underlying condition, employers were not only given the right to request more information and more assessment (especially in safety sensitive situations) but it was expected that the employer would "reasonably be aware that there was a need for more information".

So employers are left wondering. . . what can I ask, what is my responsibility and how can I ensure that I have the RIGHT information to fulfill the duty to accommodate?

12.5 — Confidentiality Issues

a) — Respect Confidentiality of Information under the Guidelines of Ethical Code, Laws, and Regulations

Most ethical codes contain a principle related to confidentiality,[4] which is an essential element of disability management and return to work practice. Without assurance that a human resources professional will maintain health information confidentially, workers would certainly be reluctant to discuss or disclose that information or to develop a trusting relationship with the human resources professional.

---

[3] *Ontario Workplace Safety and Insurance Act*, S.O. 1997, c. 16, Sched. A.

[4] "Establishing Criteria for Excellence in Canada". Occupational Standards for Disability Management, 1999. www.nidmar.ca.

In spite of the presence of the confidentiality principles in ethical codes, human resources professionals are often confronted with requests from management for medical or health information on their workers. Medical or health information should not be received / released without the written and informed consent of the worker.

Informed consent cannot take place without the worker receiving information about the following:

- what information is being received / released;
- who it is being received / released to;
- why it is being received / released;
- who is receiving /releasing the information;
- how long the consent will remain in effect.

A written consent form should have a clause indicating that the worker understands all of the above points, a signature line for the worker and a witness, and the date that the form was signed. Remember, the worker has a choice whether to give consent or not and consent must not be coerced.

Several statutes guide the management of health related and employment related information in the employment setting.

- Under the *Freedom of Information and Personal Privacy Act* covers an employer's management of all employee records;[5]
- Bill 159 the *Personal Health Information Privacy Act*[6] for the health care sector proposes new ways to ensure confidentiality of health information and improve sharing of information between caregivers to improve care;
- Under Bill C-6[7] indicate that management of health information in an insurance company will be guided with more stringent regulations;

5 www.accessandprivacy.gov.on.ca/english/act/index.html

6 http://www.e-laws.gov.on.ca/html/statutes/english/elaws_statutes_04p03_e.htm

7 http://www2.parl.gc.ca/HousePublications/Publication.aspx?pub=bill&doc=c-6&parl=36&ses=2&language=E

- Under the *Regulated Health Professions Act*[8] each regulated health professionals will have individual guidelines for health records;
- Under the *Occupational Health and Safety Act* and subsequently the ministry of Labour has developed guidelines covering the management of health records.
- Under the PIPEDA the protection of personal information is regulated for all businesses.[9]

Health information that is provided by the employee should remain confidential. In addition, prior to contacting any medical practitioner, the signed written consent of the employee should first be obtained and any information provided by the medical practitioner should remain confidential.

Under the *Regulated Health Professions Act*, a physician or health professional who gives information regarding a patient's medical condition to another person without the patient's consent unless required to do so by law, constitutes professional misconduct.

12.6 — Gaining Consent for Communication With The Team

Prior to attempting communication with the treatment team it is essential to communicate with the worker and gain consent for communication on functional capabilities:

- Inform the worker of the reason for the contact with the treatment team;
- Inform the worker that the discussion is about function and work activities that meet his/her needs;
- Show the worker all of the documents being sent to the treatment team;
- Ask the worker if there are any concerns with the communication;

---

8 http://www.e-laws.gov.on.ca/html/statutes/english/elaws_statutes_91r18_e.htm

9 http://laws.justice.gc.ca/en/P-8.6/

- Obtain a signed consent form;
- Have all parties complete a Commitment to Confidentiality form.

Commitment to Confidentiality
As a participant in the Return to Work Program, I understand that I may be in receipt of personal information of workers at (Company Name) via the Functional Abilities Form completed by the treating practitioner. This information may include address, birth date, social insurance number or medical information of individuals being accommodated in the workplace. This information is to be kept in confidence and not shared with others. I understand that confidentiality is a requirement of my participation in the Return to Work Program and promise not to discuss any personal information I may obtain. Signed: ______________________________ Please Print Name: ______________________________ Date: ______________________________ Witness: ______________________________

a) — What Can I Ask When Planning Return to Work?

There is a constant battle about what information is needed to plan return to work. Should an employer know the diagnosis? What information is truly necessary? Can I send an employee to an independent medical examination? There have been many arbitrations which debate these questions, but none that are the final answer.

An arbitration in Alberta provided a clear list of the kinds of medical information that an employer would require to plan return to work.[10] It suggested that medical information should include:

(1) The nature of the illness: a description of the illness, although the actual diagnosis was not required;

(2) permanent or temporary: whether the condition was likely to stay the same, worsen, or improve over time, along with the estimated time frame for any improvement;

(3) restrictions and limitations: what the employee can and cannot do in relation to current duties and possible alternative duties, in as much detail as possible;

(4) how the medical conclusion was reached: whether diagnostic or other objective tests were performed, or whether the information was self-reported. Neither test results, x-rays nor clinical notes need to be provided; and

(5) treatment or medication: any treatment or medication that could have an impact on the accommodation or the employee's ability to perform the job should be disclosed.

There is nothing inherent in the employer-employee relationship which vests in an employer a discretionary right to compel employees to compromise their right of privacy through the disclosure of personal medical information.", the employer can only intrude upon the privacy of an employee if it has a legitimate business purpose tied to the employer-employee relationship which justifies the intrusion."

Once in possession of medical information which clearly establishes a returning employee's fitness to return, safely and productively, an employer is not entitled to rely on its doubts about the legitimacy of the absence to deny the grievor the right to work." Does that mean that an employer cannot ask for an independent medical examination? The answer is "that depends . . ."

So what information is meaningful, that allows an employer to ensure fitness for work in a safe manner but does not intrude on the privacy of the employee?

[10] *United Nurses of Alberta, Local 33 v. Capital Health Authority (Royal Alexandra)Alberta Grievance Arbitration, Allen Ponak, Arbitrator* (October 11, 2006).

It is suggested that the most reasonable question to ask yourself as a human resources professional is:

1. Why am I asking for the information?
2. What will that information contribute to safe and timely return to work?"

Basic rules to follow:

1. Focus on functional capabilities and restrictions (use a standard format that will apply to your work duties and situation)
2. Ask about any medical precautions or risks (Is there a risk or is it symptom based and how was that risk determined)
3. Is this temporary or permanent?
4. How often will these capabilities change (improve or worsen)?
5. Are there any medical treatments (medications, etc) that will impact the safe completion of work duties? (detail specific work issues such as safety issues for the health professional)

Remember that the health professional providing the answers does not know your workplace, your work risks or your work processes so ask for information that will allow you as a return to work coordinator to adjust the work duties to meet both the employee's functional abilities but also your business needs.

Prior to attempting communication with the treatment team,

- Inform the worker of the reason for the contact with the treatment team
- Inform the worker that the discussion is about function and work activities that meet his/her needs
- Show the worker all of the documents being sent to the treatment team
- Ask the worker if there are any concerns with the communication
- Obtain a signed consent form
- Have the employee deliver the information to the health care professional and bring back the form directly to avoid any feeling that information is being hidden and heighten the transparency of the process

Asking the right questions of health care professionals

The direction of the current case law is that the employer is entitled to request, and receive, an adequate analysis from the employee's physician concerning his or her fitness. Otherwise, it is not in a position to adequately assess the employee's accommodation needs

Unions should ensure that employees are forthcoming about their disability. An employee's position is strengthened if evidence can be presented to the employer that there is minimal risk of reoccurrence and rehabilitation is well underway. It will be more difficult to deny accommodation to an employee when the employer is informed of the positive steps taken by the employee to recover.

While an employer is entitled to medical information regarding disabled employees, it must choose the least intrusive means and only seek information that is required. The employer is not entitled to the specific diagnosis, or the specific treatment. Other information is allowed only if it is necessary and reasonable in the circumstances.

It is important, in all cases, to manage the case with the correct information and functional needs of the employee. How can you expect to accommodate without the correct objective information on the abilities and restrictions for the worker. Employers do not need to know "diagnosis" but they do need to understand the functional capabilities of the worker.

b) — Formulation of Questions[11]

All questions to the health care provider should be as specific to the job duties as can be discerned. Remember that the physician can provide answers that are related specific to a medical impairment. Keep letters/questionnaires for the health care provider simple, clear and short.

Are there risks that indicate that the disability would be medically NECESSARY?

What are the current medical contraindications to return to work

- Is the worker contagious?
- Any risk to recovery if performing work?
- Any need for attendance at treatment during work hours?

[11]ACOEM Guideline "Preventing Needless Work Disability by Helping People Stay Employed" 2006.

- Any need for hospitalization?
- Any risk if commuting to and from work?

What are the current reported tolerances for work that would be DISRETIONARY?

- Tolerances for physical movements that may require limitations due to medical diagnosis
- Tolerances for cognitive activities that may require limitations due to medical diagnosis

Any side effects of medications or treatments that might impact safety in:

- operation of a motor vehicle
- use of fire arm
- work around motorized equipment
- other

Duration of contraindications/risks:
Prognosis for recovery?
Any further barriers to return to work?

Arbitrations demonstrate that the employer has a right to ask for additional assessment if the physician's note is insufficient or lacks objective information.

Ensure that you access information from the right health care professionals in order to understand the functional abilities. In most cases, the auxiliary professionals may have a better understanding or functional capabilities once the medical risks are identified by the physician.

- Physiotherapist — ask about endurance, tolerances for activities such as walking, stairs, etc and safety in performance of certain activities based on the treatment program
- Psychologist — ask about emotional risks and strategies to improve coping skills at work
- Psychiatrist — ask about safety to self and others at the workplace, risks for relapse
- Occupational therapist — ask about functional capabilities and strategies to overcome functional barriers at the workplace

- Speech language pathologist — ask about cognitive and speech related function

Once you have the information: Match the functional capabilities to your objective job demands.

c) — Communication with Physicians / Treaters

A physician's view to the speed at which an ill worker returns-to-work often has little to do with medical healing, but more to do with the patient's personal circumstances. Oftentimes, the physician gets involved with the patient's personal relationships with family or the employer, instead of concentrating on the patient's disability. If the patient tells the physician about problems associated with his or her supervisor, the physician will likely place the patient on temporary disability for a few additional days, weeks, months, or even years to protect the employee from the "stressors".

Stressors in a person's life may manifest into pain. When an employee complains of pain to a physician, the doctor may feel a moral obligation to agree with the patient and place the individual on disability. The physician-patient relationship is a very strong bond. When dealing with a patient who suffers from pain, the physician will err on the side of caution.

The direction of the current case law is that the employer is entitled to request, and receive, an adequate "nature of the condition" from the employee's physician concerning his or her fitness. Otherwise, it is not in a position to adequately assess the employee's accommodation needs.

It is important, in complex cases, to manage the case with the correct information and functional needs of the employee. How can you expect to accommodate without the correct objective information on the abilities and restrictions for the worker. Employers do not need to know "diagnosis" but they do need to understand the functional capabilities of the worker.

There are several guidelines available with respect to the role of the physician in return to work including; the Ontario Medical Association's Role of the Physician in Return to Work and the Canadian Medical Association's Role of the Physician in Return to Work. The American College of Occupational and Environmental Medicine provides the newest offering of these guidelines in the *Preventing Needless Disability Guidelines.*[12]

12.7 — Functional Assessments — Are They Really Worth The Money?

Functional Assessments (better known as FCE/ FAE/ PCE/ FAA) are used in the return to work planning process to help to determine an employee's abilities. A recent controversial discussion was held online with our workplace partners on when to use functional assessments.

a) — Why Not just Ask the Doctor or the Employee?

Generally an employee will underestimate their capabilities or over estimate their capabilities. An interesting research study was shared by S. Brouwer et al (2005)[13]. This research compared the employee limitations outlined in each of the processes. *Self report* provided the greatest number of worker limitations, *clinical examination by a physician* provided less limitations but the *functional testing* provided the most capabilities and the least worker limitations. This allows for more opportunity to offer work that the employee can do.

b) — What is the Purpose of a Functional Assessment?

A functional assessment should be used to clarify objectively what a person can do safely upon return to work and to provide recommendations on ways to improve the return to work process.

c) — When Should you Use a Functional Assessment?

Research completed by Strong, et al (McMaster Work Function Unit)[14] in 2003 provided some additional understanding of the state of the evidence on the reliability of functional assessments and when

[12] ACOEM *Preventing Needless Disability Guidelines*, 2005.

[13] S. Brouwer et al (2005) "Comparing self-report, clinical examination and functional testing in the assessment of work related limitations in patients with chronic low back pain" Disability and Rehabilitation, 2005; 27(17): 999–1005.

[14] Functional Assessment Network, McMaster Work Function Unit, 2003 http://www.fhs.mcmaster.ca/rehab/research/workfunctionunit.html.

they should be performed. A multi-stakeholder group developed some guidelines on when to use the functional assessment in return to work. The team also developed a systematic process for performance of functional assessments.

We have attached the functional assessment algorithm for your use and reference.

For more information on functional assessments you can refer to the McMaster Work Function unit's research completed in 2003. The documents can be found at: http://www.fhs.mcmaster.ca/rehab/research/workfunctionunit.html

d) — How to Make Sure the FA is Valuable

- Prior to the FA, the initiating party should meet with the employee to:
    - Review the reasons and objectives for the FA.
    - Evaluate the current Physical Demands Analysis (PDA).
    - Provide written information about the FA (what is involved, how to prepare.)
    - Share how the FA information will be used to develop a RTW plan.
    - Obtain consent from the employee for the release of FA information to each party.
    - Explain how the employer will receive the FA finding.
    - Address any concerns the employee may have about the process.
- For an effective FA process, there needs to be respectful dialogue, collaboration, and trust between all parties involved.
- From the very beginning, efforts need to be made to establish communication between the employee, FA user and assessor.
- The initiating party is responsible for providing appropriate background information to those involved in the FA process.
- The employee should remain informed and involved throughout the process.

e) — What Should you Look for in a Functional Assessor?

- An experienced professional with expertise in real work settings and rehabilitation.
- The ability to ensure that there is dialogue with the worker throughout the process
- The ability to understand your work setting and expectations and apply those in the assessment process

f) — How Much Will a Functional Assessment Cost?

That depends on the length and breadth of the assessment and the experience of the professional . . . Realize you are asking for a professional opinion to assist with return to work planning.

The cost may vary between $750 and $2500 depending on the length and the professionals involved.

Match the functional capabilities to your objective job demands.

The next step in the process is to ensure that there is a good job match. Once you have received the medical restrictions or functional capabilities it is the employers next step to see if there the employee can do their own job demands or the employee may require modified work. It is important to understand how to break down the job tasks and define each step and tools. You can hire a professional to perform a full physical and/or cognitive demands analysis in more difficult and complex cases and assist with return to work planning and job match.

12.8 — How to Perform a Job Analysis

By asking the following questions you can analyze each job in an employment setting.

a) — Purpose

1. What are the specific contributions of the job toward the accomplishment of the overall goals and objectives of the work unit or organization?

b) — Essential Function

1. What three or four activities actually constitute the job? Is each really necessary? (For example, a secretary types, files, answers the telephone and coordinates billing)

2. What is the relationship between each task? Is there a special sequence that the tasks must follow?

3. Do the tasks necessitate sitting, standing, walking, climbing, running, stooping. kneeling, lifting, carrying, digging, writing, operating, pushing, pulling, reaching, talking, listening, interpreting, analyzing, seeing, coordinating, etc?

4. How many other employees are available to perform the job function? Can the performance of the specific function be distributed among any other employees?

5. How much time is spent on the job performing the particular function? Are the tasks that are performed less frequently as important to the success as those done more frequently? Which part of the day is the specific task performed and can this time be altered.

6. Would removing a function fundamentally alter the job?

7. What happened if the task is not performed on time?

c) — Job Setting

1. Location. Where are the essential function do the job carried out? What are the characteristics of the room size?

2. Organization. How is the work performed for maximum safety, efficiency and productivity? How do the employees obtain the necessary equipment and materials?

3. Movement. What movement is required of employees to accomplish the essential function of this job?

4. Physical conditions. What are the physical conditions of the job setting (hot, cold, damp, inside, outside, underground, wet, air-conditioned, dirty, greasy, noisy, etc.)

5. Social conditions. What are the social conditions of the job (works alone, works around others, has contact with the public, works under close supervision, supervises others, works under deadlines, work pressure is constant/variable, etc.)?

d) — Worker Qualifications

1. What are the physical requirements (lifting, driving, cleaning, ability to handle pressure, ability to perform repetitive tasks, etc.)?
2. What are the general skills needed for the job (ability to read, write, type, compute, etc.)?
3. What specific training is necessary (apprenticeship, high school diploma, certification or license, etc.)?
4. What previous experience, if any, may replace or be substituted for training requirements?

e) — How to Use Job Analysis Information

Once job analysis information is available the employer will be in a better position to:

1. Develop current and accurate job position descriptions. Job descriptions should be updated on a regular basis and a job analysis performed if any duties, tasks, or responsibilities detailed above have been altered.
2. Conduct an objective performance appraisal of all the workers.
3. Validate any pre-employment assessments that may be used as screening tools when recruiting for a position.
4. Determine if accommodations can assist a person with an injury or disability to perform a job.
5. Make medical decisions about the person's ability to perform the demands and requirements of a job.
6. Develop a job bank of tasks to be used in implementing transitional work programs.

f) — Physical Demands Analysis (PDA)

A Physical demands analysis is a detailed, objective analysis of the job components and the physical requirements to perform that job. Training on how to perform a physical demands analysis is important and you can find consultants who are experienced in this area to assist you.

This is a systematic procedure to identify and document the physical, psychological and perceptual requirements of a specific job. It is more complete and detailed than the job analysis and will allow you to ensure that you understand all of the physical components of the job.

g) — Cognitive Demands Analysis (CDA)

The Cognitive demands analysis is the objective assessment of the cognitive and behavioural demands of job tasks. The cognitive demands analysis is becoming more important as individuals are returning to work after dealing with brain injuries, mental health conditions and conditions that impact cognition such as chronic pain.

h) — Visual Demands Analysis (VDA)

Every day we use our eyes to perform activities of daily living and work activities. With health conditions and as we age our eyes' capabilities adjust and change, making it a challenge to perform our work activities. Visual ergonomics is the ability to adjust the work, work processes, work station and the environment to match the ability of our eyes. In some instances this may involve simple adjustments to lighting, computer screen colours and fonts to more extensive accommodations such magnification tools and screen readers. As occupational therapists we work closely with the optometrist and the employer to develop ways to accommodate so that the employee can continue to perform the work activities.

The Visual Demands Analysis is the comprehensive outline of the visual requirements of the job. It provides the documentation of the visual demands of the essential job duties for legal compliance, accommodation, pre-placement and return to work planning

12.9 — Determining the Job Match and Gaps

Once all of the information is received about the employee's capabilities and the job demands it is important to take a methodical approach to each task to determine if there is a good job match.

This table helps to outline the steps and areas for accommodation needs.

Job tasks	**Employee functional abilities**	**Gaps and mismatches**	**Possible accommodations/ tools**
Log into computer	Able to mouse and key for log in	None	None required
Process reports using MS Word (2 hours)	Unable to key repetitively for greater than 10 minute periods	Keying time (10 minutes vs. 2 hours)	Regular breaks and alternate into other tasks *OR* voice recognition software
Answer calls	Able to answer calls and record messages	None	Headset recommended

12.10 — Purchasing Assistive Devices or Ergonomic Equipment

In some situations you may need to purchase assistive technology, devices or equipment to support the return to work and accommodation process. When you decide that you must purchase assistive devices or equipment to support return to work or accommodation it is important to follow the right process for discerning what device is most appropriate and then ensure that you have a reliable supplier to provide the device. There is an endless supply of devices and the technology changes often. You need to ensure that the tool that you choose meets the needs of the employer and the employee productivity standards.

The process steps should include:

1. Request to Manager
   - employee's job description;
   - request if there has been a job tasks analysis (to understand where are the performance barriers that could be present, as well as the overall process and goals of the job) conducted, if not, we would recommend to have one done (if the expertise is already available in the workplace than this individual would do it and if not, you would use a consultant do to it.

An occupational therapist is a great resource for you in determining the needs of the employee and the devices that would fit. Also for specialized issues such as low vision, the CNIB can be a resource or for assistance with hard of hearing, the Canadian Hearing Society can be helpful.

2. Has an initial meeting taken place with the worker (easier for him to share some information that would not take place with the employer)

- what are his goals & priorities?
- find out is attitude toward technology & accommodation
- how his performance his impacting by his functional limitations
- what devices have been recommended by your health care team?

3. Gathered information about the worker and his work environment — questions

- what are the worker's functional abilities
- what are his needs
- what are his personal preferences
- what processes are you unable to perform and are there any devices that you have used in the past to support you?

4. Environmental barriers

- Has an Ergonomic assessment been done? If not, it would be recommended that it take place by someone who might have the expertise in the workplace, if not, have a consultant to complete an assessment. Find the right expertise for this type of assessment
- If the company does not have the expertise to conduct an assessment, you would require an occupational therapist or a consultant with a background in ergonomics and human factors engineering.

5. Next step would be to start the research on potential technology or devices for the worker

- Does the device solve the problem?
- Does it do more or less than is required?
- Does it fill the gaps that were identified when matching the worker's capacity to the tasks required?
- Does the device work as it is supposed to and is it reliable?
- Was it tested before at your company? Who would test it now?
- Has it been used in a similar work setting?
- What is the durability of the device? How often will it require replacement?
- Is training required and who will be providing the training? Onsite or offsite training? Cost of training?
- Does it meet internal health and safety standards?
- Would the maintenance be completed onsite or not? Is there back up equipment available (loan, purchase)? Is it in stock? Are there restocking fees if we return it?
- Does it fit the actual work environment? Does it generate noise/ heat/ vibration? If the equipment is too bulky can it be hidden to take away the attention to the employee with the disabilities?
- Is the service and support provided inside the organization, if not, is the expertise available outside the company? Cost of support services?
- Is their any rating available to get a sense if it is worthy to buy the equipment?
- Is it compatible with the actual software used by the organization?
- Can the costs be shared between the insurer, employer and government agencies?

6. Exploration of alternatives (have I kept it as simple as possible — does it meet the worker's needs and values?
   - individual personal — does it meet the worker's skills and capacity;
   - social (co-workers) — Is the device an intrusion on the work or can it be an asset for the organization — will it improve the working relationship or productivity of the area?

7. Meeting with Management as to share the result the research.
   - Bring in the other players (occupational therapist to educate manager and employee on what would be more suitable upon RTW and why;
   - With high tech assistive devices the company representative should explain the purpose and how it is used and implemented in the workplace; what are the positive outcomes for the company, if any and the costs involved.
   - Address what other alternatives (simple solutions) can be implemented to reduce the cost.

8. Information session with the co-workers (education process)
   - If the device is to be used by the whole team then they should be involved in the choice of devices. Explain to the team why the modification will occur;

9. Prior to the RTW, a meeting should take place with the worker and the employer to review the RTW Program. This will validate that all parties are aware of their roles and responsibilities and understand the purpose of the accommodation.

10. PRIOR TO RTW the device should be in place and all technical concerns addressed.

11. On the first day of RTW the employee should have assistance for any technical or set up issues and reduced productivity should be expected until the employee is trained on the device and its use and has a chance to work with it.

12. Device Evaluation
- What is the utilization of the device?
- Does it improve the worker productivity, independence within the workplace?
- Does the device need fine-tuning?
- Is the device cost effective?
- What is the device's impact on the workplace?
- Has this device reduced lost time, health care, disability benefit utilization?

12.11 — Pitfall Prevention

In order to prevent pitfalls in your return to work process follow these steps:

1. Perform an accurate and thorough assessment of the situation
2. Develop a realistic plan
3. Communicate first with the treating physician
4. Set team goals and approaches
5. Perform regular evaluations and monitoring of the plan
6. Make regular contact with the employee and the supervisor
7. Keep communication open and transparent
8. Set solid target dates and ensure that the goals are adhered to
9. Proactively deal with barriers and performance issues
10. Take a client centred goals and approach

12.12 — Documentation Principles

Documentation is the key to a solid return to work program and your due diligence in this process. All stakeholders in the process should maintain good documentation of the activities and actions that have been taken. Remember that what is written is your record of the process should there be any questions or disputes. All documentation including emails and written notes can be used in a dispute, arbitration or tribunal and therefore make sure that each stakeholder understands how to maintain accurate and objective records.

- Keep documents clear and objective
- Ensure that each step and call is written
- Keep medical information separate from the human resources file (all medical notes should not be maintained in a supervisor or human resources file but should be sent on to the carrier or benefits administrator file)
- Ensure supervisor documents their conversations and corrections in the workplace. This will assist with progressive discipline or performance issues should this become an issues later in the case
- Obtain objective reports on duty to accommodate and functional abilities
- If the case management is outsourced, ensure that appropriate consents have been signed for exchange of information
- Document the process and the results
- Document your systematic review of all work options and why or why they may not be appropriate.
- If there is a decision that the accommodation is "undue hardship" for the employer ensure that all documentation is clear and outlines the process and communication that has occurred throughout the process and who has been involved
- Obtain an expert opinion on any decision that may lead to your duty to accommodate.
- Use consistent documentation forms and checklists to support documentation — some organizations may also maintain electronic copies (see toolkit for sample forms and documentation outlines)

12.13 — Qualities of a Return to Work Plan

Your individual return to work plan lays out the steps that need to be taken to return an employee to their pre-accident job. It is normally developed jointly by the return to work program manager (who co-ordinates the process), the worker, the worker's treating practitioner (through the provision of restrictions), the worker's supervisor, and the union (if applicable). Supervisors from other areas, the medical department, or staff from the WSIB/carrier may assist in the process when the need arises.

Your return to work plan should include the following:

- The goals of the plan -These goals set out milestones for the worker to achieve until they reach the final goal: a return to pre-accident employment.
- Actions required to achieve these goals. This includes the responsibilities of the worker, the supervisor, and any co-workers who will be assisting the worker.
- Time frames for achieving these goals so that there is a yardstick to measure the worker's progress. It is important that the plan has a beginning and an end, as modified/graduated work is a means to achieve a return to pre-accident work, and is not an end in itself.
- A clear definition of what is considered progress (e.g., the worker can work five hours a day by week three, or the worker can assume tasks by week five).
- Health care needs — If, for example, the worker is going to attend therapy during working hours, these visits must be co-ordinated with the requirements of the proposed work placement. Staff that will be impacted by these health care needs will also need to be advised -with the worker's permission.

A return to work plan that has well defined parameters and sets measures or productivity goals can be a tool to help monitor progress, give concrete parameters for graduating activity, quickly identify potential barriers, and help distinguish between medical and non-medical performance concerns.

- Goal oriented — what is the overall goal of the program and what are the weekly and daily goals

- Targeted — is the person transitioning back to full hours and regular duties?
- Time limited — 6–12 weeks for 75 per cent of cases; up to 6 months for complex cases
- Individualized — directly speaks to the employees abilities and work duties
- Recognize any risks and restrictions clearly
- Ensure that there is no compromise to recovery
- All stakeholders develop the plan together
- All stakeholders receive a copy
- All stakeholders sign the return to work plan in commitment to the goal
- Copies are always provided to the treating health care provider and carrier/WSIB
- Flexible — all return to work plans need monitoring and reworking — be prepared to adjust the plan as needed
- Meaningful and productive work — always include only meaningful, productive and suitable work
- Include performance standards in the plan (include work productivity expectations where possible)
- Ensure that the schedule has a consistent routine and progression,
- Clearly identify the days to be worked, including start and end times (and any breaks required),
- Ensure duties and work expectations are detailed and reflect both the capacities of the employee and the rehabilitative intent of the plan,
- Identify manager, employee and human resources role throughout the program
- Double check once the plan is developed that all stakeholders agree!

12.14 — The Return to Work Meeting

A meeting with all stakeholders should occur in order to plan and organize a return to work program. The meeting may include just the employee, supervisor, union representative and HR or it may include more stakeholders such as health and safety, benefits, the carrier or WCB RTW Specialist, etc. The purpose of the meeting is to ensure that all stakeholders agree to and understand roles and responsibilities in the plan.

Here is a sample meeting agenda:

12.15 — Return to Work Meeting Agenda

The following outlines the communication during a reintegration, return to work meeting. Each employee has different needs that will require accommodation or communication. This is only a guideline for a return to work meeting agenda. It is important that the agenda is flexible in order to allow collaboration with the employee when developing the plan:

1. Welcome employee back to the company and express the company's commitment to have the employee back into the workplace.
2. Review the information that has been provided from the health care provider with the employee (restrictions, return to work date)
3. Ask the employee what they feel they will be able to do on return to work, what they will have most difficulty performing in the job, and how it can be changed so that they can do the tasks.
4. Discuss the accommodation
    a. Is the accommodation feasible for your department? If not what other options exist?
    b. Who will do the tasks that the employee cannot?
    c. What should the employee do if concerns arise?
    d. When will you meet on return to work plan?
    e. What productivity expectations will there be for the employee?

f. How long will the plan be and how will it progress (i.e. when will they do the additional tasks)?

g. What will be discussed with the coworkers and team?

h. Who will order any equipment needed?

i. How is Organizational Health involved in the return to work program?

5. Adjust or agree to the accommodation

6. Discuss the importance of communication during return to work

7. Set the return to work plan and confirm the return to work date

8. Thank the employee for their involvement in the meeting and express your commitment to make the return to work plan successful.

Sample Return to Work Outline

Name: ______________________ Phone Number: ....

Employer: ____________________ Phone Number: ....

Supervisor: ____________________

Job Title: ______________________

Date of Plan: __________________

Return to work restrictions:

Return to Work Goal:

Return to Work Schedule:

Week dates	*Hours*	*Duties*
1		
2		
3		

4		
5		
6		
7		
8		
9		
10		
11		
12		

Review Schedule:

Approved by:

________________________ ____________________

Employee Supervisor

Therapist Physician (optional)

Parameters of the Return to Work Program

The Employee is responsible for:

- Reporting any concerns to the supervisor and therapist as the concerns arise
- Being on time
- Performing all duties as assigned
- Contacting the therapist as outlined

The Supervisor is responsible for:

- Ensuring job duties meet employee's capabilities as outlined
- Reporting any concerns to the employee and therapist as they arise
- Monitoring job performance
- Providing feedback to the employee on job performance

Parameters of the Return to Work Program
The Disability Management Professional is responsible for: • Ensuring all ergonomic equipment is in place prior to return to work • Ensuring job duties are appropriate for employee's capabilities • Monitoring any concerns brought forth by supervisor or employee • Reviewing return to work plan are schedule intervals. • Providing education to employee on proper body mechanics and work pacing

Sample Return to Work Plan

Date Plan Prepared April 17, 2010
On: ________________

Name of Employee: __________________________
Date of Injury/Illness: (off work since) October 22, 2009

Company Name: ABC __________________________

Company Contact Person and Phone Number: MS. HR __________________________

Function Capabilities & Limitations *(based on most current physical demands analysis/functional abilities form)*:
The doctor has not yet provided the PDA/FA form however based on discussion today must limit walking, no lifting over 10lbs., and work reduced hours with a gradual increase. She must be able to elevate her foot from time to time and continue with Physiotherapy 2-3 times a week.

Estimated Date of Return to *FULL DUTIES*: May 26, 2010 ________________

Description of employee's regular job and regular hours:

START DATE	LEVEL	DURATION	DESCRIPTION OF WORK ASSIGNMENTS (including time assigned & special equipment needed)
April 15, 2010	3 days/week	2-weeks April 15, 16, 17 April 22, 23, 24	• Nurse on-call assignment. • Limit walking • No lifting of supplies • Elevate leg when needed
April 29, 2010	• Medical appointment with physician		
April 29, 2010	4 days/week	2-weeks April 29, 30, May 1,2 May 6–9	• Nurse on-call assignment • Limit walking • No lifting of supplies • Elevate leg when needed • Increase duties if tolerated
May 1, 2010	• Meeting to discuss update from doctor and make any necessary adjustments to work plan.		
May 13, 2010	5	2-weeks May 12–16	• Nurse on-call assignment. • Limit walking • No lifting of supplies

START DATE	LEVEL	DURATION	DESCRIPTION OF WORK ASSIGNMENTS (including time assigned & special equipment needed)
	days/week	May 19–23	• Elevate leg when needed • Commence working some clinics
May 26, 2010	Return to full duty	N/A	• N/A

This early & safe return to work plan has been prepared based on the employee's functional abilities evaluation and the physical demands analysis and reviewed by the employee, manager and the health professional in consultation with the Manager, Human Resources. This plan can be adapted according to the recovery of the employee. Changes may be made dependent upon the tolerance level of the employee to the above plan. The manager and the employee will consult weekly and/or periodically to review the employees recovery. Should an issue arise prior to a scheduled meeting it is the duty of the employee to report it to the manager. A copy of the plan will be provided to human resources for the employee's personnel file. The employee will consult with her/his health professional on a *biweekly* basis and prior to her/his return to full duties.

Signature & Date:	____________________	(Employee)
Signature & Date:	____________________	(Manager)
Signature & Date:	____________________	(Manager, Human Resources)

START DATE	LEVEL	DURATION	DESCRIPTION OF WORK ASSIGNMENTS (including time assigned & special equipment needed)
Signature & Date:	____________		(Union representative)
Signature & Date:	____________		(Health Professional)

12.16 — Monitoring a Return to Work Program

The monitoring of a return to work program is as important as how the plan is developed. Most plans will require adjustment and changes. If the plan is not monitored closely then it can become a failure before you start.

a) — Who should monitor the program?

The Human Resources Professional or return to work coordinator should monitor the plan through regular communication with the manager and the employee. To start this may be on a daily basis in more complex cases or weekly basis and then wean off to biweekly and even monthly.

The manager should be asked to meet with the employee for short touch base sessions daily until the program is underway and the communication channels are open. Then the employee can be instructed to contact the manager if there are concerns.

b) — How should the monitoring occur?

Face to face monitoring is crucial initially to ensure that all the plans are being followed as laid out and that the plan is working. The Institute for Work and Health indicate that ergonomic worksite visits improve the success of return to work.[15] This can be a strategy to monitor the plan. Go and see that all the equipment, processes and modifications are in place. Encourage the worker at the worksite and address any co-worker or manager issues immediately.

c) — When should the monitoring occur?

As noted above, a manager/employee spot check daily at the end of the shift is important and can be reduced as the plan progresses.

Biweekly meetings (or whenever new functional abilities information is provided from the treating health care team) with the manager, human resources and employee to adjust or change the plan is important to consider.

The employee or manager should be told that at any time between meetings, the expectation is that if concerns arise they are addressed immediately with the return to work team. This will avoid an employee getting frustrated with the program or a manager not addressing issues until the end of the program.

12.17 — Return to Work Planning and Performance Management

An important part of proactive return to work planning and management is to identify, explore and address any performance issues which may impact the plan's potential success as early as possible.

a) — When Pre injury or illness performance issues are identified

Performance issues may have occurred prior to the current work absence, or may arise during active participation in a return to work plan. Regardless of when concerns arise, one of the first steps in addressing a performance issue is to determine whether it is attributable to a medical condition. Knowing whether the performance issues are medically based or not will help determine when and how to address them. In reviewing this point consider:

---

[15] E. MacEachen, J. Clarke, R-L Franche, E. Irvin *"The process of return to work after injury: findings of a systematic review of qualitative studies."* Scandinavian Journal of Work, Environmental & Health 2006; 32(4): 257–269.

- the types of performance concerns raised (e.g. absenteeism, reduced productivity, inability to perform specific activities, etc.);
- the timing of the onset of the difficulties;
- the condition(s) the employee encountered and how they would impact functionality; and
- the timing of the onset of the medical condition(s).

b) — When performance issues are identified prior to the return to work

If the issue(s) were the result of a medical condition:

- review the medical information and speak with the employee to determine whether the impairments which impacted performance have resolved, or whether they are expected to continue;
- identify any necessary supports, modifications or accommodations which would address residual performance impacting impairments;
- explain to the manager that any deterioration in performance could be / was the result of a medical condition.

If the issue(s) are not attributable to a medical condition:

- advise the manager of the nature of any limitations, or restrictions that can reasonably be accounted for by the medical condition(s), and that performance issues which do not fit the identified parameters should be brought to the attention of the human resources professional who will then review / investigate for a possible medical basis with the treating provider;
- If the manager had commenced a formal performance management process, encourage them to address any identified non-medical performance issues in the same manner as they would for other employees;
- when pre-absence concerns existed but were not formally documented, encourage the manager to begin a documentation process;
- explain the return to work plan and process to both manager and employee so that all parties have a clear understanding of their

expectations and the repercussions of not meeting the expectations.

c) — When performance issues arise during the return to work

Any difficulty the employee has in achieving expectations should not be immediately construed as a performance problem. Instead both parties should be encouraged to discuss issues with the human resources professional as they arise so that support and feedback can be provided. The human resources professional should immediately investigate concerns to determine whether they are attributable to a medical condition.

If the performance concern is medically based:

- assess whether performance impacting limitations will continue, and for how long;
- determine whether any workplace modifications can be implemented to help address the difficulties;
- consider revising the return to work schedule, work duties, etc. to allow for adaptation to the impairments, or time for further recovery;
- consider whether progressive return to work planning can continue based on the information available;
- advise the manager that departure from expectations supported by medical or clearly linked to disability are not to be considered for performance management.

If the difficulties are not medically based:

- immediately address the issue with employee and reinforce the expectations of the plan;
- advise the manager of the issue and determine whether formal (written) reinforcement of the expectations and repercussions should be provided;
- encourage the manager to manage any non-medical performance issues in the same manner as they would with any other employee;

- If documented in a performance assessment or a performance improvement process had been initiated, inform the manager that the procedure(s) should continue;
- If no performance improvement process has been initiated, encourage the manager to begin a documentation process and review the HR procedures for performance management.

d) — Additional Considerations

At times, it can be difficult to determine if deviations in performance or behaviour was a result of disability/medical issues. This is especially true during the onset of a condition or at the initial stages of a return to work. When it is difficult to determine if performance issues are medically based

- Prior to the return to work: treat performance/behaviours as though they are medically based in the development of the return to work plan, but additional medical would be required to substantiate further incidents. If not medically supported it would be managed as performance and past incidents may be re-considered by the human resources professional.

Ultimately, absences and performance concerns should be explored by the Human Resources Professional for the impact of disability and determine if supports, adjustments to the plan, or job modifications are indicated. Otherwise the manager should address performance problems as they arise through documentation and feedback.

CHAPTER 13: MANAGING COMPLEX RETURN TO WORK ISSUES

13.1 — Introduction

Although most return to work plans proceed without concerns, some may involve complex issues that require further interventions or management. It is important to identify complex issues early and develop a plan that will prevent the complexities from derailing the return to work process.

13.2 — 5 Strategies to Manage Complex Cases

1. Identify the "complex case" early — Red, Yellow, Black, and Blue flags[1]
2. Open the communication to employee, union, managers and health care professionals early — engage a case manager if needed
3. Gain objective information about capabilities and accommodation needs — Update as needed
4. Implement steps to reduce each barrier — be creative, monitor the implementation of each step and evaluate the steps
5. Focus on function, solutions and a strong problem solving model

Make sure that your documentation of the process is clear and objectively written.

a) — When to Refer for Case Management?

In 20–25 per cent of cases you may require the assistance of an expert case manager either internally or externally to assist with medical management and return to work planning. It is important to refer

---

[1] AD Leckie & MK Grewal, *Disability Claims Management*, Second Edition. (Toronto: Butterworths Canada, 2002); Ludeke C Lambeek, researcher, Willem van Mechelen, professor, Dirk L Knol, statistician, Patrick Loisel, professor, Johannes R Anema, senior researcher "Randomised controlled trial of integrated care to reduce disability from chronic low back pain in working and private life" BMJ 2010;340:c1035

early if you see any of the flags noted below. Here are some other things to consider in this referral process.

Worker has not returned to work within 28 days: All cases should be referred for case management if the worker has not returned to work within 28 days, unless the employer has a clear reason why case management is not needed.

Increased Risk for Future Bad Outcomes: Cases that have been identified as "at increased risk" for a FUTURE bad outcome are the ones that should be referred. There is no generally-accepted way of evaluating risk at this time, although there is a lot of "common sense" about how to do it. There is also a lot of market experimentation going on with evidence-based vs. common-sense based early assessment tools and methods. Use the checklist to determine if there are flags that may indicate chronicity.

Involvement will have a good outcome: Cases should be referred to case management any time it looks like there is a clear opportunity for a case manager to make a difference in the situation's outcome. You should only refer the case IF YOU ARE CONFIDENT that the case manager has a decent shot at actually making something good happen. Employers may want to ask a resource (medical consultant) whether making the referral makes sense, and what the case manager should be asked to do.

b) — Pitfalls of Improper Case Management

There are occasions where managing cases through case management does not work.

- *Referred too late*. If there is a clear need for case management the earlier that this is engaged the better the outcome. When the employer has been trying to hold down administrative cost — pennywise and pound foolish, the likelihood of a good outcome is GREATLY reduced, and the longer it takes to start the case management process.
- *Cost outweighs result*. It is important to spend the money on the expertise that you require early in the process to avoid long term and costly claims. Case managers often get handed cases very late in the game when they are nearly hopeless.
- *Case Managers who don't understand the employer's culture and program goals*. Case managers too often act like regular health

care professionals instead of situation managers. They are not comfortable outside the strictly medical arena and are not effective conflict resolvers and disability managers. Case management involves negotiation and hands-on managing of the case. Make sure that the case manager understands your program goals and corporate culture.

- *Communicate with the Case Manager*. Employers, Insurers and TPAs have become unsure about the value of case management. It is easier, at times, to get an IME and surveillance than spend money on case management. You must be able to trust your suppliers and work together as a team. You can gain trust of the supplier by asking them to educate you on their protocols, experience and past outcomes. Communicate regularly so that you understand the next step in the process and can ask questions as needed.

13.3 — Definitions of Flags[2]

Red Flags — potentially significant physiological risk factors for developing chronic low back pain if not appropriately assessed

Yellow Flags — potentially significant psychosocial risk factors for developing chronicity following an MSD

Blue Flags — Perceived occupational factors believed by patients to impede recovery

Black Flags — Objective occupational workplace factors that may initially lead to the onset of MSD and may promote disability once the acute episode has occurred

a) — Complex Return to Work Red Flags[3]

When identifying the complex flags there are specific strategies that can be used to intervene and manage the complexity. Note that just because a red flag exists, it does not mean that the employee is purposely attempting to take longer time away from work, but it does

---

2 *Disability Claims Management*, above note 1;The Australasian Faculty of Occupational Medicine, report *"Workplace Attendance And Absenteeism"* Royal College of Physicians, December 1999.

3 Red Flags as outlined by Leckie & Grewall, adapted by Gowan Health, 2005.

signal a need for more assistance or a different approach in return to work.

(i) — High rate of absenteeism

Documented absences:

- When preparing the return to work program discuss responsibilities of employee with respect to start times, absence reporting and set up medical note requirement for single day lost;
- Continue any progressive discipline process that was in place prior to medical absence;
- Do not consider medical absence in the progressive discipline calculation of days lost.

Undocumented absences:

- When preparing the return to work program discuss responsibilities of employee with respect to start times, absence reporting and set up medical note requirement for single day lost. Begin recording absences and set expectation of attendance with the return to work program. Begin progressive discipline process as documented absences meet standards for attendance program.

(ii) — Performance problems

- Address expectations during the return to work program with respect to work duties;
- Provide feedback to employee regularly throughout the program;
- The manager should deal with performance problems as they arise;
- Note that performance problems may have been a symptom of medical issues prior to the absence.

(iii) — Pending Litigation

- Work with regular consistent return to work program and expectations;
- Copy legal representative on correspondence only if you have signed consent from the employee.

(iv) — Expected Duration of Disability Greater Than Two Months

- Determine reason for delay in return to work;
- Find suitable accommodation or modified work to meet needs;
- Use independent assessors if insufficient information is provided.

(v) — Delays in Expected Return to Work Date

- Determine reason for delay in return to work;
- Offer in writing suitable accommodation;
- Use independent assessor or expert to improve return to work.

(vi) — Disorders Lacking Observable Clinical Evidence

- Ensure that you have clear functional abilities of employee;
- Match with suitable work situation;
- Offer support programs for symptom management;
- Set realistic goals and expectations with employee.

(vii) — Multiple Diagnoses

- Ensure that you have clear functional abilities — use independent functional assessment if required;
- Develop suitable return to work plan with modified work;
- Allow for potential longer return to work process;
- Ensure clear and proactive monitoring to address new issues as they arise.

(viii) — Pattern of Doctor Shopping

- Maintain communication with health providers, physiotherapists if involved for consistency;
- Develop communication with each health provider as they arrive on scene with history of return to work issues outlined;
- Employee may continue to "shop" for a cure but this should not delay return to work.

(ix) — Non Compliance with Treatment Plans

- Signed and Written contracts for all return to work and treatment plans;

b) — Yellow Flags for Complex Return to Work

(i) — Hurt vs. Harm Concepts

- Is the employee in a proactive treatment program with her health professional's i.e. Active physiotherapy, occupational therapy, pain program;
- Communicate with the health professionals to ensure that they have provided employee with education on capabilities and hurt vs. harm;
- Perform a functional assessment for baseline capabilities to educate employee on capabilities and have assessor educate throughout assessment;
- During return to work planning have onsite consultant to provide education on proper body mechanics, the duties that match the capabilities of the client;
- Perform a clear job analysis to ensure that job meets client's capabilities.

(ii) — Passive approach to health care

- Communication with health care providers to ensure programming is active;
- Focus on ways employee can manage symptoms at work;
- Do not offer hot packs, massages or other passive modalities at workplace;
- Written goals and objectives with assigned responsibilities;
- Use of written contracts.

(iii) — Slow recovery outside of normal

- Reassess job match;
- Independent medical assessment to determine alternative treatment and rehabilitation strategies;

- Offer suitable modified work;
- Onsite assessment and intervention by an occupational therapist/ergonomist to look at any missing links;
- Communication with employee to ensure that they are compliant with treatment programs;
- Use of written and signed contracts;
- Consult with medical disability advisor time lines to determine match or complications.

(iv) — Eagerness to Return to Work After Change of Benefits

- Follow consistent return to work process;
- Ensure clear functional capabilities are outlined and matched with job;
- Start process of return to work discussions earlier to plan for change in benefits;
- Educate employee early on benefits process;
- Do not delay return to work unduly just because of change of benefits issues.

(v) — Human Resources Issues

- Review and deal with medical issues through return to work process;
- Ensure that human resources is involved in return to work planning early in the process and invited to all return to work meetings;
- Set clear expectations for return to work program;
- Use of facilitator may be necessary in unusual situations.

(vi) — Employment Changes Expected (Lay Off, Shifts, Contract)

- Manage return to work consistently with all cases;

- Ensure that there is clear PDA's and Functional abilities assessed for each person;
- Educate employee on implications of return to work and employment changes early;
- Prepare for excessive numbers of claims prior to changes;
- Implement specific programs to counteract effects of changes i.e. shift work education.

(vii) — Lack of Knowledge of Process

- Provide education packages and programs to all employees and managers.

(viii) — RTW Expectations Based on Hearsay

- Contact employee early about return to work program and expectations, roles, responsibilities;
- Ensure that employee is educated on consequences of decisions and that the consequences are implemented if appropriate.

(ix) — Low Self Efficacy

- Develop written and signed contracts that provides control to the individual and clear responsibilities of all parties;
- Do not make decisions for the employee;
- Document decisions and actions clearly.

The following checklist was created based on the evidence for musculoskeletal disorder chronicity:

Checklist to Identify Possible Predictors of MSD Chronicity[4]

RED FLAGS: (specific for low back pain)

✓ Age — less than 20 years old or greater than 55 years old
✓ A violent trauma, such as fall from height

[4] R Gatchel "Musculoskeletal disorders: Primary and secondary interventions" Journal of Electromyography and Kinesiology (2004) 161-170.

✓ Constant, progressive, no mechanical pain
✓ Presence of thoracic pain
✓ A past medical history of carcinoma
✓ Use of steroids or drug abuse
✓ Being HIV positive and or using intravenous drugs
✓ Being in poor health or physically unwell
✓ Weight loss
✓ Persistent severe restriction of lumbar flexion
✓ Widespread neurological symptoms
✓ Structural deformity
✓ Fever
✓ Severe, unremitting night time pain
✓ Pain that gets worse when the patient is lying down

Yellow Flags

✓ A = Attitudes and Beliefs about pain — fear avoidance behaviour

✓ B = patient's behaviours — reliance on rest

✓ C = compensation issues — lack of financial incentive to return to work

✓ D = diagnosis and treatment — understanding of diagnosis and presentation of assurance from treaters

✓ E = emotions — feeling hopeless or heightened awareness of body sensations

✓ F = Familial factors — social support system

✓ W = risk factors related to Work — history of manual work, significant biomechanical demands — feel work is dangerous or harmful — past job dissatisfaction, patterns of frequent job change, unsupportive work environment, low educational level and low socioeconomic status, shift work, little unavailability of modified work

Blue Flags

✓ High demand/low control work environment
✓ Perception that the style of management is unhelpful
✓ Belief that they are working under a perceived time pressure
✓ Belief that hey receive poor social support from colleagues
✓ Dislike their jobs

Black Flags

✓ Temporal characteristics (number of work hours and shift patterns)

✓ Variables pertaining to ergonomics

Black Flags are important for evaluating disability risk more than for predicting onset of pain. Although these have not led to the initial onset of pain, they appear to promote disability once the pain has occurred.

13.4 — Reintegration

The following chart provides Managers with ideas on how they can assist an employee in successfully reintegrating themselves into the workplace after returning from an STD or LTD leave.

Timing	Tasks
A few days before the employee returns	• Mention that the employee is returning during a team meeting or send an e-mail to the team with this information, whichever is more appropriate. The communication should indicate that the employee should be welcomed during their first day back and may need assistance from team members to re-orient themselves into the workplace.
During the employee's first day back	• If there have been any changes to the employee's compensation or benefits package, they should be reviewed with the employee before their return to work. • Complete a health and safety orientation checklist with the employee prior to the commencement of any work activities. The completion of this checklist verifies that you, as a Manager, have been duly diligent in ensuring the well being of your employee.

Timing	Tasks
During the employee's first two weeks back	• Complete a "new employee" orientation process. Ensure that you touch on each of the items on the list (if any of these items have changed) sometime during the employee's first two weeks back. Many of the items on this list are things that you may already know you should go over with your returning employee. The checklist is provided as a tool to catch some of those little details that may accidentally slip through the cracks when re-orienting a returning employee. • If the employee has been away from work for an extended period of time, it may be appropriate to have them attend a department specific orientation session. This will assist the employee in familiarizing themselves with any departmental changes that have occurred while they were away. • Check in regularly with the employee to see how they are doing and ask if they need any assistance.

13.5 — Preparing for a Difficult Management Discussion

Managing return to work processes can involve many difficult conversations. It is important to prepare well when entering the management discussion. Use this checklist to prepare:

Before engaging in the discussion:

TIME:

- Do I have the time to do this properly or am I going to rush this?

FACTS:

- Do I have the facts or am I responding to emotions and hearsay?

MY ROLE:

- Am I in the right frame of mind to do this?
- Am I considering my role in this situation?

FOCUS:

- Am I looking for solutions or just rehashing the problem?
- Am I focusing on new behaviours?
- Approach long term results

COWORKERS:

- Am I considering the effect on others?
- Am I looking at the big picture?
- Can I preserve the dignity of the individual and the coworkers?

SOLUTION:

- Does the solution provide energy to the employee?
- Does the approach encourage employee control and responsibility for his/her own wellbeing?
- Have I adequately addressed the fears and concerns of others?
- Is this a shared plan for success?
- Can this help the employee be successful at work?

FOLLOW UP:

- How will I monitor the plan?
- When will we meet again to review the plan?

13.6 — Guidelines for an Effective Discussion

- Hold the meeting as soon as possible after the employee returns to work or after you have received the trigger memo so that events are fresh in everyone's mind;
- Provide a setting that allows for a confidential discussion;

- Prior to the discussion review relevant policies and procedures;
- Have the attendance record present and in writing;
- Calmly and logically control the discussion;
- Focus on the behaviour, not the person;
- State your concerns in objective terms (i.e. in the past 6 months you have been absent 4 times which is above the company average);
- Explain to the employee the reason for the concerns and how it impacts the workplace;
- Ask questions;
- Listen empathetically;
- Ask the employee for a solution to the absence issues;
- Ask if you can assist in improving the attendance of your employee;
- If the employee does not offer a reason for the absence, do not pry for medical information but indicate that you may need to request information from the physician regarding the employee's ability to work;
- If the employee reports the absences are related to a medical condition ask them to contact Human Resources to discuss their needs within the next two weeks;
- Develop action steps clearly so that both you and the employee understand the next steps and any time frame for these steps to occur;
- Explain to the employee the consequences of not following through on the set action plans;
- Set a follow up meeting date at the end of the meeting;
- Ensure that the employee understands the actions and time frames;
- If the employee refuses to cooperate or provide information, remain calm and schedule a meeting with the Human Resources

Manager and employee on another occasion to develop an action plan.

CHAPTER 14: ACCOMMODATION FOR SPECIFIC DISABILITIES

14.1 — Disability Terminology and Tips

The information contained in this section is intended as a quick, general reference to certain types of disabilities. Each individual experiences disabilities differently and distinctly, therefore it is important to assess each individual and the accommodations that are best suited for the individual's capabilities and restrictions.

a) — Mobility impairments

This category can generally be divided in two: those individuals who have sustained injuries or congenital irregularities, and those with progressive disorders. In virtually all cases, the person's intellectual abilities are unaffected. The needs of an employee with a mobility impairment may change over the course of his or her employment, so open communication and flexibility is essential.

Some points to consider:

- When introduced to a person with a disability, it is appropriate to offer to shake hands. People with limited hand use or who wear an artificial limb can usually shake hands;
- Shaking hands with the left hand is acceptable;
- Never patronize people using wheelchairs by patting them on the head or shoulder;
- When addressing a person who uses a wheelchair, never lean on the person's wheelchair. The chair is part of the space that belongs to the person who uses it;
- When talking with a person in a wheel chair for more than a few minutes, use a chair, whenever possible, in order to place yourself at the person's eye level to facilitate conversation.

b) — Blind/low vision

Visual impairments can cover a wide spectrum, ranging from complete blindness to partial blindness. For some individuals, visual impairments are a natural part of aging. Open communication can avoid perpetuating common misconceptions associated with the legal definition of blindness.

Some points to consider:

- Offer assistance in a dignified manner with sensitivity and respect. Be prepared to have the offer declined. Do not proceed to assist if your offer to assist is declined. If the offer is accepted, listen to or accept instructions;
- Allow a person with a visual impairment to take your arm (at or about the elbow.) This will enable you to guide rather than propel or lead the person;
- When greeting a person with a severe loss of vision, always identify yourself and others who may be with you. EXAMPLE: "*On my right is Penelope Potts*";
- When conversing in a group, give a vocal cue by announcing the name of the person to whom you are speaking. Speak in a normal tone of voice, indicate in advance when you will be moving from one place to another and let it be known when the conversation is at an end;
- Don't be embarrassed if you happen to use accepted common expressions such as "See you later" that seem to relate to the person's disability.

Service animals

- Do not touch the Service Animal, or the person it assists, without permission;
- Do not make noises at the Service Animal; it may distract the animal from doing its job;
- Do not feed the Service Animal; it may disrupt his/her schedule.

c) — Deaf/hard of hearing

While some individuals are completely deaf, others have decreased or obstructed hearing. Some hearing impairments are associated with aging. Again, it is important to make sure that you maintain clear communication and confirm that communication has been understood.

Some points to consider:

- If an interpreter is present, speak to the person who has initiated contact, not to the interpreter. Always maintain eye contact with the individual, not the interpreter.
- Do not shout at a hearing impaired person. Shouting distorts sounds accepted through hearing aids and inhibits lip reading.

d) — Speech impairments

An individual with a speech impairment has no difficulty understanding spoken and/or written language. In some cases, the person may use other means of communication that are equally effective, such as writing or sign language.

Some points to consider:

- Listen attentively when you're talking to a person who has a speech impairment. Keep your manner encouraging rather than correcting. Exercise patience rather than attempting to speak for a person with speech difficulty;
- Never pretend to understand if you are having difficulty doing so. Repeat what you understand, and incorporate it into clarifying questions. The person's reactions will clue you in and guide you to understanding;
- If you have difficulty communicating, be willing to repeat or rephrase a question.

e) — Mental health disabilities

Mental Health disabilities have various manifestations and consequences, depending on their type and severity. Some are the result of trauma such as physical, sexual or emotional abuse. Still others are the result of chemical imbalances which affect an individual's emotions or perception of reality, but not his or her intellect. The term mental illness is used to describe a wide range of different conditions. What they have in common is that they all affect a person's emotions, thoughts and behaviours — how they see themselves, see the world around them, and how they interact in that world.

Some points to consider:

- People who have mental health disabilities have varying personalities and different ways of coping with their disability. Some may have trouble picking up on social cues; others may be hypersensitive. One person may be very high energy, while someone else may appear sluggish. Treat each person as an individual. Ask what will make them most comfortable and respect their needs to the maximum extent possible.

f) — Intellectual disabilities

Individuals with intellectual disabilities can improve their self-reliance if adequate support is provided to help them to develop social and professional skills. Most individuals with intellectual disabilities adapt well to the workplace on a social and professional level. Some individuals have case workers that can be consulted with respect to his or her skills and the level of direction and supervision required.

Some points to consider:

- Don't use baby talk or talk down to people with intellectual disabilities. Gauge the pace, complexity, and vocabulary of your speech according to theirs;
- Remember that the person is an adult and, unless you are informed otherwise, can make their own decisions.

g) — Learning disabilities

Learning disabilities are neurological in origin, and may affect an individual's capacity to receive, process and communicate information in traditional formats. An individual with a learning disability will have varying degrees of success performing reading, writing and mathematical tasks. Appropriate accommodation can ensure that a person's learning disability will not restrict or limit his or her productivity in the workplace.

Some points to consider:

- People with dyslexia or other reading disabilities have trouble reading written information. Give them verbal explanations and allow extra time for reading;
- Don't be surprised if you tell someone very simple instructions and they request that you write them down. Because spoken in-

formation gets "scrambled" as he listens, a person who has a learning disability such as auditory processing disorder may need information demonstrated or in writing;

- Ask the person how you can best relay information. Be direct in your communication. A person with a learning disability may have trouble grasping subtleties;
- It may be easier for the person to function in a quiet environment without distractions, such as a radio playing, people moving around or loudly patterned curtains.

h) — Environmental sensitivities

Individuals with environmental sensitivities react to some foods, chemicals and environmental agents, singly or in combination. Environmental sensitivities include asthma and allergies, as well as Building Related Illnesses and Sick Building Syndrome.

Some points to consider:

- Create a scent free environment policy
- Use less-toxic products when possible. If you have contact with the public go easy on fragranced body-care products like cologne, hair spray, hand lotion, and after-shave.
- Second-hand smoke can be particularly harmful to people with MCS or respiratory disabilities. Follow no-smoking regulations, including in restrooms and stairwells.

i) — Alcohol and Drug Addiction

Substance abuse is classified as a form of dependence, which has been recognized as a form of disability. Examples include alcoholism and the abuse of legal drugs (e.g. over-the-counter drugs) or illicit drugs.

Some points to consider:

- An individual who has had a drug or alcohol dependency in the past, but who no longer suffers from an ongoing disability, is still protected by the *Human Rights Code*; do not assume that perceived troubles at work are addiction-related.

14.2 — Accommodations

Definition of Workplace Accommodation

Designing work environments and procedures that include everyone so we can do our work more effectively. These are various examples that will accommodate different individuals; not all of these are needed for everyone.

Telephones

- Provide hands-free option to promote ease of use;
- Provide voice amplifiers to facilitate conversation;
- Provide TTY service, which provides voice-to-text / text-to-voice translation feature;
- Provide large button keypads, which are highly visible and easy to use.

Computers

- Provide document holders to make typing easier;
- Provide accessibility software for keyboard or mouse, to promote ease of access to computers;
- Provide large print software, which is highly visible and easy to read;
- Install screen reader software to ease access to electronic formats.

Furniture

- Arrange office furniture to compensate for right or left side dexterity; this also promotes ease of access and reach;

14.3 — Managing Mental Health Return to Work Issues

a) — What is mental illness?[1]

Most of us have heard the words mental illness or mental disorder or psychiatric condition. These terms all mean the same thing. But what do they mean? The term mental illness is used to describe a wide range of different conditions. What they have in common is that they all affect a person's emotions, thoughts and behaviours — how they see themselves, see the world around them and how they interact in that world.

Of course, all of us go through times where our world view changes, but what makes it a disorder is how long it goes on for and how much it negatively impacts your life. There are many different kinds of mental disorders including:

Mood disorders — involve changes and disruptions in a person's mood and emotions. Depression and bipolar disorder are examples of mood disorders.

Anxiety disorders — are the most common type of mental disorder. They cause people to be overly anxious and afraid of situations or events that most people consider normal. Panic disorder and post-traumatic stress disorder are anxiety disorders.

Schizophrenia — involves people losing the ability to know what's real and what isn't (this feature is called psychosis). Schizophrenia also makes it difficult for people to think, speak and interact in an organized way. Psychosis is not just a part of schizophrenia, but may also be seen on its own, or with other disorders like mood disorders.

Eating disorders — involve a distorted body image along with serious behaviours to manage food and weight, making it difficult to nourish oneself properly. Eating disorders can be life-threatening. Examples of eating disorders include anorexia and bulimia.

Personality disorders — affect the way a person acts, feels and gets along with other people. They can also cause people to be

---

1 Primer Fact Sheets, 2008, Mental Disorders www.heretohelp.bc.ca

more impulsive. Borderline personality disorder and antisocial personality disorder are examples of personality disorders.

Substance use disorders (commonly called addictions) — occur when a person becomes dependent on a substance such as alcohol, tobacco or other drugs

Dementia — involves the loss of brain cells and results in loss of memory, judgment and reasoning, along with changes in mood, behaviour and communication abilities (beyond what might be seen in normal aging). Alzheimer's disease is the most common form of dementia.

Attention deficit (hyperactivity) disorder (ADD or ADHD) — can be diagnosed in adults but is usually found in children and youth and affects their ability to focus their attention. This condition may also include hyperactivity, which is when a person becomes easily over-excited.

b) — Non-evident disabilities[2]

The nature or degree of certain disabilities might render them "non-evident" to others. Chronic fatigue syndrome and back pain, for example are not apparent conditions. Other disabilities might remain hidden because they are episodic. Epilepsy is one example. Similarly, environmental sensitivities can flare up from one day to the next, resulting in significant impairment to a person's health and capacity to function, while at other times, this disability may be entirely non-evident. Other examples might include:

- Persons whose disabilities do not actually result in any functional limitations but who experience discrimination because others believe their disability makes them less able;
- Persons who have recovered from conditions but are treated unfairly because of their past condition; and
- Persons whose disabilities are episodic or temporary in nature.

Other disabilities may become apparent based on the nature of the interaction, such as when there is a need for oral communication with

---

2 Ontario Human Rights Commission — Policy And Guidelines On Disability And The Duty To Accommodate published 05/30/01 (http://www.ohrc.on.ca/english/publications/disability-policy.shtml)

an individual who is deaf, or there is a need for written communication with an individual who has a learning disability. A disability may become apparent over time through extended interaction or simply, the disability might remain "non-evident" because the individual chooses not to divulge it for personal reasons.

Regardless of whether a disability is evident or non-evident, a great deal of discrimination faced by persons with disabilities is underpinned by social constructs of "normality", which in turn tend to reinforce obstacles to integration rather than encourage ways to ensure full participation. Because these disabilities are not "seen", many of them are not well understood in society. This can lead to stereotypes, stigma and prejudice.

c) — Mental disability

Although mental disability is a form of non-evident disability, it raises particular issues that merit independent consideration. Over the years, many employers have expressed the need for specific guidance on the issue of mental disability. Section 10 of the Code expressly includes mental disabilities. Persons with mental disabilities face a high degree of stigmatization and significant barriers to employment opportunities. Stigmatization can foster a climate that exacerbates stress and may trigger or worsen the person's condition. It may also mean that someone who has a problem and needs help may not seek it, for fear of being labelled.

The Supreme Court of Canada[3] has recognized the distinct disadvantage and negative stereotyping faced by persons with mental disabilities, and has held that discrimination against individuals with mental disabilities is unlawful. In *Gibbs v. Battlefords*[4] the Court struck down an insurance plan for employees with disabilities that limited benefits for mental disabilities to a lower level as compared to physical disabilities. It is therefore the Commission's position that such distinctions are prima fascia discriminatory.

---

3 *Ibid.*

4 *Gibbs v. Battlefords & District Co-operative Ltd.* (1996), 1996 CarswellSask 603, 1996 CarswellSask 602, [1996] S.C.J. No. 55, [1996] 3 S.C.R. 566, 2 B.H.R.C. 92, [1997] 1 W.W.R. 1, 140 D.L.R. (4th) 1, (sub nom. *Battlefords & District Co-operative Ltd. v. Gibbs))* 203 N.R. 131 (S.C.C.)

d) — Return to Work and Mental Health Conditions[5]

(Individuals with a mental illness may experience the following)

FACTORS	ASSOCIATED DIFFICULTIES	ACCOMMODATIONS
Psychological Inability to concentrate	Feelings of restlessness, short attention span, distractibility, memory/recall of information, focus for extended periods of time.	Taking short frequent breaks when attention slips; assignment of tasks in smaller segments, keep notes or request written instructions Plan for uninterrupted work time Restructure job to include only essential duties Written minutes of meetings Provide checklists Allow additional training time Increase natural lighting in your work area Work from home
Difficulty handling time pressures and multi-tasking	Setting priorities to meet deadlines; making decisions around responsibilities and projects.	Meetings at regular intervals with immediate supervisor or team leader to establish time-targets and realistic schedule for completion of projects. Daily "to do" lists

5 Adapted from LL Mancusco, 1990, Reasonable Accommodations for workers with Psychiatric Disabilities

FACTORS	ASSOCIATED DIFFICULTIES	ACCOMMODATIONS
		Divide large projects into smaller tasks/goals Electronic calendars and organizers Ask for regular reminders from your supervisor
Difficulty interacting with others	Feelings of fear, inhibitions, shyness, embarrassment in	Request to be paired with someone who could act as a mentor.
	interacting with peers; picking up on informal/unwritten rules	Educate employees/ coworkers on right to accommodate
	in the work culture	Provide sensitivity training
		Do not mandate attendance at social functions Develop strategies to deal with problems before they arise Look at possible or previous issues and consider a way to address them Ask for correspondence in writing Ask for clear expectations and the clear consequences for not meeting them Ask for written work agreements Define what constitutes a good working relationship

FACTORS	ASSOCIATED DIFFICULTIES	ACCOMMODATIONS
		Do not discuss non work related issues in the workplace Ask for the option for not attending work related social events
Difficulty handling feedback	Understanding and interpreting feedback which may be perceived as criticism, feelings of negativity, worthlessness or defensiveness, figuring out appropriate responses to feedback.	Request feedback in writing and opportunity to discuss later; request clarification on the specific indicators of improvement; Ask for guidelines on performance indicators/targets. Provide praise and reinforcement Provide written job descriptions Written work agreements
Memory		Use a recorder for discussions and meetings Write down important or complicated issues Ask for instructions in writing Ask for the minutes for every meeting Ask for assignments in writing

FACTORS	ASSOCIATED DIFFICULTIES	ACCOMMODATIONS
		Ask for additional training time
Difficulty dealing with stress and emotions		Seek help from mental health counsellors Ask employer to provide praise and positive reinforcement Ask for time off to attend counselling Ask for phone calls to doctors or others to gain necessary support during the workday Ask for clear outline of expectations to avoid misunderstandings Consider awareness training for coworkers about how to effectively interact with you Consider awareness training for all staff on mental illness
Difficulty responding to change	Changes at work — expected or unexpected, e.g., job duties, supervisor/management, coworkers, downsizing, acquisitions, new rules or	Advise the employer of any specific needs which may help to reduce stress, attend any planned meetings to deal with change; seek assistance through the employee assistance program or other support service.

FACTORS	ASSOCIATED DIFFICULTIES	ACCOMMODATIONS
	organization structure	Provide transition time between old and new managers Regular meetings re: change process
Environmental Inability to screen out environmental stimuli	Distracted by sounds, smells, sights, for example: difficulty working in an open concept office with noise, constancy interactions.	Partitions around desk, use of head pones playing soft music, good ventilation.
Physical Lack of energy or stamina	Tolerance to work a full day or for varying shifts, rising for early morning start, effects of medications.	Flexible work arrangements-job sharing, part-time work hours. Determine if the condition is permanent or if medication changes physical activities can help. Breaks Additional time for new learning Work from home

14.4 — Managing Chronic Pain

a) — Definition of pain

The most widely used definition, introduced by the International Association for the Study of Pain (IASP),[6] states: "Pain is an unpleasant sensory and emotional experience associated with actual or potential tissue damage or described in terms of such damage." This definition suggests that pain is a complex, multi-dimensional experience that is difficult for patients to describe, for clinicians to evaluate, and for investigators to study. It also implies that a direct, one-to-one relationship between the severity of tissue damage and the intensity of pain sensation is not a given.

b) — Classification by duration

Acute pain

The most widely accepted definition of acute pain states that it is "the normal, predicted physiological response to a noxious chemical, thermal or mechanical stimulus . . . typically . . . associated with invasive procedures, trauma and disease . . ." and is "generally time-limited". Acute pain may be viewed as an appropriate response to a stimulus that threatens and/or produces tissue injury.

Contemporary definitions of pain should take into account the degree of congruity between the duration and intensity of the noxious stimulus and the pain response. In general, the intensity of acute pain is proportional to the intensity of the stimulus and persists as long as the stimulus persists, or until healing of tissue injury.

Chronic pain

Chronic pain occurs in a wide range of disorders: trauma, malignancy and chronic inflammatory diseases such as rheumatoid arthritis. Chronic pain has been defined as lasting more than six months, but this definition doesn't take into account that pain and its underlying pathology may not exist simultaneously. Chronic pain may be due to a persistent process, but it also may persist after resolution of an underlying condition. In addition, the intensity of chronic pain may be disproportionate to the intensity of the noxious stimulus or

---

6 IASP Definition of Pain, www.iasp-pain.org

underlying process. These observations hint at an intriguing finding: alterations within the nervous system itself may contribute to pain. Chronic pain may be defined as pain associated with a chronic disorder, or pain that persists beyond resolution of an underlying disorder or healing of an injury, and that is often more intense than the underlying process would predict.

c) — Chronic pain as a disease in its own right

Although clinicians are relatively adept at treating acute pain, they are less successful at treating chronic pain. In chronic pain patients, clinicians often focus primarily on diagnosis and treatment of the underlying disease. This reflects the historical view that pain is a nonspecific symptom of a disease process, and "the sensory end product of an essentially passive information transmission system". The primary pathology may persist, yet the pain must be managed in the interests of the patient's well-being. Further, chronic pain may continue despite resolution of the underlying disease, due to enduring changes within the nervous system. The nervous system is clearly not a "passive information transmission system," but a "plastic" structure wherein modulation of pain signalling can occur. Effective chronic pain treatment must target underlying neurological mechanisms. This suggests that chronic pain should be viewed as an entity in its own right, apart from underlying conditions.

Treatment for chronic pain

Treatment components should involve a team approach to managing the pain symptoms and may involve:

- Physician (GP or specialist);
- Psychologist (pain counsellor);
- Physiotherapist;
- Occupational therapist;
- Other treatment team — alternative medicine, massage therapy, etc.

The main components should include:

- Appropriate diagnosis and early intervention;

- Management of medications and pain modalities (TENS, IFC, Laser, etc.);
- Cognitive behavioural strategies for managing pain (communication and assertiveness skills, managing pain flare-ups, reflective thinking, CBT thinking strategies);
- Relaxation and meditation;
- Gradual upgrading of activities, exercise and return to work;
- Ergonomic and body mechanics adjustments;
- Education on hurt vs. harm;
- Reactivation in home and work;
- Rebalancing of priorities and setting realistic expectations.

Early referral for treatment during the "potential chronic pain" phase is essential. Where possible, treatment incorporating the methods of behavioural therapy is preferred, although it is recognized that there is not a sufficient capacity in the province to provide treatment for all workers with pain disabilities/impairments.

d) — Managing chronic pain in the workplace

Chronic pain has been a continuing challenge for disability management professionals. Over 30 per cent of the population suffers from chronic pain (pain which persists for greater than 3 months past normal healing). The following demonstrates the techniques, which are essential for treatment of chronic pain.

We are reminded that the "duty to accommodate" becomes extremely challenging. It is expected that an individual with chronic pain may experience absences above the average in the organization even with appropriate accommodations in the workplace. Employers will need to ensure that a systematic process of accommodation is used to meet the "duty to accommodate".

According to research completed with individuals with chronic pain, the following components of treatment and accommodation should be considered. The Cochrane Review[7] on "Multidisciplinary

---

[7] P Cote, et al, "The Burden and determinants of neck pain in workers: Results of the Bone and Joint Decade 2000-2010 Task Force on Neck Pain and its Associated Disorders" J of

bio-psycho-social rehabilitation for chronic low back pain" there was strong evidence that intensive multidisciplinary bio-psycho-social rehabilitation with a functional restoration approach improved function when compared with inpatient or outpatient non-multidisciplinary treatments. Some programs showed improvement in work readiness but primarily the improvement was in pain and function.

e) — What is a bio-psycho-social rehabilitation program for chronic pain?

A bio-psycho-social rehabilitation program would include the following components:

1. Proper medication management through analysis of a specialist with pain management expertise.
   (a) Much of the research is leading specialists to prescribe narcotics such as Oxycocette to manage pain but still the treatment of choice has been the tricyclic anti-depressants
   (b) The treatment would be provided by the physician on the team but may involve a specific specialist in chronic pain such a physiatrist.
2. Gradual increase in activity and exercise levels to reduce deconditioning effects and increase involvement in daily activities
   (a) Involvement of a physiotherapist and occupational therapist in upgrading activity and exercise is essential to improve an individual's ability to perform functional activities
3. Sleep hygiene principles to normalize/ maximize sleep patterns
   (a) When in pain, an individual develops maladaptive sleep routines
   (b) Sleep is essential for repair and rejuvenation of the body
   (c) Developing a normal sleep routine will allow the individual to maximize the repair time

---

Manipulative and Physiological Therapeutics (February 2009) Vol. 1321 at S70-S86. Cochrane Review for Chronic Pain Management 2005, Guzman et al 2005. www.cochrane.org/reviews/en/

4. Cognitive behavioural therapy intervention to gain control over pain

(a) Delivery of the program by a trained Cognitive Behavioural Therapist (psychologist) is essential in showing success with this technique

5. Use of non-medicinal pain management techniques including relaxation, cognitive behavioural strategies, TENS Units, biofeedback, etc.

(a) An individual's ability to manage pain and control the pain response can be enhanced through the use of modalities but these should be self administered instead of those which rely on a health professional to deliver the intervention

6. Appropriate job matching to improve ability to pace, change position as needed and manage pain symptoms in the workplace.

(a) An occupational therapist would complete a physical and cognitive demands analysis to determine the demands of the job and ensure a match

(b) A gradual reintroduction (at times longer than the 8–12 week process) may be required to accommodate a return to work program

7. Proper ergonomic strategies to reduce loading of muscle groups and decrease fatigue

(a) The workstation should be designed optimally to reduce the event of flare-ups and to ensure that the individual can manage the work activities.

(b) Simple adjustment of heights, weights and process allocations can make the difference between return to work success and failure

8. Quality of life decision making to assist the individual in making decisions and taking control of life albeit with pain

(a) The key to managing pain is making decisions, which are within the individual's own control.

(b) The decisions that the individual makes may not be supported by the employer or the benefits program but must be made in order to allow the individual to gain quality of life when managing work and home life is not possible.

(c) Many individuals with chronic pain may find that flexible work hours or part time work is the best way to manage work and home demands. It is noted in arbitration decisions that employers may be required to accommodate flexible work options but the employer may not be required to compensate for the financial implications of moving to a part-time job or to a lower paying position.

Persistent pain is experienced by over 30 per cent of the population. An effective team approach will allow for improved management of pain in and out of the workplace.

f) — Accommodations for chronic pain

FACTORS	ASSOCIATED DIFFICULTIES	ACCOMMODATIONS
Fatigue	Unable to sustain the hours of work	Flexible work hours and start times, job sharing, rest break schedules, part time work
Concentration	Difficulty focusing when pain levels are high	Headsets, offices with walls instead of cubicles, recheck systems and checklists, present information in varied ways Avoid deadline based activities
Reduced endurance	Unable to complete tasks that involve repetition or static activities	Vary activity between physical and less physical activities Rest schedules i.e. short breaks throughout the day instead of longer ones
Need for position changes	Unable to sit or stand for long periods	Sit/stand workstation Proper seating

FACTORS	ASSOCIATED DIFFICULTIES	ACCOMMODATIONS
		Ergonomic consultation with equipment changes Varied work activities
Psychosocial issues	Isolation from co-workers, difficulty participating in after hours social events, depressive symptoms	Identify triggers Assist in monitoring triggers Social events/team activities during days/lunches See Mental Health Accommodations
Unpredictable pain	Absences Attendance with treatment team	Request estimate of number of days would be expected to attend appointments, or expected absences
Inability to perform physical aspects of job	Repetitive, forceful or awkward postures	Worksite assessment, ergonomics, retraining

14.5 — Managing addictions and dependencies

a) — Definition of Substance Abuse

Substance Abuse can present itself in many forms. Addictions are most frequently those with alcohol and /or illegal drugs. There are a number of other types of addictions, which may be considered but are less frequent. It is important to consider that the nature of addictions themselves may be that the employee will not voluntarily identify the need for accommodation until the end of the process. Several arbitrations and legal opinions indicate that this may be an issue even past the termination of the employee for performance or absence issues. It is important for the employer to consider if there is any causal link between the employee's disability and the misconduct.

Employers have an obligation to accommodate employees with addictions. What does that obligation include?

- Involvement of a medical expert to determine if a disability exists;
- Recommendations with respect to treatment;
- Accommodation for the treatment program;
    - Possible payment for residential treatments
    - Possible payment of Income replacement while the individual undergoes treatment
    - Possible contribution to seeking treatment i.e. pay for treatment up front but then take regular payments off pay check for treatment costs following RTW
    - It may not preclude providing some discipline for behaviours
- "Last Chance Agreements" are generally considered to be valid and enforceable against the parties, subject to human rights law. The main policy reason for enforcing a last-chance agreement is that the agreement arises out of a bargain between the employer, the employee and the union. To disturb that bargain would discourage parties from settling matters between themselves, and would increase the number of grievances referred to arbitration.

In the absence of the evidence that the employee is sincerely committed to his/her own rehabilitation, human rights decision makers will generally be prepared to uphold an employer's decision to terminate.

"The test is not whether anything else could have been done. There is always something more that could be done for a person in distress. There is always the hope that one more try or one more treatment will turn a situation around. But the Human Rights Code does not demand that disabled employees be given every conceivable opportunity. It demands that the employee be accommodated to the point of undue hardship by the employer." — Arbitrator Knopf[8]

---

8 *Toronto District School Board v. C.U.P.E.* (1999), 1999 CarswellOnt 3230, 79 L.A.C. (4th) 365 (Ont. Arb. Bd.).

b) — Return to Work and Addictions

FACTORS	ASSOCIATED DIFFICULTIES	ACCOMMODATIONS
Absences	Pattern of absences may appear	Discussion with worker outlining attendance expectations Ask if there are any issues effecting ability to attend Begin progressive discipline process
Illegal sales or purchases of drugs on work premises	Legal issues — CONSULT WITH LEGAL	Discipline Offer treatment Outline expectations
Visible signs of addiction	Safety on job	Meeting with supervisor Request clearance from physician for safety Offer EAP Send home — assisted
At work while impaired	Decreased concentration Reduced judgement	Meeting with supervisor Assess risks Send home by taxi — offer EAP Offer treatment if available
Offered Rehabilitation	Absence from work	Accommodate time off work, consider income replacement, consider payment options for treatment programs

FACTORS	ASSOCIATED DIFFICULTIES	ACCOMMODATIONS
Rehabilitation non compliance	Continued performance issues	Last chance agreement — Consult with Legal

14.6 — Accommodation for Deaf, Deafened and Hard of Hearing[9]

There are many ways to optimize communication with an individual who is Deaf, deafened or hard of hearing person. When in doubt, ask the individual to identify his/her preferred method of communicating.

Getting a Deaf person's attention:

- Ask the individual how he/she prefers to be approached;
- Approach him/her from the side or front as not to startle;
- Tap the desk or floor instead of speaking to gain attention;
- A shoulder tap is appropriate if the person is near you;
- Wave your hand if they are at a distance;
- Flash the room lights for a larger audience;
- Remember, people who are Deaf tend to rely on physical contact more for getting attention, support, asking for focus, etc.

The Environment:

- Use a well-lit room to maximize vision;
- Do not speak with the light behind you, as your face will be shadowed;
- Pick the best spot to communicate; avoid noisy background situations and areas that are poorly lit;
- If the hallway outside a room is noisy, close the door.

Technical Tips:

[9] Adapted from Ontario Hearing Society's fact sheet on Communication with the Deaf, Deafened and Hard of Hearing, 2008.

- Always have a pen and paper in public areas;
- Writing down key phrases and words may be helpful;
- Use a laptop or texting for key words;
- Take advantage of technical devices that improve communication, such as Pocket Talker or FM system;
- Ensure all technical devices are operational and all staff are trained in their use (i.e. TTY).

Interpreting:

- Use a professional, qualified sign language interpreter; not unqualified untrained, well-intentioned "signer" friend or family to fill the role of interpreter. Friends and family members of a person who is Deaf should not be used as "interpreters" even upon the Deaf person's request. Permitting a family member or friend to step into that role may violate the individuals' right to confidentiality. You must also be aware that the friend or family member has an interest different from or even adverse to that of the Deaf person. In addition, the family member, friend or well intentioned "signer" does not have the qualifications to interpret.

14.7 — Accommodation and Blind/ Low Vision

a) — Common visual impairments

Cataract — A clouding or opaque covering on the lens of the eye

Diabetic retinopathy — Disorder of the retina due to haemorrhaging caused by diabetes

Glaucoma — Disease characterized by increased pressure within the eye and damage resulting in loss of vision

Hyperopia — Farsightedness

Macular Degeneration — Age-related deterioration of the retina, characterized by loss of central vision

Myopia — Nearsightedness

Retinal Detachment — A separation of portions of the retina from the interior supporting structure of the eye

Retinitis Pigmentosa — A degenerative pigmentary condition usually characterized by slow, progressive loss of field vision and is commonly referred to as tunnel vision

Nystagmus — Involuntary, rapid, repetitive eye movements

The *Grismer*[10] *(1999) Supreme Court Case* opened our eyes to the need for accurate visual assessments and accommodation for visual impairments.

In order to maintain safety, productivity and quality, employers should begin to consider visual demands analysis for jobs and specific accommodations for visual impairments.

Visual impairments include:

- Low vision;
- Colour blindness;
- Reduced ability to perceive depth;
- Reduced peripheral vision;
- Blindness.

Some statistics to SEE clearer and LOOK closer:

- Individuals over the age of 40 years begin to have difficulty with presbyopia (impaired ability to see items close to the eye);
- Individuals over the age of 40 years suffer from dry eyes;
- Approximately 1.7 million Americans have some form of macular degeneration;
- The National Eye Institute indicates that there are 1.5 million surgeries for cataracts each year;
- Visual problems, such as eyestrain and irritation, are among the most frequently reported complaints among computer users;
- In 1992 it cost nearly $2 billion per year to diagnose and treat eye problems related to vision and computer usage.

Visual impairments in the workplace may go unnoticed as they progress. Many of the age related visual disturbances come on gradually and may appear as an increase in accidents, reduction in quality or production issues.

[10] *B.C. (Superintendent of Motor Vehicles) v. B.C. (Council of Human Rights)*, [1999] 3 S.C.R. 868 (S.C.C.)

b) — What is a visual demands analysis?

A visual demands analysis (VDA) is a comprehensive outline of the visual requirements of the job. Most Physical Demands Analyses do not consider the detailed visual needs of the jobs. A Visual Demands Analysis is completed through examination of the safety and quality requirements to perform the job. Our specialized assessors work closely with an optometrist to detail the acuity, field of vision, depth and colour perception required to perform the job.

In order to complete the VDA the assessor completes a detailed analysis of the following:

- Job tasks;
- Safety issues (operation of machinery, moving equipment, driving);
- Detail required for quality production (size of part, inspection area, colours, speed);
- Lighting (lux, type of lighting, colour of light);
- Terrain of work;
- Job related eye wear;
- Glare issues.

These are then converted into Visual Demands that can be compared to an individual's eye assessment by an eye care professional.

c) — Accommodations

Accommodation for changes to Visual Acuity:

- Enlarge font on computer screens and written materials;
- Change colour contrast on task i.e. screen colours vs. font; line belt colour vs. part;
- Include colour cues for change in activity or task;
- Ensure eye wear is kept clean;
- Ensure there are colour strips on changes to terrain i.e. yellow tape on step edges, colour differences where terrain changes height;
- Provision of specialized magnifiers on tools or at workstations;

- Use of assistive technology such as:
    - Screen readers
    - Speech recognition systems
    - Speech Synthesizers
    - Refreshable Braille displays
    - Braille embossers
    - Talking word processors
    - Large print word processors
    - Screen enlargers or screen magnifiers

Accommodation for changes in field of vision:

- Change position of equipment and tools;
- Inclusion of mirrors or specialized prism glasses;
- Develop eye catchers for high risk areas i.e. flashing lights, colour flags.

Accommodation for changes in Depth Perception:

- Provide distance markers for moving equipment
- Insert mechanical stops or alarms
- Computerized processes that provide accuracy for distance (i.e. robotic arm with
- sensors)
- Installation of coloured light to show changes in terrain
- Use of safety sensitive light sensors and light curtains in high risk areas

These are only a few of the ways that visual impairments can be accommodated in the workplace. Consideration of these issues early in your processes will assist you in dealing with an aging employee population and also ensure that every employee has the opportunity to perform at their maximum abilities.

d) — Devices

Computers are being used more and more by individuals who are blind or visually impaired. In fact, many companies have worked extensively with people with visual impairments to accommodate their special needs at school, work, and home.

There are hardware and software devices available which can provide enlarged print displays, speech output, or Braille output. As indicated by the worker's preferred medium (print, speech, or Braille), computerized equipment is available both for receiving and sending information.

Closed-circuit televisions (CCTVs) enlarge printed materials for individuals unable to read regular print. Many workers with impaired vision are able to read materials available only in regular print by placing the printed materials beneath the unit's camera and reading the magnified material from the CCTV screen. CCTVs enable the viewer to read black print on a white background or white print on a black background, depending upon which is easier for them to discern. In recent years, CCTVs have become available with color monitors as well. A CCTV can be setup over a typewriter, enabling a clerical worker to proof work produced in regular print.

Aids and appliances — There are many tools (or aids and appliances) available to facilitate the inclusion of people with visual impairments in the workforce. Some commonly used aids and appliances are:

- talking calculators (hand-held or desktop calculators with speech output);
- light probes (light-sensitive pointers which enable the user to identify blinking phone lines);
- variable speed tape-recorders (cassette tape-recorders which play and record using four-sided tapes and can be listened to at a fast rate of speed for expediency);
- Brailled measuring devices (rulers, measuring tapes, yardsticks, measuring cups with raised line markings);
- Brailled or talking timepieces (clocks or watches with Brailled numbers or speech output);
- bill identifiers (speech-output machines which can identify U.S. currency);
- Braille labeller (embosses Braille on vinyl or magnetic tape);
- postal scale (has raised dots at each ounce interval);

- talking scale (measures grams, ounces, ounces-troy, and pennyweights);
- adapted hand tools (saw guide to make 15 to 90 degree cuts, drill guide, Stanley combination square, framing square, micrometers, Stanley calliper rule);
- battery tester (audible battery checker);
- reading stand (enables reader to read with free hands as well as adjust height and angle for visual comfort);
- bold-line paper (paper with darkened lines to make for easier viewing).

Optical devices — Many individuals with limited vision can make good use of their eyesight by using optical devices. Items commonly used include: eyeglasses with prescriptive lenses for people who are nearsighted or farsighted, glasses with tinted lenses for individuals who are light sensitive, contact lenses, magnifiers (these may be hand-held, standing, or mounted in eyeglasses), and small telescopes (these may be hand-held or mounted in eyeglasses).

Scanners are hand-held or flatbed cameras which read print into a computer that utilizes specialized software to reproduce the material into text that can be imported into word processing and other programs to be managed and manipulated. Adapted scanner technology is also referred to as OCRs — Optical Character Readers. Scanners can be portable, stand-alone, or PC-based.

Adaptive hardware and software — Hardware and software designed specifically for individuals with visual impairments is known as adaptive hardware or software. Some examples are:

- speech synthesizer — A speech synthesizer is an internal or external device that provides auditory output from the computer to allow people with visual disabilities spoken access to the computer screen.
- screen reader — A screen reader is a sophisticated software program that works in conjunction with a speech synthesizer to give blind computer users access to operating systems, word processing programs, telecommunications packages, databases, and spreadsheet programs.

- Braille display — A Braille display is a device that attaches to a computer to give a blind computer user access to the screen via Braille output. Braille displays are available in portable and desktop models and display twenty to eighty characters per line of text. Many computer users who are blind use a Braille display in combination with speech output.
- Braille embosser — A Braille embosser produces hardcopy Braille from word processing files on a computer. Although it produces Braille, it operates like a standard printer.
- screen enlargement software — Several programs on the market allow people with low vision to access information on a computer screen with the assistance of a screen enlargement program. Such programs provide low vision workers with larger print on a standard computer screen. Screen enlargement programs can be used in combination with speech.

14.8 — Accommodation and Learning Disabilities

a) — A Definition of learning disabilities[11]

Learning disabilities is a general term that refers to a heterogeneous group of disorders manifested by significant difficulties in the acquisition and use of listening, speaking, reading, writing, reasoning, or mathematical abilities.

Learning disabilities:

- is a general term for a heterogeneous group of disorders;
- are manifested by significant difficulties in listening, speaking, reading, writing, reasoning, or math;
- are part of a person's make-up (they will not go away);
- are presumed to be a dysfunction of the central nervous system;
- may occur across the life span;

[11] Adapted from Bridges to Practice Guidebook 1, National Adult Literacy and Learning Disabilities Center, Washington, D.C. 1999; (National Joint Committee on Learning Disabilities, 1994, p. 16)

- may result in problems with behaviour, social perceptions, and social interactions (but they are not the disability);
- are not the result of other disabilities such as loss of sight or hearing, nor are they the result of a lack of intelligence, or deficiencies in education.

b) — Accommodation Strategies[12]

(i) — Reading Strategies

- Allow employee to seek out different sources and intensities of light;
- Allow privacy for reading aloud;
- Provide a space with minimal distractions;
- To reduce amount of reading, match employee with a peer for paired reading (taking turns);
    - Allow a peer to read material to the employee before the employee reads it
- Use high-interest/low level reading materials as a substitute for texts;
- Make shorter assignments and/or allow more time for completion;
- Rewrite difficult written material required for a job task, using simpler language;
- Provide tape-recorded instructions, messages, materials (on the job);
- Listen to books on tape or books on computer disk;
- Use scan and read software and other technology (see tools);
- Identify a friend, family member or co-worker to help with needed reading;
- Highlight or color code important information on handouts;

---

[12] http://www.aelweb.vcu.edu/publications/LDGuide/toc.htm

- Write clearly using large print subheadings to organize material, simple and direct language, and plenty of white space;
- Suggest stopping points in lengthy text, helping the employee to identify manageable "chunks" for reading and study;
- Go over all written directions orally;
- Allow and encourage the employee to read aloud so he/she both sees and hears the material;
- Minimize the need to read handwriting by providing typed directions;
- Use a consistent format in providing directions for activities or assignments;
- Provide feedback on employee's work in person or on tape;
- Provide needed background information via videotape or speakers;
- Use a variety of learning experiences: demonstrations, field trips, discussions, and group/cooperative projects;
- Allow additional time for testing or workplace performance;
- Allow test directions/test items to be read aloud to employee (when testing subject matter other than reading);
- Allow testing in private, distraction-free area;
- Provide directions for required performance on audiotape or videotape;
- Allow use of transparent coloured overlays and/or page magnifiers;
- Allow use of line markers to maintain focus on correct line of print;
- Allow marking of answers directly in test booklet (for standardized tests) to prevent tracking problems when moving from test to answer sheet.

(ii) — Writing strategies

- Provide a workspace with minimal distractions;

- Allow employee to seek out different sources and intensities of light;
- Discuss the purpose and rationale for each writing activity;
- Provide models of/practice with classroom and on-the-job writing tasks;
- Begin with small writing tasks and allow plenty of time;
- Build writing practice into the curriculum by setting aside time for daily journal entries on the subject being taught;
- Suggest that the employee use a tape recorder to dictate what he/she wants to write, then play it back and write it down;
- Encourage use of assistive technology (see tools);
- Decrease the length of assignments or number of responses required;
- Allow more time to complete writing tasks;
- Assign group work with roles for different employees, so writing is not required of everyone;
- Allow use of audiotape recorders or peer note-takers instead of making notes in class or training session;
- Use electronic dictionary, spellchecker, or special software (see tools);
- Use computer word processor to eliminate handwriting problems and simplify the organization and editing process (see tools);
- Create pocket-sized cue cards or "problem-word" lists for frequently used, hard-to-spell words;
- Use voicemail for communications at work instead of memos or email;
- Allow demonstration of knowledge/competence without writing, by explaining orally, face-to-face or on audiotape;
- Allow use of voicemail for communications at work instead of memos or email;

- Allow use of computer word processor instead of handwriting in exams;
- Allow more time for testing;
- Use multiple-choice or other short-answer format for tests instead of essays;
- Allow test answers to be spoken and recorded (when not testing writing ability);
- Allow use of other technology to facilitate the writing process (when not testing writing);
- Allow marking answers directly in test booklet (for standardized tests) to prevent tracking problems when moving from test to answer sheet;
- Encourage employee to get someone to proofread his writing before it is shared.

(iii) — Calculation strategies

- Allow use of calculators and other computational tools (see tools) to solve word problems in class or on the job;
- Allow extra time for tasks involving math;
- Reduce the length of practice assignments (number of problems) to avoid overloading memory and attention span;
- Assign group work with roles for different employees so math is not required of everyone;
- Use calculators and low-tech aids, such as pocket-sized multiplication tables, measurement equivalents, etc. (see tools);
- Identify a friend, family member or co-worker to help with tasks involving math;
- Allow employee to work computation problems on graph paper or vertically lined paper to keep numbers properly aligned;
- If employee confuses operation signs, enlarge the size of signs on practice problems or workplace documents;

- Encourage use of a calculator to check accuracy of work or problem solving;
- Encourage use of low-tech aids like lists of formulas, measurement equivalents, etc. (see tools);
- Provide models of/practice with classroom and on-the-job tasks that require math;
- Allow extra time for testing;
- Allow calculator use and other computational tools (when testing problem-solving or subject matter other than math computation);
- Allow use of transparent coloured overlays and/or page magnifiers;
- Allow use of line markers to focus on correct line of print;
- Allow marking of answers directly in test booklet (for standardized tests) to prevent tracking problems when moving from test to answer sheet;
- Allow use of computational aids for workplace performance.

(iv) — Reasoning strategies

In general:

- Build work teams to include a balance of strengths and minimize the impact of an individual with a disability.

For sequencing problems:

- Break lengthy sequences into parts;
- Provide cue sheets or prompts (schedule of events, list of jobs, steps in a process);
- Maintain regular schedules and routines in class or on the job.

For problems with recognizing important information & classifying/sorting:

- Highlight or color code written material to draw attention to critical features and show relationships;
- Establish and learn routines for regular, everyday tasks so you can focus your attention on matters that require thought and planning;

- Use a calculator or other technology, as appropriate to simplify some of the steps in a complicated process;
- Work with a partner who has strengths where you have difficulty.

(v) — Organizational skills strategies

- Seat employee in area free of distractions;
- Use preferential seating;
- Allow the employee to select his/her seating;
- Help keep employee's work area free of unnecessary materials;
- Provide opportunities for movement;
- Help employee develop an organized space (notes on one subject kept together, study supplies kept together, file folders for organizing, etc.);
- Break work into smaller amounts;
- Allow employee to decide what task to do first, second, third, etc.;
- Help employee set time goals for each task;
- Help employee develop a checklist for each step;
- Assign peer coaches;
- Help employee identify a study buddy;
- Use mnemonic devices (see "Memory" for examples);
- color code or visual cue to organize tasks;
- Work on one subject at a time.

CHAPTER 15 — EVALUATION OF DISABILITY PROGRAMS

15.1 — Perform Evaluations to Measure Disability Management Program Outcomes

The evaluation of the Disability Management program is an integral part of the disability management process. It ensures that the program is constantly evolving to meet the needs of the workers and other persons directly involved with the program such as supervisors, shop stewards, union officials and the management team. Other rationale for evaluating the program includes:

- Ensure program objectives are being met;
- Evaluates costs and demonstrates the cost/benefit;
- Demonstrates program benefits;
- Identifies program successes and failures;
- Provides for program improvements.

Because a return to work program may have many objectives, employers will find that the evaluation process should measure outcomes, the process itself and even the workers perception or satisfaction with the program. Evaluations should address both "qualitative" issues, such as worker satisfaction, as well as "quantitative" issues, such as the cost benefits of the program. Either qualitative or quantitative evaluations may be part of the process or the outcomes of the program. An evaluation designed in a continuous quality improvement framework will provide for a continuous evaluation of the program with the ability to modify the program as required.

a) — Track costs of disability management programs

All organizations make decisions based on financial implications. It is for this reason that Human Resources Professionals must express program proposals and annual program summaries in such a way that clearly identifies the benefits in terms of cost. Cost-benefit analysis is a method of identifying all costs, both direct and indirect, that are incurred in through a process or program and comparing these costs with all the potential benefits that would directly affect the process or program. It is a technique for comparing the costs and benefits of a particular intervention and/or development and implementation of a program.

It compares:

- the cost of implementing the measure;
- the benefit of the intervention in terms of potential costs.

The purpose of Cost Benefit Analysis is to show whether the benefits of a measure or intervention outweigh its cost.

b) — What are costs?

Costs are the solutions to the problems. Identify and cost out all possible solutions and choose the solution that gets the best result for the least money. In general, there are both administrative and engineering solutions that are cost effective to implement. Examples of costs include:

- Costs directly associated with the intervention i.e. construction project, equipment purchases;
- Costs of installation of equipment (secondary);
- Training costs associated with new equipment.

c) — What are benefits?

"Benefits" are the cost of not doing something about the problem. Try to document all applicable costs. Use accident, illness, absenteeism, turnover, training time, quality control, WSIB, and personnel data to quantify the impact of the accommodation and subsequent heightened worker performance. Examples include:

- Wages;
- Costs of disability (WSIB, STD, LTD);
- Benefits.

d) — Calculating the cost benefit

Total of primary Benefits (B1)
÷ Total of all primary costs (C1)

OR

Total of B1 and secondary benefits (B2)
÷ Total of primary (C1) and secondary costs (C2)

What does the answer mean?

If the ratio is 1:1 or greater, then the decision is economically efficient.

15.2 — The Cost Benefit of Individual Accommodation

The goal of accommodation is to alter the work, the environment or the work tools in order to allow disabled employees to accomplish the outcome of the job.

Research studies completed in Canada and the US have found that the average cost of an accommodation was well below $500.[1] Most accommodations do not involve purchasing items or services, but involve alteration in the work process or duties. This involves indirect costs instead of a cash layout. (Indirect costs may include supervisor time, paperwork, HR time, monitoring, documentation, co-worker education and support) When reviewing the cost benefit of accommodation generally you will be looking at cost avoidance.

a) — The Costs to be considered are

- Worker and Workplace Assessment costs (internal or external);
- Tools or ergonomic environmental changes;
- Accessibility changes made;
- Administrative costs (supervisor time, HR time, paperwork costs).

---

1 ML Baldwin & WC Johnson, *Dispelling the myths about work disability* (Ithaca, NY: Cornell University Press, 2000).

These costs do not consider the indirect costs that you and your employee will experience.

b) — The Savings to be considered are

- Reduction in lost time income replacement costs (WSIB, STD, LTD and sick leave) including NEER costs and potential premium and administration increases;
- Improved productivity (per cent of productivity improvement);
- Improved sales (if your employee is a salesperson or account manager this can directly be seen in the bottom line);
- Retention of a trained employee (the cost of recruitment and training of new employees has been reportedly anywhere from $2000 to $20,000 depending on the position and skill).

These savings do not consider the indirect benefits such as employee morale and union support.

It is important to understand that having a disabled employee at home on income replacement benefits means that you are paying, not only for the income replacement, but you also are paying someone else to complete the work at your workplace or you are losing that absent employee's productivity and sales. The Manufacturer's Association in collaboration with WSIB has prepared a document to help employers determine the cost of injuries.[2] An example to help you with the cost avoidance equation follows.

Scenario one:

> John is off work for 6 months on short-term disability at 75 per cent of his salary if not provided with accommodation within the first month. John makes, on average, $250 per day, averaging 20 workdays a month, as a production line worker. Overtime employees replace him at 1.5 times his hourly wage.
>
> Johns' Income replacement = $250 × 20 days × 6 months = $30,000 × 75 per cent = $22,500

[2] "Business results Through Health & Safety Guidebook" WSIB, 2004; Emile Tompa, Claire Oliveira, Roman Dolinschi, Emma Irvin, "A Systematic Review of Disability Management Interventions with Economic Evaluations" J Occup Rehabil (2008, 18:16-2). See also their website: www.wsib.on.ca

John's replacement workers = $250 × 20 days × 6 months = $30,000 × 1.5 = $45,000

Administrative fees for short term disability average 15 per cent = $3375

TOTAL COST = $70,875

Scenario two:

If John had been accommodated back into his regular job after one-month absence (or less, ideally) the cost would include a workplace assessment, ergonomic tools and a gradual return to work of 4 weeks (4 hours for 2 weeks, 6 hours for 2 weeks and then 8 hours for 2 weeks).

John's Income replacement for one month = $250 × 20 days = $5000 × 75 per cent = $3750

Administrative costs for STD at 15 per cent = $562.50

Overtime workers for gradual return and absence = $250 × 20 days + 60 hours ($1875) × 1.5 = $10,312.50

Assessment costs = $500

Ergonomic tools = $250

TOTAL COST = $15,375

Cost Avoidance Equation

Scenario One ($70,875) - Scenario Two ($15,375)

= COST AVOIDANCE of $55,500

Note: This is a simplified example meant to demonstrate the basic cost avoidance of accommodating disabled employees. This does not include the productivity gains and indirect savings associated with his successful return to work.

Accommodation of more complex cases will involve a more detailed review of the costs, but in most scenarios return to work with accommodation saves employers and employees significant costs, which will go directly to the bottom line — the difference, in some companies, between profits and losses.

c) — Identify and implement realistic cost containment strategies

For employers, injuries, illness and disability can have significant costs. Time lost from work due to injuries has a financial cost in terms of both direct and indirect costs. Direct costs are the costs that are most easily tabulated. They include medical costs, compensation and insurance. Indirect costs are also costs to an organization, although they are a little less obvious. Indirect costs include costs related to time spent investigating incidents and injuries, re-training staff, overtime costs for replacement workers, reduced service and care. It is estimated that the indirect costs of a workplace injury could be as high as 4 times higher than the direct cost of an injury[3].

Most employers will realize that injury prevention is the best way to prevent any of these workplace injury costs. Furthermore, following an injury, an aggressive approach to an early and safe return to work through a well-structured, comprehensive disability management program is the only means available to employers to limit the costs of injuries. The introduction of an effective return to work program was able to reduce the total number of days lost to injury by half.[4] The potential for cost savings with reduced time lost is obvious. In addition to potentially reducing costs due to injury, an employer with a return to work program can also minimize the risk of paying fines or penalties that may result if a return to work program or accommodation of a disabled worker is not provided.

d) — Conduct Qualitative Evaluations

Qualitative analysis deals with subjective information that is collected from sources such as audits, case studies, interviews, focus groups and surveys. They are useful to understand perceptions, feelings and knowledge of people and are generally used for the following purposes:

- Process evaluations (such as the Disability Management Checklist at the end of this chapter);
- Evaluate individualized outcomes;

---

3 WSIB Annual Report, 2004.

4 These concepts are supported by: Mercer, "The Total Financial Impact of Employee Absences" October 2008; Emile Tompa, Claire de Oliveira, Roman Dolinschi & Emma Irvin, "A Systematic Review of Disability Management Interventions with Economic Evaluations" (2008) 18 J Occup Rehabil at 16–26; RL Franche et al. "Workplace-based return-to-work interventions: A systematic review of the quantitative literature" (2005) 15:4 J Occup Rehabil. at 607–631.

- Examine unusual successes/failures;
- Evaluate implementation strategies and training;
- Describe diversity across program sites;
- Improve programs;
- Evaluate quality.

The validity and reliability of the evaluation is dependent on methodological skill, sensitivity & training of evaluator. This evaluation method tends to generate new ideas, elaborations, explanations or meanings.

e) — Conduct Quantitative Evaluations

Quantitative Analysis deals with clearly measurable objective information. Information is collected and analyzed from existing data and presented in a way that allows for decisions to be made. Such information can be:

- Incident reports;
- First Aid logs;
- Accident investigation reports;
- Injury analysis;
- Sick leave reports;
- LTD/STD reports;
- Benefit payout records;
- Insurance premiums (Compensation).

f) — Evaluate worker/supervisor satisfaction with program

It is important to determine whether both the worker's and the supervisor's needs are being met. This requires an evaluation of the perception, opinions and experiences of the individuals directly involved in the program. A variety of qualitative methods can be used to gather this information. Examples include:

- Surveys or questionnaires with carefully framed, simple questions;

- Focus groups or interviews: collection of participants comments, responses, feelings;
- Follow-up interviews: face-to-face discussion of specific return-to-work program strengths and weaknesses;
- Review of program records/documentation.

The questions should focus on the important elements of the return to work process. In addition, survey a representative group of all programs, including programs that are successful, ones that have been unsuccessful and programs that were complex. The purpose of ascertaining the satisfaction of the persons directly associated with the program is to enhance and improve the program based on the feedback received.

g) — Consider audits for benchmarking

There are several organizations that can provide you with evidence based auditing services to compare your current results to the best practices. As part of your continuous improvement process or in your start up phases a disability management audit will provide the organization with an understanding on the key components of the program that should be implemented and the gaps of your program as compared to the benchmark.[5]

[5] DE Shrey, *Effective Work-Based Disability Management Programs*. In Phyllis M. King. (Ed); Sourcebook of Occupational Rehabilitation (New York, NY: Plenum Press, 1998) at 389–409; see also www.nidmar.ca for the Disability Management Audit developed based on the disability management standards.

CHAPTER 16: OUTSOURCING TO CONTRACTORS

16.1 — Introduction

Many organizations are now considering that disability management is not a part of their core business and are moving towards outsourcing all or a part of the disability management services. This decision holds with it the following concerns:

- Lack of control by the employer in the duty to accommodate. Remember the employer always holds the legal obligations and liability;
- As the provider is external to the organization they will have difficulty fully integrating into the workplace culture. Workplace culture is one of the keys to the success of a disability management program;
- Continuous need for communication links within the organization. When there are changes within the organization such as manager changes or department restructuring the external provider will need to be kept informed and understand the reasons for the changes;
- The external provider can appear to provide a shield to the organization around difficult benefit or return to work decisions but this is only a false shield and ultimately the employer holds the responsibility;
- Lack of control over the individual processes within the external providers' personnel and training. As the human resources professional for your company you have final decision over who is hired and what continued level of qualifications they may maintain. With an external provider you will need to ensure that you have set the ability to screen personnel and the auditing processes within your contract so that you can maintain control over the

external organization's recruitment of skill and level of expertise in the program;

- Hidden costs. There may be many hidden costs that you may not realize within an outsourcing situation. Make sure that your contract is clear about expectations, disbursements, extra costs within the process that may be masked in initial contract verbage;
- Disability management requires internal expertise and training. Even if the process for monitoring or planning the return to work is outsourced, the company continues to require management training, a conduit onsite to translate company information, changes, review processes and reports and maintain internal communication on the program. This can be the most time consuming piece of the process and therefore it is important to set internal responsibilities for the program and allocate appropriate internal resources in implementation of an outsourced program.

The external consultants or outsourced programs may include:

16.2 — External Consultants or Outsourced Programs

a) — Legal firms

Legal firms provide detailed advice regarding employment law and duty to accommodate — ensure that the firm specializes in labour relations and employment issues. This resource is valuable and can provide your organization with the latest expertise when making difficult employment decisions regarding an individual with a disability. Having a legal firm which specializes in this area on retainer is a good use of funds.

b) — Third party adjudication services

There are several organizations that can provide third party adjudication services for your sick benefits, short term disability/weekly indemnity or salary continuance programs. This service provides the ability for the employer to have limited access to medical information and lets a trained organization adjudicate and determine eligibility for benefits based on medical information and job demands. They can facilitate return to work planning and medically monitor an ill employee to determine the timing and requirements for return to work.

This is a worthwhile service to consider as it allows the opportunity for the employer to have an arm's length from these decisions. Note that in self-insured programs the employer will continue to hold the decision of whether to pay or not in complex situations but this program allows for consistency and fairness in managing benefits.

c) — Disability management consultants

In the development of your programs it is recommended that you consider consultation on policy and procedure development and implementation from a consultant that can provide objective evaluation of your programs and offer advice on program development. This will shorten your time for development and implementation and ensure that you have considered all of the processes and nuances of the management of disability.

d) — Case management firms

This type of consultant provides case management of complex cases or return to work cases. They do not adjudicate the claim but work with the employee, their treating practitioners and your managers to design a return to work or accommodation process. They will help to delineate the difference between medical and nonmedical issues and bring the non-medical issues to your organization for resolution instead of "medicalizing" the performance or relationship issues that complicate return to work. It is important to clearly outline your expectations and when you will choose to use this service as it can be costly and should be used for only your most complex disability issues.

e) — Carriers / insurance companies

Most organizations will have a carrier to administer your long term disability benefits, short term disability benefits and healthcare benefits. Their role is to follow the policy that you have contracted to adjudicate and administer the benefits. Many of the carriers will have services to enhance early return to work but you need to understand their role and limitations based on your contract as they have contract provisions which may inhibit their ability to work with all of the return to work programs.

f) — Independent assessment and evaluation firms

In complex situations where you are unable to obtain clear restrictions or limitations from an employee's treating health professional there may be a need to have access to assessment services. These assessment services would provide independent medical and functional assessments. You will require this in less than 10 per cent of situations and they can be very costly. Setting up and interviewing the roster of assessors, prior to you requiring the services can save you time and unwanted expense at the time of the request. Be sure that the assessors understand your program and your purpose and ask the right questions in order to use the services well.

g) — Occupational health physician consultants

In some situations during return to work planning there is a need for assistance from an occupational health physician to ensure that the information from the treating physician is clear and objective and that the individual is safe to return into the workplace. Some organizations choose to have everyone cleared by an occupational health physician prior to return to work but this can delay return to work and be a costly alternative to having a smooth workplace based program. The best use of an occupational health physician's expertise is in gaining support for return to work through a doctor to doctor communication in complex situations and clearing return to work safety issues.

h) — Occupational health nurses

There are many firms that outsourced occupational health nursing services to your organization. Having an occupational health nurse placed onsite can allow you to manage medical surveillance programs, perform health and wellness education services, arrange for vaccinations and manage return to work issues. It is important to outline the scope of the services and ensure that the return to work processes are consistent with your policy and procedures. Note that having an occupational health nurse onsite does not allow you to have access to the medical information but only allows you as the employer to have a professional onsite to manage that information and translate it into functional information that can be used by the management team to plan return to work or stay at work programs.

i) — Health care organizations

Many larger organizations have arranged for employees to have early access to occupational therapy, ergonomics, physiotherapy, chiropractics, massage therapy either onsite or in a local external clinic. This service can expedite an employee receiving the care that they require at the time of injury or illness and reduce the time away from work to get treatment. Many of the clinics can also provide work hardening and work simulation and functional assessments. It is important that the health care provider understands your organization, the work that you do and facilitates early and safe return to work with their treatment processes and provision of functional information to you in a timely manner.

j) — Mediation services

In some disability management processes non-medical issues prevent return to work. Attempting to manage those non-medical issues may be difficult internally and having access to a mediation service can help to develop a practical plan that works for both the employer and the employee. It can also be used for legal documentation in the cooperation process for mediation of return to work, employment and labour relations issues.

16.3 — Steps to choosing an external consultant

- Define your need clearly — you may wish to undergo an audit to truly understand your need and the gaps in the current service. This will avoid the issue of choosing a service which truly does not fill the gap;
- Explain your reasons for choosing an external consultant;
- Define the expectations that you would have of that consultant;
- Choose the right type of consultant;
- Determine if you will approach this with a "Request for Information" or "Request for proposal" process;
- List the potential consultants — consult with other employers on their experience, who they use, consult with professional associations to determine if they have lists of providers, network;

- Outline the objectives for the service i.e., adjudicate sick leave, reduce absenteeism, facilitate return to work, manage complex cases;
- Document your request for services;
- Contact appropriate service providers for a proposal;
- Review proposals and narrow down your choices to the top three to four;
- Interview the service provider (ensure that you have the actual provider of service in the room not just the marketing person). Have key personnel in your organization interview the proponents (include senior management, frontline management, union representatives);
- Determine fit with your corporate culture, objectives, expectations and needs;
- Ask for customization of services to your specific needs — look for flexibility, the ability to look at your unique issues and quality and detailed answers;
- Examine the costs of the service — make sure that you understand all of the costs including flat fees, hourly fees (how many hours would they expect to provide?), disbursements, travel costs, extra administrative fees, risk based fees, bonuses or surcharges;
- Examine the sample contract — consider the length or contract and ensure in a process such as this that you have a length of contract to allow for adequate evaluation of the services (3–5 years);
- Define the expectations of the program in depth. Define the process steps and roles and responsibilities;
- Choose the best proponent for services;
- Now begin the true work of integrating this service provider into your corporate culture and processes . . . this can take 2–6 months of implementation time prior to delivery of some of the more complex programs.

GLOSSARY OF TERMS

Accommodations: Includes assistive devices, equipment, modifications to the work environment and/or modifications of job tasks to enable individuals to perform the essential duties of a job.

Alternative Employment: Employment that is comparable to the worker's pre-injury work in its nature, earnings, qualifications, opportunities and other relevant aspects.

Assistive Device: Any special equipment, tool, device or clothing that modifies the limitations caused by physical impairments.

Bona fide Occupational Requirement: The essential requirements of a job. They outline necessary pre-requisites that are required for a person to be able to perform the job safely and competently.

Certifications: There are various certifications related to managing disability in the workplace these may include:

CDMP — Certified Disability Management Professional
CRTWC — Certified Return to Work Coordinator
CRSP — Canadian Registered Safety Professional
COHN — Certified Occupational Health Nurse

Cognitive Demands Analysis: The objective assessment of the cognitive and behavioural demands of job tasks.

Compensable Injury: Any injury or illness that is deemed to be occupationally or work-related. The WSIB form (form # 2647a) called a "Functional Abilities Form for Timely Return to Work" must be completed by the Health Care Provider. A compensable injury can result from these incidents: First Aid, Medical Aid or Health Care Claim or Lost time.

Direct Costs: Costs directly related to a disability, and are related to medical compensation and insurance costs of the event. These usually can be directly tabulated into dollars.

Disability: Any restriction or lack (resulting from an impairment) of ability to perform an activity or task in the manner or within the range considered normal for a human being. The relationship between body structures and functions, daily activities and social participation, while recognizing the role of environmental factors. (WHO, ICF)

Disability Management: The process of implementing strategies to prevent and manage absence from work thus minimizing the impact of an impairment (resulting from injury, illness or disease) and protecting employability.

Disability Management Coordinator: The person assigned the responsibility for carrying out the objectives of the workplace-based disability management program. This person is also responsible for supporting workers with disabilities and coordinating multi-disciplinary efforts to facilitate an early and safe return to work.

Ergonomics: The science of the relationship between human beings and the working environment. Matching work to a worker's capabilities, (physical, psychological, cognitively) workplace and workstation.

Essential Duties: Core functions of a job. The duties necessary to the performance of the job and to the production of actual job outcomes.

First Aid Injury: A work-related injury at such minor nature that it can be treated onsite by the first aid attendant. These are not reported to WSIB but are kept on file.

Functional Abilities Assessment (FAA, FAE, FCE): An assessment of functional, physical, mental or emotional capacities of an injured/ill individual performed by a doctor, specialist, occupational therapist and/or physiotherapist trained to objectively measure function. An assessment of a worker to determine his or her ability to work under various circumstances. Ideally, the conditions under which the evaluation is done should mimic the job for which the worker is being considered.

Graduated Return to Work: Involves the gradual increase of work hours and/or duties, slowly increasing both the frequency and duration until the regular job can be performed.

Hazardous Situation: An incident that occurs at work by an unsafe act or condition or both that a potential to result in a property loss or physical harm to the person. These are not reported to WSIB but are kept on file.

Health Care Claim: A work-related injury/illness incident, which requires treatment or services such as a visit to the physician or health care provider off the worksite. This type of incident requires the employer to complete a form 7 within 3 days of the incident. Health Care Claims do not result in any lost time from work. This is sometimes referred to a "medical aid form".

Hierarchy of Return to Work: Process of determining the job that the employee would consider return to work to best facilitate return to suitable and comparable employment.

- The original job at the original worksite (with no accommodations or temporary accommodations);
- The original job at the original worksite (with permanent accommodations);
- A similar job within his or her original department or work unit;
- A new job within the organization (identify transferable work skills);
- A new job in another organization or to self employment with retraining as necessary.

Impairment: Any loss or abnormality of psychological, physiological or anatomical structure or function.

Independent Medical Assessment (IME): Where there are discrepancies or differences in opinions around the employee's prognosis or functional abilities, the employer may request that an independent medical assessment be completed in an attempt to resolve the issue. The employer pays for the cost of the IME. There are many different types of Independent Medical Assessment such as those completed by internist, orthopaedic surgeons, rehabilitation specialist, psychiatrist and rheumatologist.

Indirect Costs: Costs associated with an accident, injury or incident that are related to the event but are not part of the medical or compensation costs. Indirect costs include costs related to damages, interrupted service, uninsured costs, investigation costs, opportunity costs etc. General assumptions are that indirect costs are four (or more) times greater than direct injury costs to an organization. These are generally more difficult to tabulate in costs.

Job Accommodation: Any adjustment or addition to the workplace that improves the ability of an individual to perform the tasks required.

Job Coaching: The process of a professional engaging the worker in meaningful tasks while facilitating an action-reflection-learning process tailored specifically to the client within the goal of resumption of work roles.

Joint Labour/Management Disability Management Committee: The group of individuals who represent the return-to-work stakeholders and who develop, implement, organize and monitor the RTW program.

Lost Time Claim: A work-related injury or illness that results in lost time from work beyond the day of injury. A form 7 needs to be completed by the employer within 3 days of the incident to apply for compensation or benefits.

Modified Work: Any changes in the job tasks which allow an employee to do meaningful, productive work within his/her capabilities (e.g., physical changes to a work area, reduction or elimination of tasks changes in equipment used).

Non-compensable injury: Any injury or illness that is not work related. This is often referred to as a personal condition.

Permanent Disability: A disability that continues to exist once the employee has reached maximum medical recovery. This should be evaluated on a yearly basis. In WSIB this is a legal term and triggers a change in obligations on the part of the employer/employee.

Physical Demands Analysis: A systematic procedure to identify and document the physical, psychological and perceptual requirements of a specific job.

Pre-injury Work: The job performed prior to the date of a worker's injury/illness. Includes all the duties, functional demands, qualifications, earnings, etc. associated with this work.

Regulated Health Professional: A member of a College of a Health Professional as defined in **The Regulations Professions Act, 1991** (i.e. Includes physicians, chiropractors, physiotherapists, occupational therapists, etc.).

Return to Work Coordinator: Person primarily responsible for the implementation of the return to work program and for ensuring that individual return to work plans are developed, monitored and brought to appropriate conclusions.

Return-to-Work Plan: An individualized plan designed to assist an injured/ill worker to successfully return to work. This plan is transitional and has specific time frames.

Suitable Job:

- Job demands match employee's capabilities and consider employee's restrictions;
- Job uses the skills and talents of the employee;
- Employee has the necessary education, training and skill set for the job demands;
- Job keeps employee as close to own work group as possible (own department);
- Does not displace another employee;
- Job matches where possible the hours of work and compensation of pre-illness job (NOT required if all other criteria are met).

Temporary Disability: An injury or illness which is expected to improve with time or treatments.

Total Temporary Disability: The term used for income replacement benefits provided to an employee on WSIB.

Transferable Skills: Separate skills acquired during the performance of jobs or hobbies that can be used in other jobs.

Transitional Work: Any group of tasks or specific jobs that are not intended as the final outcome of a worker's return-to-work but are set according to employee capabilities to assist with return to regular work.

Undue Hardship: Evidence of detrimental impact on the productivity or profitability of an employer's business. A legal threshold used in connection with duty to accommodate and the employer's responsibility to alter the duties of the work, or the work environment, to facilitate an injured worker's return to work. The onus is on the employer to show adequate evidence of undue hardship if they determine that they are unable to accommodate an employee with a disability.

Visual Demands Analysis: A comprehensive outline of the visual requirements of the job.

Work Hardening: A series of carefully designed, controlled job tasks used to build strength and endurance to assist an injured/ill worker to return to work.

Worklessness: Being off work due to injury or illness or inability to work.

BIBLIOGRAPHY

Akabas, S.H., Gates, L.B. & Galvin, D.E. (1992). Disability Management: A Complete System to Reduce Costs, Increase Productivity, Meet Employee Needs, and Ensure Legal Compliance. New York: AMACOM

Baldwin, ML & Johnson, WC, Dispelling the myths about work disability, Ithaca, NY; Cornell University Press, 2000.

Bird, F.E. and Germain, G.L. (1996). Loss Control Management. Practical Loss Control Leadership (Rev. ed.). Loganville, Georgia: Det Norske Veritas Inc.

Bloswick, D.S., Villnave, T. and Joseph, B. (1998). Ergonomics. In Phyllis M. King (Ed.), Sourcebook of Occupational Rehabilitation. New York, NY: Plenum Press.

Canadian Human Rights Commission. "A Place for All: A Guide to Creating an Inclusive Workplace" Minister of Public Works and Government Services 2006 Cat. No. HR21-62/2006

Canadian Human Rights Commission (2000). Bona Fide Occupational Requirements and Bona Fide Justifications under the *Human Rights Act*. Ottawa

Canadian Council on Rehabilitation and Work; Workplace Employment Equity

Campolieti, M. & Lavis, J.N. (2000). Disability expenditures in Canada: Trends, reform efforts and a path for the future. Canadian Public Policy Vol. 26(2) pp. 241–263

Diller, J.V. (1999). Cultural Diversity: A Primer for the Human Services. From Chapter Two: What it means to be culturally competent. Toronto, ON: International Thompson Canada

Dyck Dianne E. (2002). Disability Management: Theory, Strategy and Industry Practice, Second Edition. Butterworths Canada.

Franche R-L, Cullen K, Clarke J, Irvin E, Sinclair S, Frank J. et al. Workplace-based return-to-work interventions: A systematic review of the quantitative literature. J Occup Rehabil. 2005. Vol. 15, no. 4, p. 607–631.

Humprey, B.G. (2002). Human Resources Guide to The Duty to Accommodate. Aurora, ON: Canada Law Books

Institute for Work and Health; Seven Principles of Return to Work (2007)

Janlert U. Unemployment as a disease and diseases of the unemployed. Scand J Work Environ Health 1997;3:79–83.

Leckie A.D. & Grewal M.K. (2002). Disability Claims Management, Second Edition. Butterworths Canada.

MacEachen E, Clarke J, Franche R-L, Irvin E. The process of return to work after injury: findings of a systematic review of qualitative studies. Scandinavian Journal of Work, Environmental & Health 2006; 32(4): 257–269

Margoshes Barton (1998). Disability management and occupational health. Occ. Medicine: State of the art reviews. Vol. 13, no. 4.

National Institute of Disability Management and Research (1995). Disability Management in the Workplace: A Guide to Establishing a Joint Workplace Program. Port Alberni, BC: NIDMAR

National Institute of Disability Management and Research (1999). Ethical standards and professional conduct. Occupational Standards in Disability Management. Port Alberni, BC: NIDMAR

National Institute of Disability Management and Research (2000). Code of Practice for Disability Management. Port Alberni, BC: NIDMAR

Ontario Human Rights Commission Website Policy and Procedures for duty to accommodate for employers. www.ohrc.on.ca

Rankin, N. (2001). An Employers Guide to Disability Management. Aurora, ON: Canada Law Books

Riessner, S., Shrey, D. & Zimmermann, W (Eds.) (1997). Strategies for Success: Disability Management in the Workplace. Port Alberni, BC: National Institute of Disability Management and Research

Shain, M. (2000). Best Advice on Stress: Risk Management in the Workplace. Ottawa, ON: Health Canada

Shrey, D.E. and Lacerte, Michel (1994). Principles and Practices of Disability Management in Industry. Winter Park, FL: GR Press, Inc.

Shrey, D.E. (1998). Effective Worksite-Based Disability Programs. In Phyllis M. King (Ed.), Sourcebook of Occupational Rehabilitation (pp. 389–409) New York, NY: Plenum Press

Spector, R.E. (2000). Cultural Diversity in Health and Illness (5th ed.). Upper Saddle River, NJ: Printice Hall Health

Statistics Canada: Physical Activity Limitation survey 2006

Watson Wyatt (2000/2001) & (2004/2005). & (2007) Staying at Work Report

Web Resources

Canadian centre for occupational safety and health information service www.ccohs.on.ca

Canadian Human Rights Commission www.chrc.org

Disability Management Employer Coalition: http://www.dmec.org

Health Canada: www.hc-sc.gc.ca

Human Resource Development Canada www.servicecanada.gc.ca

Institute for Work and Health www.iwh.on.ca

International Labour Organization: http://www.ilo.org/public/english/employment/skills/disability/draftcod.htm

National Institute of Disability Management and Research www.nidmar.ca

Ontario Human Rights Commissions www.ohrc.on.ca

Workplace Safety and Insurance Board www.wsib.on.ca

INDEX

NOTE: All references are to section numbers of the Guide.

B

C

E

Carswell Order Form

MY ORDER: Please send me the following:

☐ YES, I would like my HR Manager's Guide at 50% off.
Please make me a Standing Order Subscriber and send me new titles automatically.

QTY	PRODUCT	ORDER NUMBER	PRICE	STANDING ORDER SUBSCRIBER PRICE
	HR Manager's Guide to Project Management - NEW	981451-68096	$70	$35
	HR Manager's Guide to Governance and the Human Element – NEW	982271-68096	$68	$34
	HR Manager's Guide to Discipline and Termination, 2nd Edition – NEW	982272-68096	$70	$35
	HR Manager's Guide to Health and Safety, 3rd Edition (Ontario)- NEW EDITION	982273-68096	$70	$35
	HR Manager's Guide to Applied HR Strategy	9282484-68096	$70	$35
	HR Manager's Guide to Non-Competition and Non-Solicitation Agreements	9283286-68096	$70	$35
	HR Manager's Guide to Human Resources Management Systems: A Practical Approach, Third Edition	980007-68096	$80	$40
	HR Manager's Guide to Background Checks and Pre-Employment Testing	9282794-68096	$70	$35
	HR Manager's Guide to Profit Sharing in Canada	9282816-68096	$70	$35
	HR Manager's Guide to Attendance Management	981452-68096	$70	$35

Shipping and handling are extra. Prices subject to change without notice and subject to applicable taxes.

Deliver To:
Name: ______________________________

Company: ______________________________

Address: ______________________________

City: ____________ **Prov.:** ____________ **Postal Code:** ________

To Place Your Order
Call Toll-Free: **1-800-387-5164**
In Toronto: 416-609-3800
Fax Toll-Free: **1-877-750-9041**
In Toronto: 416-298-5082

Online: www.carswell.com/email

PAYMENT METHODS:
☐ **Cheque** ☐ **VISA** ☐ **MasterCard** ☐ **American Express**

Card #: |__|__|__|__|__|__|__|__|__|__|__|__|__|__|__|__| **Expiry Date:** |__|__|__|__|

☐ **Bill my Carswell Account #:** ____________________ **P.O. #:** ____________________

Telephone #: (____)____________________ **ext.**______ **Fax #:** (____)______________

Signature: ______________________________

Orders must include signature and telephone number to be processed.

One Corporate Plaza, 2075 Kennedy Road, Toronto Ontario Canada M1T 3V4 | carswell.com | thomsonreuters.com

CARSWELL®

THOMSON REUTERS